A Different Distance

Also by Marilyn Hacker

Presentation Piece
Separations
Taking Notice
Assumptions
Love, Death, and the Changing of the Seasons
Going Back to the River
The Hang-glider's Daughter: New and Selected Poems
Selected Poems: 1965–1990
Winter Numbers
Squares and Courtyards
Desesperanto
First Cities: Collected Early Poems 1960–1979
Essays on Departure: New and Selected Poems
Names
A Stranger's Mirror: New and Selected Poems 1994–2014
Blazons: New and Selected Poems, 2000–2018
Calligraphies

Also by Karthika Naïr

Zon-Mai : Parcours nomads (co-author)
Bearings
DESH: Memories inherited, borrowed, invented
The Honey Hunter
Until the Lions: Echoes from the Mahabharata
Over and Under Ground in Mumbai & Paris (co-author)
Amirah ou la Princesse intrépide (adaptation of the opera
La Princesse arabe from the libretto by Paula Fünfeck)
Electric Birds of Pothakudi

A Different Distance

Marilyn Hacker
and Karthika Naïr

First published by Milkweed Editions, USA, in 2022

Published in India by Context, an imprint of Westland Books, a division of Nasadiya Technologies Private Limited, in 2024

No. 269/2B, First Floor, 'Irai Arul', Vimalraj Street, Nethaji Nagar, Alapakkam Main Road, Maduravoyal, Chennai 600095

Interior design by Tijqua Daiker and Mary Austin Speaker

ISBN: 9789360457730

10 9 8 7 6 5 4 3 2 1

Typeset by Jojy Philip, New Delhi

Printed at Parksons Graphics Pvt. Ltd

For Julie Fay, Mimi Khalvati, Karyn London, Deema Shehabi, and Kim Vaeth, who all kept the lights on at 'a different distance'. For Golan Haji, Norbert Hirschhorn, and Fady Joudah, physicians of the heart.

—MH

To the kith—near and far, white-coated and not—who kept me safe and (somewhat) sane through these last years.

—KN

LINKS AND TIES

It was end-March 2020. Yes, that moment when Covid-19 transformed, almost overnight, from a mysterious and highly contagious new disease to a global scourge that brought countries to a standstill. Borders closed like snares. Mortuaries began to overflow. Entire sectors of activity became redundant ... I don't need to itemise the list of unimagined changes the pandemic brought in its wake. They are hard to forget.

An email arrived from Marilyn Hacker, who had barely managed to return to France from Lebanon (where she had been teaching) before the abrupt and full lockdown in both countries. Marilyn, who has been one of my literary heroes since poetry entered my life, and from whose work I learn something new each time, whether it is the ghazal's ability to inhabit all languages and themes, or how political the act of repetition can be within a pantoum. Marilyn, who was now inviting me to join her in writing renga around this strange new life.

Her choice of renga might seem bitingly ironic in the context of the pandemic. This ancient form of collaborative poetry (literally, linked poem)—originally written in imperial courts in Japan, then around dinner tables of monasteries, or in public gardens—had always been associated with a gathering, with revelry. Yet, there we were, physically cut off from each other despite being just a few kilometres away, thanks to the stringent rules of the lockdown.

Other differences exist in our pandemic-era correspondence. Traditionally, to create a renga, poets take turns to write stanzas (now called tanka) of 5-7-5 then 7-7 sound units (*mora*) and—much like in *antakshari*—absorb or include a word or words contained in the last line of one person's tanka into the opening line of the next one's. In English, we tend to substitute the mora with syllables and retain the structure of the tanka as the basic building block. Marilyn and I each chose to write two or three stanzas before handing over the baton to the other.

Marilyn's invitation proved to be a creative lifeline. I was in Paris, shuttling between home and hospital those days, having just begun chemotherapy, following surgery for a recently diagnosed tumour—all of it complicated by RDEB, a chronic disorder which reduces the skin and mucous membranes to something like wet tissue, easily torn and hard to protect. The nights brought long, gut-tearing bouts of nausea, and internal lesions. The subsequent pain and exhaustion made me doubt my ability to write again. Marilyn's gesture of quiet solidarity—she had undergone chemo years ago—gave me purpose and restored a sense of self outside the tyranny of the body. It was a sanity-saver.

We wrote to each other across the year: *A Different Distance* comprises 114 poems covering the period from 29 March 2020 to 31 March 2021. They are a chronicle of everyday existence, that of our countries, of our loved ones, near and far: the uncertainties, the fears, but also the unexpected boons. They map distance, how different life could be across continents, but also across neighbouring districts in Paris, and how languages—even similar ones—jostled differently around us: French and English, Arabic and Urdu and Hindi, and more.

It was a time scarred by open displays of discrimination and power imbalances, a time when mortality and pain invaded every home. But it was also one blazoned by generosity, by selflessness—from strangers as much as from kith. *A Different Distance* celebrates these people, these acts of kindness—beginning with that email on 29 March 2020.

Karthika Naïr
29 November 2024

A DIFFERENT DISTANCE

Crocus, primroses,
in locked-down Square Léopold
Achille. The plague spring.

Rana sent me a photo
of police on Hamra Street

enforcing curfew.
The boy I watched on the roof
of the refugee

squat was locked down already,
daily, among washing lines.

—MH, 29 March 2020

Daily lines burgeon
on Louis Blanc pavements, each sprout
five feet from the next:

human unblossoms outside
baker-butcher-grocers' doors.

One out for one in;
gloved, masked, sanitised before
and after each yield.

The pigeons strutting the same
sidewalks heed no distancing.

—KN, 30 March 2020

"Distance between us ..."
she wrote long ago, and then
made it permanent.

Charpentier, *Vêpres à la Vierge*
(while I'm doing the dishes)

on the comforting
old squat black CD player:
for a moment, there's

connection, if only with
that perplexed self, desiring.

—MH, 30 MARCH 2020

That desire for self
to be more, more than terra
firma for virus

settlements, begets fresh creeds.
Parisians grunt and wheeze praise

to Lord Jogging, while
roaming forlorn as our streets.
Romans hymn and drum

Volare from balconies.
Jack Bernhardt downs ten thousand,

yes, minutes of *Bones*—
libation of eyes and wits
to fair Agent Booth.

The right mantra for lúc lác
spurs my quest across the net.

—KN, 31 March 2020

Across the street, a
girl stands lengthily at the
window, smoking and

looking at empty sidewalks,
sun-soaked on April first.

I wished the tourists
would disappear. Now they're gone.
Watch what you wish for!

In purdah, in quarantine,
I dice one more aubergine.

—MH, 1 APRIL 2020

Aubergine, once more.
Braised, bartha-ed, basil-and-beef-
fried, in any form ...

The thought invades aurous noons,
leaves sharp pugmarks on my dreams

these still-wintry nights.
Preschoolers play COVID-Age
tag in our courtyard:

not more than two at a time,
and 'catch' with an out-flung glove.

—KN, 3 April 2020

We drove out to the
place they called Karantina
where crews of ships from

Europe once waited forty
days to be declared plague-free.

Desolate still, but
in a lonely high-rise, in
a vast gallery,

the ninety-year-old painter's
new gouaches, texts, tapestries.

Afterward, a huge
Armenian lunch in Bourj
Hammoud with my two

young friends, nobody knowing
quarantine was just starting.

—MH, 3 April 2020

Bedlam just started
here, N writes from New Delhi's
migrant worker camps.

How will they lockdown millions
who have neither doors nor roof?

Millions who must walk
many moons to reach a home
to self-isolate.

Prime Minister Modi bids
his nation to light candles.

President Macron,
meanwhile, warned us off facemasks
unless really ill.

Spring: the dearth, in my two lands,
of roses for all the graves.

—KN, 4 April 2020

Rose garden hidden
in the Square du Grand Veneur—
it's starting to bud,

but the gates are locked, only
kids from the logements sociaux

in the enclosure
peer through the grates, in strange,
bright April sunlight.

Here's a petition against
euthanizing the sick old.

—MH, 5 April 2020

Sick and old: for Laure
and Serge, teens from Block D, I
now tick both boxes.

L—four-inch heels keen across
cobblestones—rushes to hold

open all our doors.
Their mom, though, no longer hails
me with nod and smile:

chemo-shorn, brow-less beings
in masks could spell one more germ.

—KN, 6 April 2020

One more spell, one more
incantation—it's only
The Art of the Fugue

or Hildegard of Bingen
or Alice Coltrane: music

calms anxiety.
Abida Parveen sings
a Hafez ghazal,

cross-legged, eloquent hands ...
I pick out a word or two.

—MH, 6 April 2020

Two words, now, for me:
Hum dekhenge—We shall see.
Iqbal Bano soars

skyward on Faiz's refrain, and
something steelier than hope

lights the heart once more.
Heart that fluttered last evening,
stalled a few instants:

a frog in the throat these days
hearkens to beasts less winsome.

—KN, 9 April 2020

Ego, clawing beast:
with or without our selfhood,
beasts try to survive,

as does each isolate I,
newly dispensable, or

in the equation.
Lock up these, those, forever,
then open the doors.

I open late windows on
unnatural bright April.

—MH, 10 April 2020

Bright as this April:
Isa, flushed after cycling
from Pantin—risking

dour fines we none can afford—
brings me dorayaki, home-

made, with sweet red beans
crushed and flour ground by Nico,
who'd foraged for weeks.

Balm for my bile-deluged gut,
swaddling for sleep-deprived dreams.

Wajdi Mouawad writes
to his infant, unknowing
son: *Quoi dire de plus*

urgent que l'amour? Sometimes,
pancakes will do just as well.

—KN, 13 APRIL 2020

Pancakes, not huîtres,
phone calls, texts, instead of wine-
flavored exchanges

in the public privacy
of a café. Sautéed snow

peas, shallots, chicken,
wine anyway, but for one,
yesterday's bread, a

departing moon above roof-
dormers, now my horizon.

—MH, 14 April 2020

My horizon, each
week: the poppy-printed, teal
hair cap of Nurse Rose

(handstitched, the florets for cheer)
as she disinfects—'secures,'

in the martial cant
so dear to our president—
my portacath site.

She, of calm hands and raptor
gaze, snags any truant vein.

—KN, 15 April 2020

I play truant when
I go to the bakery,
or Russian roulette

for a baguette tradition,
une réglette de macarons.

I should be indoors.
Back inside I'm dizzy with
fear, but I eat one,

two, caramel macaroons.
"Look, we have come through." Who knows?

—MH, 15 April 2020

Who knows anything
today? Prefects, priests, pressmen,
physicians ... no one.

Yet, wait, everyone we know,
or don't, dons shades of prophet.

Sun-drenched flowed the Quais
de Valmy and de Jemmapes
these last afternoons

while I brooded indoors with
Coke as cure and company.

—KN, 18 April 2020

Wolves accompany
me, a dream I'd like to have,
lope across a steppe,

howl an ode to the half-moon,
break bread with al-Farazdaq,

hunt mice if we must.
Overarching, the night sky
blankets the city

we're immured in, or opens
it up to ghazals of rain.

—MH, 19 April 2020

A rain of ghazals,
petrichor from verse by long-
lost poets, crumble

many sabre-toothed daymares,
if just for a rainbow while.

Ghalib, Faiz, Firaq,
Sahir (always Sahir), then
the doyen, Khusrau:

sufi, secular or plain
kafir; their ghazal, nazm, and

sher, the first to strike
my early, unlearned ears;
demand rebellion

yet earn adoration from
a resolute nastik heart.

—KN, 20 April 2020

My atheist heart's
an impatient physician,
has no words to calm

vertigoes, palpitations
provoked by a sentence in

a news brief, or just
the sameness of spring days that
lengthen, out of reach.

No words then, music, numbers
and feeling, metal, thoughts, reeds:

oud, violin, or
saxophone, behind them
a mind, hands, a mouth

unseen as a friend's face now.
Today, the doctor's Mozart.

—MH, 21 April 2020

My doctors Bourrat
and Blazy—Amazons with
spines of carbon steel,

shafts marked truth and solace,
fingers the envy of neat

goldsmiths—take the time
to write and ring, to enquire,
and devise relief,

with bad puns, in pandemics,
covering for painkillers.

—KN, 23 April 2020

Covering her face
with the mask she'll wear all night,
my daughter goes to

meet the patient first in the
queue: midnight in the ER.

Through nights in Aceh
after the tsunami, in
a hospital tent,

she saw herself back in school,
saw herself the physician.

I imagined her
then, now, at a different
distance, think of her

unmasking in the morning,
driving home to walk the dogs.

—MH, 23 April 2020

Home with the dogs—four—
and spouse of five-odd decades,
my dad (veteran

of three wars; child, too, of World
War II, famines, a blood-steeped

Partition) thunders
at the virus, the lockdown,
the distance from kin ...

the years of command futile
before this covert agent.

—KN, 24 April 2020

Before, I covered
my head to enter a mosque.
I cover my face

now, to go down to the street.
Niqab's forbidden in France,

but masks like the ones
the kiné gave me will be
obligatory.

I sent a photo of my
solo atheist iftar

to Samira in
Algiers, to Maryam in
London. Next year will

we sit down together to
break bread for anyone's feast?

—MH, 26 April 2020

Stale bread: feast for one
gleaning breath from rotting peel
and near-empty cans

of red beans from garbage bins
around the local Mono'p.

Streets abandoned by
traffic and pedestrians
find homes with vagrants.

Vagrants left unfed, unsafe,
even as the cops slap fines

on their unhoused hands,
and leaders applaud our state-
wide lockdown success.

Some deaths never figure, not
even as nameless figures.

—KN, 28 April 2020

Known, nameless faces,
figures, throw open windows
up and down the street

each night at eight to applaud
doctors, nurses, éboueurs,

and to show ourselves
to each other at the end
of a locked-in day.

I wave to the girl in the
fifth-floor dormer, she waves back.

—MH, 29 April 2020

Her sixth-floor dormer,
a cigarette, the much-loved
view of our skyline:

Claire—critical-care intern—
sighs for one, after twenty

hours on breathless feet.
Evening applause is sweet, but
she'd choose PPE

over the President's praise—
and eggs on grocery shelves.

—KN, 1 May 2020

Shelves in the G20
are still filled with coffee, cheese,
brown eggs, garriguettes,

Greek yogurt, milk, wine—but I
hurry, forget tomatoes,

get out of harm's way
(masked, gloved) as fast as I can.
Food shopping once was

community, communion.
Poison in the chalice now.

—MH, 2 May 2020

In my chalice, now,
on good days: mouthful of fresh
cirrus and sapphire,

sometimes nimbus, with falling
sheets of vitreous heaven.

That daily ramble,
required to expel Taxol
and its unkind ilk,

impossible alone, yet
forbidden in company.

Once more, Doctor B
rides to the rescue, handing
armour to my knights:

Isa, Nico, Claire, Philippe
bear her letterhead as shield.

—KN, 4 May 2020

A facemask as shield,
or he hopes so, bearing wine
and some news, Hisham walks

along the Corniche, open
now, toward Raouché,

his mother's flat, where
he hasn't been in three months.
Scholarship, maybe,

fall term in London, maybe.
Freekeh bil dajaj tonight.

—MH, 4 May 2020

Tonight, an empire
of pain reigns over attempts
to write, think; to be.

Fall, even *summer*, graze past
ears as would submerged boulders.

RDEB—four
horseless, shapeless, ageless words—
must play first fiddle;

second, third, and last, as well,
while all others earn exile.

—KN, 5 May 2020

Home becomes exile
in the punished city. Leaves
green beyond grillwork,

Nâzim Hikmet's postcard from
prison poems on the sill.

Locked-in lovers make
love until it bores them. Once,
through a hurricane

in Crete ... but that was three days,
decades ago, two of us.

—MH, 7 May 2020

This, decades ago,
was how I gaped at the sea.
Reaching Rue Manin,

the years sublime, suddenly-
much-younger selves drink from this

downpour of gloaming,
we gasp at the carnival
corralled within Parc

des Buttes-Chaumont. Cedar, elm,
and linden; pine, plane, and beech

arch towards the sky.
Hazelnut and cherry trees
flaunt wanton blossoms,

and the cascades underground
serenade us from afar.

—KN, 8 May 2020

From afar, but it
wasn't, thunder, rush of dark
clouds, then crash of rain,

just after I noticed, no
gates blocked the berges of the Île

Saint-Louis. No way
but, run under the torrents,
no café shelter.

Strip off once indoors, shower.
Flu, or worse, I'm on my own.

Later, on my own,
I slice shallots and mushrooms
into olive oil

and begin to imagine
I might not cough tomorrow.

—MH, 9 May 2020

Tomorrow might bring
the unknown—new foes, allies
of Taxol; blitzkrieg

within the chest; skull afire
(the mind sentinels one front

alone, these days)—but
also Philippe, bonne fée, by
the hospital doors,

strafed by showers or barraged,
joyfully, by vernal sun.

—KN, 12 May 2020

Lengthening vernal
afternoons to evenings,
sometimes we would walk

Bastille to Concorde, halfway
back, talking, stop for coffee

in a nondescript
café, touching each other's
arms for emphasis.

Where the métro took someone
home's a foreign country now.

—MH, 13 May 2020

Foreigners but both
home: this body and Paris,
the only ones I

have known dearly for thus long,
inconstant, heedless satyrs,

but mine, always mine.
Now, though, they turn hesitant,
unfamiliar to

their mirrors, shorn of birthmarks
and lush with other beings.

—KN, 14 May 2020

Budding, lush, wilting,
lilacs, then roses, behind
iron grills: locked gardens,

each with some reminiscence.
There, we ate ham sandwiches

on a bench, talking
about Homs, and Aleppo.
There, a France Inter

reporter interviewed me
two months after I finished

chemo. I stared at
green leaves, blue sky, found something
more appropriate

to say than "I'm still alive."
And am, outside the gates, now.

—MH, 15 MAY 2020

Outside now, the sun
beckons—Piper whose descants
play louder than full

orchestras. Parisians hear
and obey, disregarding

dictates by doctors,
ministers, coppers, and throng
canal quays and squares.

Masks hang from chins, kiss pockets.
Distance is a banished land.

—KN, 17 May 2020

Banished from London
streets as over seventy,
Arij remembers

her mother's joy walking through
Zamalek, head bare, at last,

and going back nine
years ago to interview
Tahrir Square students.

She wraps an ironic scarf
to mask her face, and goes out.

—MH, 17 May 2020

"A face, a hand, or
chest: how long since I felt one
other than my own?"

Caregiver C, whose hugs could
lull most breeds of pain, sounds lost.

Back home for a few
prized hours, she cannot snuggle
her two young children,

just as distressed. Lou, the cat,
alone rubs against her feet.

—KN, 19 May 2020

I sip it alone,
Italian coffee with a
little cardamom.

Last time I drank coffee with
someone: my best student, at

Kaza Maza in
Hamra, before she left for
the mountains, with friends,

to play out the quarantine.
After she'd gone, I lingered.

—MH, 21 May 2020

Lingering after
the sun dives down nacreous
rooftops, I trace them—

chimney pots, dormers, the slate
tiles, the lead guttering—all

with distant, blackened
fingers that recall other
lines and curves. Breathing,

speaking ones, that reach out, and
not merely to note a pulse.

—KN, 22 May 2020

A day's pulse measured
sometimes in outgoing calls.
A voice but no face

accompanying. If I
meet a friend in the street, we're

both masked. Yesterday
Nahed bused to the Bastille—
we'd walk on the port.

Locked. On the Opéra stairs,
eyes, hands, enlivened masked words.

—MH, 24 May 2020

The words, unmasked, bear
serrated edges: "Relapse,"
says Doctor MM,

referring to her cancer.
It is I who flinch from them,

wishing I had not
just named the demons she'll have
to dispel once more;

named them and recounted all
their lurid powers at length.

—KN, 25 May 2020

The length of my life
now defines me like my skin
color, sex, or faith.

It's meant little since, aged five,
judged too young to read and write,

I said I could, did.
Again infantilized, should
I be locked up so

the young can go about their
business, getting and spending?

—MH, 27 May 2020

This business called
life got spent (say it: drained) on
just a glass of milk

at Muzaffarpur railway
station. Maqsood Alam—house

painter in Delhi,
banished back to his Bihar
by statewide lockdown,

by national uncaring—
"ran pillar to post" to save

his ailing Ishaq,
aged four. The boy's breath ran out
sooner than columns

to fill in the government-
drafted forms for sustenance.

Same day, same station:
a babe tries to wake his dead
mother. Police state

both died on trains. And that kin
still get ex gratia aid.

—KN, 30 May 2020

Still point of morning,
discarded masks on the street,
riots' detritus.

Not a morning of roses.
Patients on ventilators

echo "I can't breathe,"
or might if they could speak.
What's your death sentence—

counterfeit bill, métro ride?
The knee comes down on your throat.

—MH, 31 May 2020

Throats, knees, lungs, kidneys—
dispensable, when cased in
black, brown ... Dalit skin?

Ask Bondy-based Gabriel,
fourteen, who might lose an eye:

lawless justice from
Castaner's cops. Names, too, are
a kind of hide for

Larbi, their shades litmussed in
grillings at border control.

—KN, 3 June 2020

Borders were porous
with the right passports
or a titre de séjour.

Danes can go to Norway now,
but Swedes can't. When Nahed got

her French passport, we
drank champagne. She can't see her
sister in Stockholm.

She's job-hunting in Toulouse,
going masked to interviews.

—MH, 5 June 2020

Unmasked interview
on Crowdcast—isle of brief joy,
its sole borders those

carved by broadband access, land
with no COVID contagion—

where Meena and I
speak at the US launch of
her book *When I Hit*

You; speak of verse, fiction, caste
killings, murderous husbands,

and more; speak, across
Boston, London and Paris,
with gracious Shuchi,

host from Brookline Booksmith, to
readers, unseen, round the world.

—KN, 8 June 2020

From around the world,
Lebanese expats are flown
back to al-watan—

Moscow, Rio, Montreal,
Paris—bringing the virus

to their homecomings
in Beirut or the Beka'a.
Numbers leap. Katia

wrote to me a month ago:
Our epidemic's over.

I know she follows
the news ... Cafés reopened,
clothing shops, crèches.

As for the money changers,
were their counters ever closed?

—MH, 10 June 2020

Close encounters, let's
call them, of the fifth or sixth
kind: in Bareilly,

returnee migrants get soused
with liquid bleach—yes, the kind

bottled with danger
to eyes and skin—as a cure,
by the State, no less,

while Delhi shuts hospital
doors on its nonresidents.

—KN, 12 JUNE 2020

Resident of a
city, body, state of mind
I shrug off under

shadows and sun on the Quai
Saint-Bernard. A yoga class

salutes the river;
a portly couple tangos
to their own cassette.

I walk without a mask, as
far as the Jardin des Plantes.

—MH, 13 June 2020

Assemblage, as far
as the eye can feed: litchi,
melon, mint, mango,

moka, peach … corps de sorbet
(and ice) glimmer and curtsy,

preen, swirl in their trays
to carouse with me, Isa
and Nico—plotters

of my first sortie outside
home and hospital. Lambent

this dusk, like our blithe
reunion at Berthillon,
Île Saint-Louis, still

mecca for bon vivants, each
palate worshipful in queue.

—KN, 15 June 2020

In a queue for bread
outside the bakery on
the boulevard: it's

almost normal. An almost-
normal Sunday market with

hand sanitizer
dispensers at entrance points.
Almost no distrust

of the masked person next in
line for cherries, shrimp, courgettes,

hummus, samosas.
Which merchants have disappeared?
Which shoppers I knew

vaguely by sight won't I see
again? It's chilly for June.

—MH, 21 June 2020

June, now, is the month
of solstitial nights, roses,
and two presidents

convinced the grandeur of their
nations—flanking, from north and

south, the Atlantic—
resides in statues of dead,
all-too-fallible

men, to be safeguarded far
more than the breath of today's

denizens; convinced
naming evils of the past
would be a crime (mine

christened it separatism).
How frail must they find our lands?

—KN, 27 June 2020

Old, frail, nonetheless
I walked home from Montparnasse,
invulnerable

for the moment, pink K-way
against the drizzle. Almost-

midnight streets full of
mostly local, mostly young
drinkers and flâneurs

as if nothing had happened.
I kept my mask on, except

on the Pont Sully
where there was no one, only
reverberations

of music on the quais, next
Decamerons, next clusters?

—MH, 29 June 2020

Clusters of colour—
reign of aestival blossoms—
caper on Philippe's third-

floor balcony. They join us
and a madcap even breeze

to celebrate this,
my first visit in many
months; first touch of drink

(organic) outside home and
hospital since early March.

—KN, 4 July 2020

"Since we want to march
from the hospital to the
BDL and set

up our tent, we should wear scrubs
and masks," Rachid said. Interns,

medical students
were planning one more sit-in.
"We'll be wearing masks

anyway," said Nour. "They found
forty new cases last night."

—MH, 6 July 2020

Another new case,
in our land: Martine Landry,
all of seventy-

six, Amnesty activist,
acquitted after three years

of legal nightmares
for her solidarity
to teen refugees

who'd have been wrongly expelled.
Oh, we take pride in being

playwrights of the great
Declaration of Human
Rights—but, it's a show

we'd rather tour or license
abroad than produce at home.

—KN, 10 July 2020

At home, my brain or
my blood churn out symptoms: stress,
swellings, dizziness,

unhinged by solitude and
anxiety. Telephone

calls replace dinners,
long walks down known, unknown streets.
We're free, but who's "we"?

It was a challenge in March.
Is it perpetuity?

—MH, 11 July 2020

"Is it already
the end?" That was from Nurse D,
distractedly, while

finetuning the drip flow to
my chest. *Already?* Six months,

or twenty-four weeks
and three days; I can spare you
the hours, but let's throw

in a pandemic for change.
Our laughter rings verdigris.

—KN, 18 July 2020

The grey-green eyes of
the floundered revolutions,
hers and his and hers,

wolves' eyes in a dream fading
to a blurred image of hills,

apricot orchards,
Beka'a Valley vineyards I
never visited—

Bukra fil-meshmesh, these years'
harvests of gone tomorrows.

—MH, 19 July 2020

Tomorrow has gone,
I learn, for Hasdeo Arand—
forest in central

India, haven for Gond
tribes, eighty-odd species of

trees, scrubs (thirty-eight),
herbs (nineteen), birds (one-one-one) ...
sloth bears, elephants,

leopards: larynx of a land.
Coal mines emerge. Through lockdown.

Standing committees
lie down, governments traffic
reserve forests, and

Adani makes hay while a
virus shines—blinding nations.

—KN, 20 July 2020

Four o'clock sunshine
on the Seine: the bookshop's a
beehive. Karthika

is here and I'm here, first time
we've met since January.

In a room above
the river, we record for
the Bengaluru

festival she can't attend.
Then we sit at Panis, with

hot chocolate, black
coffee. She takes off the mauve
silk scarf round her head

and lets the sun soothe the scars,
tease the hair-stubble to grow.

—MH, 26 July 2020

Stubbly the teasing,
the banter, the laughter—sweet
nothings we had grown

unused to, locked down all these
months. This reading-recording

first, with Marilyn
and Adam, and an unseen
pianist, upstairs

at Shakespeare and Company.
My favourite Wednesday

this year. Then, a slew
of retrouvailles—its English
sibling feeble—all

week, spotlit by the same sun
and, often, hot chocolate.

—KN, 31 July 2020

Foot, hot in its brace
for a stupid broken bone,
propped on a cushion,

I'm back and forth on WhatsApp
for six hours; two explosions

on the port, half of
Beirut blown up: Gemmayzé,
Bourj Hammoud ... "We're safe,

in shock, the windows shattered ..."
War-zone cell-phone videos.

The bride in white lace
hijab, blown down in her gown,
is a doctor who

was in an ER six hours
later, triaging stretchers.

—MH, 6 August 2020

The triage stretches
through the night on Kozhikode
Airport's tarmac, then

in ERs of hospitals
across two neighbouring towns.

Volunteers—battling
manic rains and a raging
virus—seek voices

beneath the debris of one-
ninety lives fleeing COVID-

19 from Dubai.
Eighteen dead, and one-twenty
injured. "Amma, were

there people you ...?" She replies:
"They were all someone's blood, child."

—KN, 9 August 2020

Someone's child, someone's
uncle, sister, son: were they
blasted, infected?

The disasters converge. While
Katia sends me a WhatsApp

photo, bottle of
white wine I left in the fridge
on Makdisi Street.

"I've packed your books and clothes. We'll
drink the wine when you come back."

—MH, 17 AUGUST 2020

"When you come next, we'll
drink a beaker of sunset
by Vellayani

Lake!" Then his voice clouds, "That won't
be likely this year, will it?"

Buoyant since birth, my
dad held on to hope all these
months: a surefire cure,

tests, vaccines ... His belief, now,
flags after the morning news.

—KN, 23 August 2020

No more rainbow flags—
Les Mots à la Bouche bookshop
has been replaced by

another Doc Martens store,
and the Moroccan grocer

by Princesse Tam.Tam
underwear, one of three clones
in ten blocks. I don't

want to walk down the rue Sainte-
Croix de la Bretonnerie,

where sometimes I'd go
near midnight and browse, come home
with that new novel

by Nina Bouraoui and
grapefruit juice for the morning.

—MH, 23 August 2020

Grief stains the morning
like grape, overripe, the tongue:
purple, glutinous.

Grief stains their voices: Achan
and Amma live, relive, loss

each time I call. Three
deaths in two days: old, dear friends;
forty- and sixty-

year-old kinships; their markers
of being. Grief edged by new,

enforced distance, by
the lack of touch, of last rites.
Grief clogs, till Swaroop

YouTube-streams a funeral.
Life seeps back into their chords.

—KN, 31 August 2020

Who'll get their life back?
Although no one ever does.
Iva says the last

trip she took was seven months
ago, to a friend's wedding,

classmate from med school,
and no one's come to their house
since February,

though the big garden's in bloom.
You're the risk factor, I tease—

nights in the ER.
It's two years since I've seen her,
Beirut, night shifts, now

pandemic intimacies:
WhatsApp, FaceTime, telephone.

—MH, 4 September 2020

The old telephone
holds Larbi's voice, which holds me,
gently, as he says:

"Ron is no more. The end was
sudden." We'd thought, like him, *cure*

was a real word;
so is *relapse*, we learn. Ron,
wind beneath many

wings; our own counter-cliché—
the finance pro who loved dance.

"His eyes shimmied when
he spoke of performances
watched with you": gauche, my

words to Marcel, Ron's husband,
who brings me comfort instead.

—KN, 8 September 2020

Instead of teaching
online in the ruins of
Beirut, Rana flew

to Norway with her two kids,
back to her fourth language, their

school days, her research.
Abou Rana and his group
of leftist thou'ar

are on the street every night,
masked in the late summer heat,

clearing rubble in
Gemmayzé, whose tragedies
a year ago were

lovers leaving, or leases
with exorbitant new rent.

—MH, 11 September 2020

Exorbitant, new
fears raise Raavan-heads every
where; vie for first place

in the mouths of ministers
and media. We make room

for "séparatisme,"
and then "ensauvagement." My
parents taste "urban

naxal": should I tell them that
is bhakt-speak for folks like me?

—KN, 17 September 2020

Devotee of do-
nothing, the minister does.
In one another's

arms, faces, masks on chins, wrists,
the young crowd late-summer streets,

drinking Cokes or beer,
eating sandwiches. I wish
this were fine. I'd like

to mind my own business, read
film reviews, not virus charts.

—MH, 18 September 2020

I read film reviews,
famished for the cinema—
land unvisited

since March. And theatre, word
that makes me weep: patria,

no less, touchable
only during virtual
meetings, rehearsals

recorded and 'WeTransferred'
(new terms that yield bread, though not

quite butter). Shambling
home from hospital, I watch
hounds, pugs, mutts, and pups

raise happy Cain by the quai:
enfin, a show safe for all!

—KN, 22 September 2020

For all the good it
does, the mayors say "Stay safe,"
with no restrictions.

It's your fault if you're fat, old,
diabetic, asthmatic,

or having chemo.
Stay indoors. We'll keep the bars,
gyms, playgrounds open.

It's fall, it's started raining,
and the river says, "Elsewhere ..."

—MH, 28 September 2020

Rivers of sunlight
flood Joëlle's studio, much
like faces, voices,

fill her screen—from Bangalore,
Delhi, Dhaka, Calcutta.

All gathered to fête
eighty years of Alliance
Française du Bengale.

And J and I, with demon-
tiger and forest-goddess,

join the party from
Ivry. Through verb and line, curve,
morpheme in three tongues.

The Sundarbans fill our mask-
less minds, and laughter, our ears.

—KN, 28 September 2020

Our minds, our ears, eyes
are dulled with grim statistics.
Not much else, except

the train wreck of the world as
we thought it might be: well-oiled

dictators, would-be
tyrants, armed thugs. Wildfires
blaze through rainforests.

We pretend it's la rentrée
here. Masked kids flutter like bats

in the street when school
lets out. Badauds throng
café terrasses for what may

be last times, before wind, rain,
or closure and confinement.

—MH, 1 October 2020

Confinement closes
in, rusty-tongued this time, but
still raptor: reminds

Dr B, warning me of squalls
ahead. Her first respite in

nine months, "capsized," she
sighs, "by the rising caseloads."
Yet she can find cheer

in my reborn lashes and
brows, and laugh at poor sallies—

this week, mine feature
filet de breast, grilled extra rare
but served, alas, sans

sauce teriyaki (slathered
with bicain lotion instead).

—KN, 7 October 2020

Lotion on my cheeks,
forehead, and neck—anything
soothing and calming.

Now that I can walk again,
take a walk after dinner.

Darken all the screens.
Drink red wine instead of white,
or no wine at all.

Tisane à la verveine be-
fore bed, harpsichord music,

maybe a hot bath,
though I had one at seven,
changed the bed linens.

Awake at three, five, at six
I get up, say it's morning.

—MH, 9 October 2020

Morning can get no
more rutilant than this. I
have seen it after

long. After seven months, three
weeks, a night. I counted each,

on the trail that led
here, to A. Boutrous's *One
More Thing*, at Théâtre

des Abbesses, to dancers, to
selves arcing, tumbling, torquing,

crouching ... to twined limbs
and huddled heads and ragged
breath that invites mine

to sing, to thrill, to be once
more, once more be this instant.

—KN, 13 OCTOBER 2020

An instant implodes
the insouciant afternoon.
It could be the bike

that glanced me crossing the street.
It could be long, honed knives.

My writing hand is
in plaster. The closing of
a mosque distracts from

the city under curfew.
Commuters rush home from their

obligatory
work to fixate on more screens,
complexions of fear.

I write on a screen, too, look
with longing at my notebook.

—MH, 20 October 2020

Notebooks and longing:
I think of notebooks, little
smudged, lined notebooks that

waited for aeons to gleam
with this chronicle, a date

and a name: 7
November 2020;
Kamala Harris.

Vice President-Elect. Light
streams into this year, in skeins.

—KN, 9 November 2020

Trout streams or jet streams,
duffel bag, binoculars:
life of “the wild old,”

as Marie imagined and
lived it in her seventies,

eighties. Stroke-silenced
her last decade, she didn’t
live to see “old” mean

indefinite confinements,
wild like a wolf in a cage.

—MH, 11 November 2020

Uncaged, like wolf cubs
in the wilderness, bounded
our smiles. Last Thursday:

we met after four whole months,
only the third time this year.

Virtual, though, this
reunion, with our faces
mosaicked across screens

in UK by Zoom at the
Achates Philanthropy

Prize ceremony.
We read poems to honour
heroes who brought art

to homes through the pandemic.
#artfeltthanks, no mere slogan.

—KN, 18 November 2020

Slogans, jokes, went round
the first time, recipes for
iftars solitaires,

photos of cassoulet or
couscous, window-framed landscapes

of unconfined trees,
berges de la Seine, the Corniche,
Riverside Park dogs.

No one's clapping in windows
this time. Winter is coming.

—MH, 22 November 2020

This time, winter comes
to Paris on stockinged feet,
no fuss, no fireworks,

until she's layering breath
with frost and the pipes with gnarls.

In Vellayani,
my parents greet their wedding
anniversary

by bracing their windows and
ears for Cyclone Burevi.

—KN, 3 December 2020

Ears attuned to sounds
at three in the morning that
are irrelevant:

techno party down the block,
wine shop delivery truck,

the pulse in my ears.
And sleep is over again:
dream conversations

on the Corniche, Raouché's
wave-lapped rocks, kitchen table

that might be here or
some unvisited city.
Conversations stop

with the dreams; night continues
with its noises, my silence.

—MH, 5 December 2020

The noise, the noise shreds
all thought to silence. Inside
the dazzling white drum

("a cylindrical super-
conducting MR scanner,"

the radiographer
corrects softly), I am mere
atoms of water,

each captained by protons of
hydrogen, hurtling earthward.

Mere mass, off-kilter,
of drops rushing, lining, re-
aligning between

magnets and radio waves,
between rhythm and discord.

—KN, 12 December 2020

Discordant darkness
of curfew-emptied streets.
Saint Lucy's Day past,

daylight will linger longer,
but when will sidewalks refill

with people heading
to movies, theatre, dinner,
ou que pour flâner?

On a screen, I watched white-robed
girls crowned with candles, singing

'Santa Lucia'
in another country, in
another language,

another year, when voices
wove, anodyne, in the air.

—MH, 16 December 2020

They weave the air gold
today, the voices that brought
breath and heart this year.

Namesake-publisher at four
a.m.; then Jai and P, all

from Delhi. L ships
snowflakes from Boston; Honji
and Seb, red roses,

berries, and Lindt from Berlin.
Philippe, with choux à la crème,

lights up my landing.
Sankar, two decades on, smiles
his wishes by ten.

d, you'd said: "I know you know
you're loved." More than ever, d.

—KN, 18 December 2020

What I loved more than
wine, pomegranate juice, or
cardamom coffee

was conversations. Her face
or his face, preferred language—

(mine was, often, a
shorba of three that seemed to
have its own grammar)

—and history, none the same.
I called Mimi today (she's

locked down in London)
and saw her silver mane, im-
perious nose, grin.

Thought of coffees and curries.
Voices, pages, feed us now.

—MH, 20 December 2020

Your voice on the page—
well, screens of laptop and cell
phone, if precise, not

poetic, we should be—feeds
me, d, with mirth, thought, joy, doubt,

absurdity, much
needed, through the galloping
months of this fearsome

time. Not everyone knows why
I have eluded faces—

Skype, Zoom, FaceTime, Whats-
App, whatever—whenever
possible. Last week,

I lost my voice. Tears unspooled,
instead, across video.

—KN, 23 December 2020

Lights out across the
street, five stories of windows:
the young black-bearded

man at his computer screen,
the small, long-dark-haired woman

I remember as
a twenty-years-ago bride,
all eclipsed. And you

aren't far away, but the
Gare du Nord might be Beijing,

though if I launch a
bottle of syllables, one
will return on the

tide of the internet, in
one more possible morning.

—MH, 26 DECEMBER 2020

One more loss to mourn:
Ousmane Sy, stage name Babson.
Soft-hearted giant,

says the press. King of the style
christened *House*, master mover,

choreographer,
champion of girl power.
Your *Queen Blood*, paean

to women, with eight danseuses-
dynamos, scythed space and time—

and a much-esteemed,
international jury's
presumptions. Come back:

you'd just begun, your brick-red
beats must sear sightlines for long.

—KN, 31 December 2020

Wouldn't the lines be long
at any clinic if they
vaccinated there,

and wouldn't it be worth the wait!
Instead, attente prolongée

alone, in winter,
nervous, in a cluttered flat,
waiting for the light

of day, of the next season,
of another person's face.

—MH, 4 January 2021

"Wear another face
this year," I tell two thousand
and twenty-one, "one

we'll fear less, if not quite love
at first sight." It lengthens, this

wait to be shielded,
like shadows at dusk. Or is
this the cotangent

the sun casts at dawn? The streets
of Paris, cobblestone and

bitumen and spit,
have no answers to give me,
as I tread from 10th

to 11th, 4th to 5th,
but they console: *We've seen worse.*

—KN, 8 January 2021

No worse, there is none.
Of course there is, but Hopkins
voices my mood at

three in the morning, awake
with head throbbing, sharp pain in

the small of my back.
Symptoms of distress, wanting
out, of confinement,

of laptop-screen dialogues.
Nahed's bright sublet, over-

looking cobblestones.
Mutabbal, bamya, Fairuz:
familiar, now so

strange I felt sick. Nahed walked
me, arm in arm, to a cab.

—MH, 11 JANUARY 2021

Let us arm ourselves
with memory, lest all trace
be swept under the new

bordel-de-merde level
of current chaos

with variant strains,
stagnant vaccination drives
and other tumult.

Before sunrise, January
9, outskirts of Calais: it's

minus three degrees
(Celsius) and masked police
are tearing up tents

of refugees, chasing them
to a hopeless, frozen dawn.

—KN, 13 January 2020

Hopeless to wait for
vaccine registration or
search for hours online.

A few fortunate ones signed
up: places filled in twelve hours.

So live your life in
suspension. Claire went for a
pedicure in a

Haussmannian flat, bought a
scone on the rue du Cherche-Midi

where we'd had lunch in
possible September. She's
ninety-five, seen worse,

unshelves Montaigne to reread
after she watches the news.

—MH, 26 January 2020

The news watched me back,
pleased, more pleased than Mister Punch
had ever been: *I' d*

dance with you if I could. Mark
the date, Rachid Ouramdane's

been named future head
of Théâtre national
de Chaillot, mecca

of dance in France. The heart sings.
Son of French-Algerian

parents, Rachid's coat-
of-arms at Chaillot for the
lustrum is one word,

hospitality, which he's
probed all these years. The heart sings.

—KN, 13 February 2021

My heart sinks as night
falls, minutes later daily.
Soon, March, spring again,

but *curfew, confinement* still
menace. "All this for a few

old farts who'd die soon
anyway ..." comments in *Le*
Monde. I remember

the AIDS epidemic, shunned
gay sons. I'd rather be shunned

for flamboyant life
than "for my own good," I think
eating a salad

alone at nine o'clock for
the three hundredth COVID time.

—MH, 15 February 2021

The COVID Age: that
may be the Anthropocene's
gift to the planet.

My thoughts are dark, sometimes dour,
these vaccineless days and nights,

especially nights,
already overrun by
triffids, viciously

potent, tsars of vast terrains
of my body—mucous, skin,

breath—now venturing
to occupy the lands I've
tried hard to defend

all these years. That space where word
meets page, that grand blank expanse.

—KN, 2 March 2021

Expanse, constriction ...
Marwan Barghouti has been
in jail for how long?

The Gazaoui student, at
Harvard on a fellowship,

goes out, gets coffee,
walks to the library, thinks—
but I don't know what

he thinks, only that he's there.
And I'm here, a constriction

round my temples, not
an occupying army,
only my weakness;

my body's vain protest at
its prolonged isolation.

—MH, 7 March 2021

It's been a prolonged
cosmic spoof, the quest to get
vaccinated: I'm

new kin to Don Quixote,
one whose windmills keep shifting.

Hospitals, barely
equipped to protect their own,
can't inject chronic

patients, despite trifectas
of RDEB, cancer,

and chemo, if we're
ambulatory. Vaccine
centres asked I turn

seventy-five. Today, I
savour post-vaccine fatigue.

—KN, 16 March 2021

“Fatigue, regrets ...” a
quote from Adrienne Rich in
a notebook margin.

Once, twice a week, evening
conviviality, banned now.

One friend in the Lot,
one in the Vaucluse, with a
spouse/friend, watch seasons

change, take up gardening, hike,
ride bikes, study Italian—

Voltaire’s dream? COVID
shuts the city down again,
possibilities

contingent on—but who knows?
Not budding trees, locked cafés.

—MH, 19 March 2021

Budding hope gets locked
once more. Caseloads skyrocket;
caregivers, frontline

workers fight, feet on quagmire,
less equipped a year later,

not more, despite all
the tedious talk of war and
wartime effort. Talk

comes cheap to our government,
talk that's a perfect smokescreen

for failure, torpor,
electoral ambition.
Islamo-gauchisme

gains screentime: great game
plan for twenty twenty-two!

—KN, 29 March 2021

Two hours before dawn,
I give up on sleep, turn on
the bedside lamp, pick

up the book I put down at
midnight, attempt escape to

Algiers, another
decade, history, someone's
struggle who's not me

getting old in a quagmire
city, "Unfortunately

it was paradise ..."
Solitary confinement
now. Food shopping the

only vestige of human
exchange, though daylight lingers.

—MH, 29 March 2021

What lingers, through day,
month, and year, will be kindness—
kindness that kept me

sane and safe, yes, even with
the same unsought trifecta

snapping at my heels,
noisy and unfunny, save
during our chats, d.

Scaffolding to laugh (and weep)
at this, the théâtre de

l'absurde of our own
grandly defective bodies.
In this almanac

of blessings, laughter became
you, d, and somehow, spring tide.

—KN, 31 MARCH 2021

ACKNOWLEDGMENTS

We thank the editors of the following publications in which certain poems from *A Different Distance* first appeared:

Shakespeare and Company
Los Angeles Review of Books
Open Magazine
Rusted Radishes
Manhattan Review
New England Review
Michigan Quarterly Review

KN: Words prove annoyingly inadequate here, as I attempt to thank the people who made this book possible. Some, directly, by bolstering the writing. Some held me together during this time, fraying threads, torn seams and all. Some did both. Then there are those whose names I might not have caught, or retained: my fissures of memory or attention notwithstanding, their help mattered, mattered much. Among them all, in no defined order:

Marilyn Hacker: for the very idea of the renga—and the invitation, which transformed this year; for patience, encouragement, and poetry that has been an inspiration for years;

Fady Joudah: for the early, intent read, the impassioned discussions, and the catalytic belief in what would become *A Different Distance*;

Daniel Slager, Bailey Hutchinson, Mary Austin Speaker, Joanna (Yanna) R. Demkiewicz, Claire Laine, Milan Wilson-Robinson, and their teammates at Milkweed Editions: for welcoming the renga with warmth and certainty, and producing this book with elegant expertise;

Sarah Yake of Frances Collin Literary Agency and Anjali Singh of Ayesha Pande Literary: for, once again, being our bridges across the ocean; and, once again, for priceless counsel;

Karthika V.K. and the team at Context/Westland for bringing *A Different Distance* to farther latitudes—both old and new; for holding on to their promise through the pandemic years, through the vagaries of terminations and resurrections; for the joyful reunion with familiar faces and line-break discussions: I missed you all. It had been a while!

Adam Biles: for organising a joyful, memorable recording session of the renga at Shakespeare and Company in July 2020; for the equally joyful afternoons, with little

Anouk, of flânerie and literary dissections around Parc des Buttes-Chaumont through the 'third wave';

Dr Anne Blazy: for unstinting support, unsparing honesty, understanding; for startlingly inventive ways to beat or—at least—take on RDEB-triffids and chemo-gremlins; for the cheer, the shared fondness for wicked puns, the choice of orange-tinted footwear and accessories to brighten chemo-days, to assuage pain;

Rose Boudan: for her presence, through miles and miles of appointments, tests, surgery, chemo, radiation ...; for reorganising her holidays to ensure that presence through those miles; for the tact and gentleness deployed—across several departments of a large hospital—to get procedures programmed at the earliest, all without scuppering a long-awaited book tour; for gentle skill in finding elusive veins; for transfusions of optimism;

Dr Emmanuelle Bourrat: for being a captain extraordinaire in EB research and care; for her rigour and dedication in coordinating that care across several departments and hospitals; for her attentiveness to all the related EB-critters, big and small, nipping at heels; for trying to ensure, always, that the disease does not submerge identity; for her delight in patients' achievements outside hospital;

Christine Chevrier, Hafsoiti Hassan Djohar, Isabelle Lafay, Christine Laborde, Célia Liron, Dr Arnaud Rigolet, and their colleagues at Hôpital Saint-Louis; Dr De la Dure-Molla, Judith Juste, and Dr Paul-Armand Chaudru de Raynal at Hôpital Rothschild; Dr Florence Zembra: for continuing to keep me somewhat functional, even these last eighteen months; for prompt help and resourcefulness in dealing with the triffids, which pullulated during this time; for immense generosity of time;

Dr Mallika Amellou, Isabelle Assier, Dr Bethsabée Benadon, Dalia Cissako, Dr Hélène Corté, Hawa Dial, Samira Mezouar, Nadja Sondarjee, Honorine Villard, Dr Stéphane Villiers, and others at the Sénopôle of Hôpital Saint-Louis: for joining forces with the teams above; for kindness and great reactivity; for shaping cancer treatment around the spiny contours of RDEB, as far as possible;

Dr Golan Haji and Mr Bhaskar Gopakumar: for breadth and generosity of knowledge; for the ability and patience to break down their knowledge into digestible bytes for non-professionals; for quiet support all through my mulish reactions to test results;

Philippe Bruguière: for being there, week after week, by hospital doors, after surgery, chemo, radiation, pain management . . .; for staying back in Paris during all three lockdowns just for that; for farsightedly sourcing N95 masks right before they became rarer and dearer than a unicorn's mane; for endless treats of artisanal chocolate to mark each milestone of treatment; for engrossing discussions on Connected History and Indo-Persian syncretism through the music and miniatures, and so much more;

Sabine Kasbarian: for ensuring hospital pick-ups and drop-offs pre- and post-surgery these twenty-four years, despite their tiresomely increased frequency since 2020; for homemade tiramisu and crêpes as incentives for treatment; for taking me along to COVID-regulation-friendly, limited-access performances and dances whenever possible;

Isabelle Pichon-Varin and Nicolas Renault, Claire Delcroix, Stéphanie Harvier, Philippe Crespin, Martine Depagniat, Marielle Morin, Johanna Blayac: for vital, practical help and countless hours of vibrant discussion; for walking with me, literally and figuratively, since February 2020, armed with medical certificates—through lockdowns and fines, curfews and enthusiastic cops; for ensuring laundry- and pharmacy-runs, home maintenance, and grocery supplies while I could not; for scouring town to find essential provisions during the first, panicky phase of the lockdown; for a steady stream of delicacies, from homemade dorayaki to brioche to matcha cubes encased in dark chocolate, in a bid to retrieve the kilos lost to chemo.

Françoise Gillard: for bringing *Le Tigre de Miel* to magical life on the digital platform of the Comédie-Française; for frequent reminders that there was still more to the year than a dysfunctional body; for supplies of excellent confectionery and thought;

Mélanie Aron, Éric Auzoux, Marion Bastien, Chantal Berthoud, Willy Cessa, Awatef Chengal, Ginette Dansereau, Caroline Delaporte, Lies Doms, Oonagh Duckworth, Emmanuelle de Varax, Fabienne Gaudin, Christine Gurreri, David Jays, Girija Kaimal, Mira Kamdar, Wanjiru Kamuyu, Christine Lalou, Charlene Lim, James O'Hara, Daisy Phillips, Marek Pomocki, Dawn Prentice, Sunithi Bhandari and Lakshman Rao, Nicolas Six, Isabella Spirig, Laurie Uprichard, Françoise Vanhems, Cécile Vasseur, Honji Wang and Sébastien Ramirez, Laetiţia Zecchini: for being only a phone call, or parcel, or—whenever possible—a sanitised visit or rehearsal away, whatever the latitude; for sending food for laughter and thought and, inevitably, taste buds;

Christine Cornet, Bruno Plasse, Jill Schoolman, Emma Raddatz, Sophie Giraud, Joëlle Jolivet, Dominique Vitalyos: for exciting new literary projects and suggestions, all through this time; for vast reserves of cheerful energy;

David Shulman: for the solace and music of *The Inner Life of Dust*; for a glimpse of the magical realm of Panchabhuti kriti; for the quiet, sustained inspiration that he and his comrades at Ta'ayush and the shepherds and cave-dwellers in the South Hebron Hills embody, against all odds, in the face of increasing violence and systemic injustice;

Claire Verlet, Delphine Dupont, Alexia Pick of Théâtre de la Ville: for access to some of the year's most unforgettable moments of dance; for the heady rush of being a tiny, writerly, translatorly cog in the brave, bespoke world of a digital Danse Élargie;

Farooq Chaudhry: for the carte blanche that led to *Where Dragons Dance* taking shape in my head, which is what matters the most;

Gert Van Overloop, Irina Levskovskaya, Jonas Schildermans, Christine Tinlot, and my other colleagues at Eastman: for keeping me embedded in Larbi-land all through the trifecta of Cs; for the biggest box of Pierre Marcolini chocolates to go astray twice before arriving in Louis Blanc three months after dispatch from Antwerp, adding weight to our own variant of Murphy's Law—and to general merriment; for good-heartedness;

Sidi Larbi Cherkaoui: for continuing the tradition of six impossible things before breakfast; for the beauty and chaos, the doubt and the conviction; for making work that—nearly two decades of familiarity later—provides oxygen, punches the gut, and brings a song to my heart, sometimes (as with the timeless *Faun*) all at once;

Eva Kleinitz, Svetlana Rouveure, Ron Deckers: for the courage and grace and honesty they exemplified, even on the worst of days; for having been a part of my life, and shaped it; for still, in many ways, being there;

Swarup B.R.: for irreverence and uncondescending wisdom; for volunteering to keep alarmingly sociable parents out of trouble during a pandemic; for tracing, and liaising with, architects and accountants and tile-layers, for two sets of distant, fastidious kin;

Pramod Kumar K.G.: for being, encore et toujours; for celebrating this book although none of it, for once, was written at his dining table; for all the book hampers sent for fabular research—and solace;

Anand Murty, Rahul Soni: for happy misanthropy and terrible music videos, and the ability to hold long, droll conversations through iMessages;

Sankar Mohan Radhakrishnan: for the reliable regularity of our conversations, which were a soothing reminder of things the pandemic did not upend;

Jai Arjun Singh: for continued Mahabharata-obsession, this time transmuted into a course on its stage and celluloid adaptations; for the many hours spent preparing for the course, especially those marvelling together at *Mayabazar*; for reading, and insightfully responding to, myriad writing, from galley proofs to early, unfinished drafts;

Nilanjana Roy, Salil Tripathi, Prem Panicker, Karthika V.K., Ajitha G.S., Anita Roy: for writing and calling, systematically, caringly, from various parts of the globe; for roping me into their literary ventures, long-distance;

Amma and Achan: for reading Vaikom Muhammed Basheer's *Mathilukal* to me over Skype, thus bridging both distance and time; for their unconscious reminder that the pandemic should not determine some equations;

Deepak Unnikrishnan: for prose that coruscates, each time; for gallons of Apple Cloudy and anecdotal goodies that alchemised a six-hour airport wait; for the ghastly awesomeness that is Onam Bo-Che, and other unusual—yet effective—analgesics, like a post-post-post-modern photo portrait of Casper-the-ghost-via-Munch to combat nausea; for the space and time, the breath, to acknowledge exhaustion, despair, and galactic levels of unknowing;

Sanjoy Roy: for remaining my 3:00 a.m. person, the pandemic notwithstanding, not just on design and layout and form and structure, whether in poetry or dance or now prose, but when triffids strike; for the wicked blood-brain barrier breaches; for the dispatch of fictional chocolate/dragon delights, in the absence of shared meals in either of our cities.

Alison Harris

MARILYN HACKER is the author of fourteen books of poems, including *Blazons* and *A Stranger's Mirror* (longlisted for the 2015 National Book Award); a collaborative book, *Diaspo/Renga*, written with Deema K. Shehabi; and an essay collection, *Unauthorized Voices*. Her eighteen translations of French and Francophone poets include Samira Negrouche's *The Olive Trees' Jazz*, Jean-Paul de Dadelsen's *That Light, All at Once*, and Claire Malroux's *Daybreak*. She is a former editor of the *Kenyon Review* and of the French literary journal *Siècle 21*. She received the 2009 PEN Award for Poetry in Translation for Marie Etienne's *King of a Hundred Horsemen*, the 2010 PEN/Voelcker Award for her own work, and the international Argana Prize for Poetry from the Beit as-Sh'ir/House of Poetry in Morocco in 2011. She lives in Paris.

Koen Broos

KARTHIKA NAÏR is a poet, playwright, fabulist and librettist. *Until the Lions: Echoes from the Mahabharata*, her reworking of the foundational South Asian epic in multiple voices, won the 2015 Tata Literature Live! award for Book of the Year (Fiction). *Les Oiseaux électriques de Pothakudi* —illustrated by Joëlle Jolivet—won the 2023 Prix Felipé for 'ecological children's literature', and was shortlisted for the 2023 Jugendliteraturpreis.

The performances she has scripted and co-scripted include Urja Desai Thakore's *ROOH: Within Her* (2024); *PETTEE: Storybox* (2024) with novelist Deepak Unnikrishnan; Carlos Pons Guerra's *Mariposa* (2022), a queer reimagining of Puccini's opera *Madame Butterfly*; and Akram Khan's multiple-award-winning *DESH* (2011), whose central, animated sequence adapts her book *The Honey Hunter*.

Naïr is the co-founder of choreographer Sidi Larbi Cherkaoui's dance company, Eastman. In 2012, she blueprinted the biannual Prakriti Excellence in Contemporary Dance Awards (PECDA) for Prakriti Foundation, a unique initiative for dance in the Indian subcontinent, and she remained its artistic director across four biannual editions.

»Hören Sie nicht auf die verlockenden Versprechen von Vermögensverwaltern oder Investoren – lesen Sie dieses Buch!«
WARREN BUFFETT

Das kleine Handbuch des VERNÜNFTIGEN INVESTIERENS

An der Börse endlich sichere Gewinne erzielen

JOHN C. BOGLE
Gründer von Vanguard, dem zweitgrößten Vermögensverwalter der Welt

FBV

Bibliografische Information der Deutschen Nationalbibliothek
Die Deutsche Nationalbibliothek verzeichnet diese Publikation in der Deutschen Nationalbibliografie. Detaillierte bibliografische Daten sind im Internet über https://dnb.de abrufbar.

Für Fragen und Anregungen:
info@m-vg.de

7. Auflage 2025

Türkenstraße 89
80799 München
Tel.: 089 651285-0

Die englische Originalausgabe erschien 2007 bei John Wiley & Sons, Inc. unter dem Titel *The Little Book of Common Sense Investing*.

Übersetzung: Petra Pyka
Redaktion: Marion Reuter
Umschlaggestaltung: Melanie Kretschmer, in Anlehnung an das englische Original (Coverdesign: Wiley)
Satz: Daniel Förster, Belgern
Druck: GGP Media GmbH, Pößneck
Printed in Germany

Wir produzieren nachhaltig
www.m-vg.de

ISBN Print 978-3-95972-132-5
ISBN E-Book (EPUB, Mobi) 978-3-96092-236-0

Inhalt

Lobende Stimmen zu *Das kleine Handbuch des vernünftigen Investierens*

»Jack Bogles Ausnahmekarriere deckt die gesamte Bandbreite ab, vom einsamen Bilderstürmer bis zum gefeierten Rockstar. Seine Vision und die Entwicklung der Indexfonds veränderte die Investmentwelt – für Privatanleger ebenso wie für institutionelle Investoren. Jack ist es zu verdanken, dass Abermillionen von Anlegern Indexfonds **gekauft** haben. Doch es reicht nicht, nur einen Index nachzubilden. Erfolgreiche Investoren verinnerlichen auch die Prinzipien, die Indexfonds zugrunde liegen, und durchschauen die Fallstricke, die der effektiven Ausführung eines Investmentplans entgegenstehen. *Das kleine Handbuch des vernünftigen Investierens* liefert das nötige Rüstzeug für die Umsetzung einer erfolgreichen Portfoliostrategie. Lesen Sie es und gewinnen Sie!«

DAVID. F. SWENSEN,
CHIEF INVESTMENT OFFICER, YALE UNIVERSITY

»Was Gutenberg für den Buchdruck war, Henry Ford für die Autoproduktion und Shakespeare für die englische Sprache, das ist Jack Bogle für Finanzen. *Das kleine Handbuch des vernünftigen Investierens* fasst auf nur 267 Seiten die Genialität der 70 Jahre zusammen, in denen er den Prozess für alle revolutioniert hat, vom kleinsten Sparer bis zum größten Pensions- und Treuhandfonds. Ein Lesespaß, von dem Sie nebenbei gewaltig profitieren können.«

William J. Bernstein,
Autor des Bestsellers *The Investor's Manifesto: Preparing for Prosperity, Armageddon, and Everything in Between*

»In hundert Jahren werden die Historiker nur mehr zwei Investoren aus unserer Zeit kennen: Warren Buffett und Jack Bogle. Und welche Bücher? Buffets Bibel, *Intelligent Investieren* von Ben Graham und … alles von Jack Bogle. In einer Welt der Anlagefüchse ist Jack nach wie vor der unerschütterliche Igel. *Das kleine Handbuch des vernünftigen Investierens,* in dieser Auflage aktualisiert, wird sich als zeitlos erweisen, weil es Bogles große Idee artikuliert – nämlich, wie sich Anleger den Anteil am Marktertrag sichern können, der ihnen zusteht.«

Steve Galbraith,
geschäftsführender Gesellschafter, Kindred Capital

»Jack Bogles *Kleines Handbuch* steckt voller Weisheit. Es ist informativ, kenntnisreich und unkonventionell – und darüber hinaus auch noch zutreffend! Wie Bogle deutlich macht, ist die Straße zu Anlageverlusten gepflastert mit teuren Ratschlägen, teuren Investitionen und teurer Werbung (für teure Ratschläge und teure Investitionen). Bogle empfiehlt Anlegern einen ganz anderen Ansatz, der den Anlageerfolg praktisch garantiert.«

TED ARONSON,
GRÜNDER, AJO PARTNERS

»Das beste Buch zum Thema Geldanlage, das ich je gelesen habe. John Bogles bodenständiger Anlageansatz ist leicht nachvollziehbar und äußerst lukrativ. Ich wünschte, ich hätte ihn vor 25 Jahren gekannt! Sehr zu empfehlen!«

DUANE MEYERS,
EINZELANLEGER AUS WEST RICHLAND, WASHINGTON.
AMAZON-REZENSENT DER ERSTEN AUFLAGE 2007

Zur Erinnerung an den verstorbenen
Paul A. Samuelson, Wirtschaftsprofessor
am Massachusetts Institute of Technology,
Nobelpreisträger und Investmentexperte

Als ich 1948 an der Princeton University studierte, machte mich sein Lehrbuchklassiker mit der Wirtschaftswissenschaft vertraut. 1974 entfachten seine Schriften mein Interesse an der Indexnachbildung als Anlagestrategie neu. 1976 äußerte er sich in seiner Kolumne in der *Newsweek* beifällig zu meiner Einführung des weltweit ersten Indexfonds. 1993 schrieb er das Vorwort zu meinem ersten Buch, und 1999 leistete er mir kräftige Unterstützung bei meinem zweiten. Er ist im Jahr 2009 verstorben, doch ist mir weiter Mentor, Inspiration und Lichtgestalt.

Vorwort zur zehnten Jubiläumsausgabe

Damit aus Gewinnern keine Verlierer werden

Erfolgreiche Kapitalanlage steht und fällt mit dem gesunden Menschenverstand. Wie Warren Buffett, das Orakel von Omaha, sagte, ist das zwar einfach, aber gar nicht so leicht. Einfache Arithmetik lässt vermuten, was die Geschichte bestätigt: Die Erfolgsstrategie für die Anlage in Aktien ist es, alle Aktiengesellschaften des Landes zu möglichst niedrigen Kosten zu halten. Das garantiert Ihnen, dass Sie in Form von Dividenden und Gewinnsteigerungen nahezu vom gesamten Ertrag profitieren, den diese Unternehmen erwirtschaften.

Diese Strategie ist im Grunde ganz einfach umzusetzen: *Kaufen Sie einen Fonds, der dieses Gesamtmarktportfolio abbildet, und halten Sie ihn ewig*. Ein solcher Fonds wird als Indexfonds bezeichnet.

Der Indexfonds ist schlicht ein Korb (Portfolio), in dem viele Eier (Aktien) liegen, und der die übergreifende Wertentwicklung des US-amerikanischen Aktienmarkts (oder eines beliebigen Finanzmarkts oder Marktsektors) nachbildet.* Der traditionelle Indexfonds repräsentiert per definitionem im Grunde den gesamten Aktienmarktkorb, nicht nur ein paar einzelne Eier. Dadurch wird das mit der Einzeltitelauswahl verbundene Risiko ebenso eliminiert wie das mit einem Schwerpunkt auf bestimmten Marktsektoren verbundene Risiko und das Risiko der Managerauswahl.

Bleibt nur noch das Aktienmarktrisiko. (Und das ist wahrhaftig groß genug!) Dass Indexfonds auf kurze Sicht wenig aufregend sind, machen sie durch ihre höchst spektakuläre langfristige Produktivität wett. So ein traditioneller Indexfonds ist darauf ausgelegt, ein Leben lang gehalten zu werden.

Der Indexfonds schaltet die mit der Auswahl einzelner Aktien, Marktsektoren und Manager verbundenen Risiken aus – bleibt nur das Marktrisiko

Doch dieses Buch ist mehr als ein Buch über Indexfonds. Es soll verändern, wie Sie über Geldanlage denken. Es erklärt, warum Ihnen langfristige Anlagen viel bessere Dienste leisten als kurzfristige Spekulation. Es erläutert den Wert der Diversifizierung, die wichtige Rolle der Anlagekosten und die Gefahren, die mit

* Sie wissen ja: Ein Index kann auch für den Rentenmarkt oder aber für weniger frequentierte Anlageklassen wie Rohstoffe oder Immobilien aufgelegt werden. Wenn Sie möchten, können Sie heute Ihr gesamtes Vermögen in ein breit gestreutes Portfolio kostengünstiger traditioneller Indexfonds investieren, in dem alle Anlageklassen und Marktsektoren in den USA und weltweit vertreten sind.

dem Vertrauen auf die bisherige Wertentwicklung eines Fonds verbunden sind, und mit dem Ignorieren des Grundsatzes der *Rückkehr (oder Regression) zum Mittelwert (Reversion to the Mean, kurz RTM)* in der Kapitalanlage. Und schließlich erfahren Sie noch, wie die Finanzmärkte funktionieren.

Haben Sie das alles durchschaut, werden Sie erkennen, dass der Indexfonds tatsächlich die einzige Anlageform ist, die Ihnen im Grunde garantiert, dass Sie Ihren gerechten Anteil an den Erträgen erhalten, die die Unternehmen erwirtschaften. Dank des wundersamen Zinseszinseffekts ist das Vermögen, das diese Erträge über die Jahre abgeworfen haben, geradezu märchenhaft.

Der traditionelle Indexfonds

Ich spreche hier vom traditionellen Indexfonds. So ein TIF ist breit gestreut und hält den ganzen (oder fast den ganzen) Anteil an der US-Aktienmarktkapitalisierung, die Anfang 2017 26 Billionen US-Dollar betrug. Für seinen Betrieb fallen minimale Kosten und keine Beratungsgebühren an. Der Portfolioumschlag ist gering, der steuerliche Optimierungseffekt hoch. Der traditionelle Indexfonds – der erste seiner Art bildete den Standard & Poor's 500 Index nach – hält schlicht die Aktien der dominanten amerikanischen Unternehmen. Er beteiligt sich an jeder Aktie auf dem Markt in Relation zu ihrer Marktkapitalisierung und hält sie dann für alle Zeit.

Die Magie der kumulierten Anlageerträge, die Tyrannei der kumulierten Kosten

Bitte unterschätzen Sie nicht den Kumulationseffekt der großzügigen Erträge, die unsere Unternehmen erwirtschaften. Nehmen wir an, die Aktien unserer Unternehmen werfen im Jahr 7 Prozent Rendite ab. Rechnet man einen ursprünglich investierten Dollar über zehn Jahre mit diesem Satz hoch, dann werden daraus zwei – und nach 20 Jahren vier Dollar, nach 30 Jahren 7,50 Dollar, nach 40 Jahren 15,00 Dollar und nach 50 Jahren 30,00 Dollar.*

Die magische Wirkung dieses Effekts grenzt an ein Wunder. Schlicht gesagt ist es dem Wachstum, der Produktivität, dem Einfallsreichtum und der Innovationsfähigkeit unserer Unternehmen zu verdanken, dass Kapitalismus Vermögen schafft – *für dessen Eigentümer ein Spiel mit positiven Vorzeichen. Die Aktienanlage bringt langfristig Gewinn.*

Die von den Unternehmen erwirtschafteten Gewinne übersetzen sich letztlich in Aktienmarkterträge. Ich habe keine Ahnung, welchen Anteil dieser Erträge Sie sich bisher sichern konnten. Wissenschaftliche Studien belegen jedoch, dass ein typischer Anleger, der in einzelne Aktien investiert, etwa 2 Prozentpunkte pro Jahr hinter dem Markt herhinkt.

---

* In den letzten hundert Jahren betrug der durchschnittliche Nominalertrag von US-Aktien 10,1 Prozent pro Jahr. Effektiv (also nach Abzug von 3,4 Prozent Inflation) lag die *reale* Jahresrendite bei 6,7 Prozent. Im anstehenden Jahrzehnt dürften diese beiden Werte voraussichtlich deutlich niedriger ausfallen. (Nachzulesen im neunten Kapitel).

Wenden wir diese Zahl auf die Jahresrendite des Standard & Poor's 500 Stock Index für die letzten 25 Jahre von 9,1 Prozent an, dann bewegt sich Ihr Jahresergebnis vermutlich in der Größenordnung von 7 Prozent. Ergebnis: Als Gruppe wurden den Anlegern nur rund drei Viertel des Marktkuchens serviert. Hinzu kommt, wie im siebten Kapitel näher erläutert: Als typischer Investmentfondsanleger haben Sie noch schlechter abgeschnitten.

Ein Nullsummenspiel?

Wenn Sie nicht glauben, dass dies die Renditen sind, die die meisten Anleger erzielen, dann denken Sie bitte kurz über die »unerbittlichen Regeln der einfachen Arithmetik« nach (viertes Kapitel). Diese eisernen Regeln bestimmen das Spiel. Wir Anleger als Gruppe erzielen den Aktienmarktertrag.

Als Gruppe – und ich hoffe, Sie sitzen gut, wenn Sie diese verblüffende Offenbarung lesen – sind wir Anleger Durchschnitt. Für jeden Prozentpunkt Überrendite über den Markt, den einer von uns erwirtschaftet, verbucht ein anderer einen Fehlbetrag in gleicher Höhe. *Vor Abzug der Anlagekosten ist es ein Nullsummenspiel, den Aktienmarkt zu schlagen.*

Ein Spiel für Verlierer

Wenn die Anleger versuchen, ihre Vergleichsgruppe zu überrunden, entsprechen die Gewinne der Erfolgreichen unweigerlich den Einbußen der Verlierer. An dem fieberhaften Handel im kostspieligen Wettbewerb um Überrenditen verdient nur, wer im Zentrum unseres Finanzsystems sitzt. Wie Warren Buffett unlängst schrieb: »Wenn Billionen Dollar von Börsianern verwaltet werden, die hohe Gebühren verlangen, dann sind es gewöhnlich die Verwalter, die unverhältnismäßig profitieren, nicht die Kunden.«

Im Kasino gewinnt immer die Bank. Beim Pferderennen stets die Rennbahn. Beim Lotto grundsätzlich der Staat. Das ist in der Kapitalanlage nicht anders. Bei diesem Spiel gewinnt in jedem Fall der Finanzcroupier. Die Anleger als Gruppe verlieren. *Nach Abzug der Anlagekosten bringt es Verluste, den Aktienmarkt zu schlagen.*

Weniger für die Wall-Street-Croupiers = mehr für die Masse der Anleger

Erfolgreiche Kapitalanlage ist daher, den Anteil an den von unseren Unternehmen erwirtschafteten Gewinnen, den die Wall Street kassiert, zu minimieren, und den Anteil, der auf das breite Anlegerpublikum entfällt, zu maximieren. (Und damit meine ich *Sie*, werte Leser.)

Ihre Aussichten auf den Ihnen zustehenden Anteil am Marktertrag steigen beträchtlich, wenn Sie den Handel mit Aktien minimieren. Eine wissenschaftliche Studie machte deutlich, dass das aktivste Fünftel aller Aktienhändler in dem kräftigen Bullenmarkt von 1990 bis 1996 einen Portfolioumschlag von über 21 Prozent pro Monat verzeichnete. Sie erwirtschafteten den jährlichen Marktertrag dieser Haussephase von 17,9 Prozent, doch die anfallenden Handelskosten schlugen mit rund 6,5 Prozent zu Buche, sodass sie unter dem Strich 11,4 Prozent pro Jahr einstreichen konnten – lediglich zwei Drittel des Marktertrags.

Auch Investmentfondsanleger haben oft verstiegene Vorstellungen von der eigenen Allwissenheit. Sie wählen Fonds danach aus, ob der Fondsmanager in der letzten Zeit – oder auch langfristig – überdurchschnittliche Ergebnisse erzielte. Oft beauftragen sie noch Berater, um ihnen dabei zu helfen (die »Helfer«, von denen Warren Buffett im Folgekapitel spricht). Doch wie ich im zwölften Kapitel näher erkläre, sind die Berater noch weniger erfolgreich. Allzu viele Fondsanleger achten überhaupt nicht auf die Kosten und bezahlen bereitwillig hohe Emissionsaufschläge, überzogene Fondsgebühren und Aufwendungen. Dabei unterliegen sie außerdem noch unwissentlich den erheblichen, aber undurchsichtigen Transaktionskosten, die bei den Fonds infolge ihres hyperaktiven Portfolioumschlags anfallen. Fondsanleger meinen, sie könnten beständig überdurchschnittliche Fondsmanager auswählen. *Doch sie irren sich.*

Fondsanleger sind überzeugt, dass sie jederzeit herausragende Fondsmanager auswählen können – weit gefehlt

Ganz im Gegenteil. Wer Geld investiert und dann aus dem Spiel aussteigt, ohne unnötige Kosten zu übernehmen, dessen Erfolgschancen sind atemberaubend. Warum? Ganz einfach: Weil er Anteile an *Unternehmen* besitzt, und Unternehmen als Gruppe mit ihrem Kapital beträchtliche Erträge erwirtschaften, ihren Aktionären Dividenden zahlen und die restlichen Gewinne in künftiges Wachstum investieren.

Richtig, viele Unternehmen scheitern. Firmen, die auf falsche Ideen und starre Strategien setzen und nicht kompetent geführt werden, fallen letztlich der *schöpferischen Zerstörung* zum Opfer, die das Wahrzeichen eines wettbewerbsorientierten Kapitalismus ist. Doch ihnen folgen andere Unternehmen.* Insgesamt aber sind Unternehmen mit dem langfristigen Wachstum unserer dynamischen Wirtschaft mitgewachsen. Seit 1929 hat sich das Bruttoinlandsprodukt (BIP) der USA mit einer nominalen Jahresrate von 6,2 Prozent gesteigert. Die jährlichen Vorsteuergewinne unserer Unternehmen sind mit einer Rate von 6,3 Prozent angewachsen. Die Korrelation zwischen BIP-Wachstum und Anstieg der Unternehmensgewinne beträgt 0,98 (mit 1,0 wäre sie vollkommen). Ich gehe davon aus, dass diese langfristige Beziehung auch in den kommenden Jahren fortbesteht.

Raus aus dem Kasino! Ein für alle Mal!

Dieses Buch will Ihnen zeigen, warum Sie nicht länger die Croupiers der Finanzmärkte reich machen sollten: nämlich, weil sie in den letzten zehn Jahren von Ihnen und Ihresgleichen jedes Jahr rund 565 Milliarden Dollar kassiert haben. Ich verrate Ihnen

---

* »Schöpferische Zerstörung« ist eine Formulierung von Joseph E. Schumpeter aus seinem 1942 erschienenen Buch *Kapitalismus, Sozialismus und Demokratie*.

auch, wie leicht Sie diese Croupiers meiden können: Indem Sie einfach einen Fonds auf den Standard & Poor's 500 Index oder einen anderen Indexfonds auf den gesamten Aktienmarkt kaufen. Und sobald Sie Ihren Einsatz platziert haben, sollten Sie das Kasino schleunigst verlassen – und zwar endgültig. Halten Sie Ihr Marktportfolio einfach unbeirrt weiter. Nichts anderes tun traditionelle Indexfonds.

Ganz einfach, aber gar nicht so leicht

Diese Anlagephilosophie besticht nicht nur durch ihre schlichte Eleganz. Ihre mathematischen Grundlagen sind einfach unwiderlegbar. Aber es ist nicht ganz leicht, die nötige Disziplin zu wahren. Solange wir Anleger den Status quo unseres heutigen flickenteppichartigen Finanzmarktsystems akzeptieren und solange es uns Spaß macht, Aktien zu kaufen und zu verkaufen (zu welchen Kosten auch immer), und solange wir nicht erkennen, dass es eine bessere Methode gibt, wird eine solche Philosophie immer unserem Bauchgefühl zuwiderlaufen. Doch ich fordere Sie auf, sich die leidenschaftliche Aussage dieses kleinen Handbuchs zu Herzen zu nehmen. Tun Sie das, werden auch Sie sich der Index-Revolution anschließen und Ihr Geld auf neue, »wirtschaftlichere, effizientere, ja, ehrlichere Weise« anlegen* – auf produktivere Weise, die in erster Linie Ihren Interessen dient.

---

* »Wirtschaftlich«, »effizient« und »ehrlich« sind die Begriffe, die ich 1951 in meiner Abschlussarbeit »The Economic Role of the Investment Company an der Princeton University« verwendete. Manche Prinzipien gelten ewig.

Thomas Paine und der gesunde Menschenverstand

Es mag vermessen von mir sein, zu hoffen, dass ein Buch den Funken auslösen kann, um eine Revolution in der Kapitalanlage zu entfachen. Neue Ideen, die allem widersprechen, was der gerade gängigen Meinung entspricht, werden stets mit Argwohn und Verachtung, ja sogar mit Angst aufgenommen. Schon vor 240 Jahren stand Thomas Paine vor demselben Problem. 1776 trug sein Traktat *Common Sense* dazu bei, die Amerikanische Revolution auszulösen. Und das hat Tom Paine geschrieben:

> »Vielleicht sind die auf den Folgeseiten enthaltenen Gedanken noch nicht modern genug, um ihnen allgemeine Zustimmung zu sichern. Dass man etwas lange Zeit nicht für falsch hielt, verleiht ihm oberflächlich den Eindruck, richtig zu sein, und löst zunächst einen wilden Aufschrei zur Verteidigung des Überlieferten aus. Doch der Tumult legt sich bald. Die Zeit bekehrt besser als die Vernunft. … Ich habe hier nur schlichte Fakten zu präsentieren, einfache Argumente und gesunden Menschenverstand.«

Wie wir wissen, setzten sich Thomas Paines überzeugende und wohlgesetzte Argumente am Ende durch. Die Amerikanische Revolution brachte uns unsere Verfassung, die bis heute die Aufgaben unserer Regierung und unserer Bürger festlegt – das Grundgerüst unserer Gesellschaft.

Ich bin überzeugt, dass sich meine schlichten Fakten, einfachen Argumente und der gesunde Menschenverstand auch bei den Anlegern im kommenden Zeitalter durchsetzen werden. Die

Index-Revolution wird dazu beitragen, ein neues, effizienteres Anlagesystem für unser Land aufzubauen – ein System, das in erster Linie den Anlegern dient.

Struktur und Strategie

Manche könnten behaupten, dass ich sowohl als Gründer von Vanguard im Jahr 1974 als auch als Erfinder des ersten Indexfonds 1975 ein persönliches Interesse daran habe, Sie von meinen Ansichten zu überzeugen. *Natürlich!* Aber nicht etwa, um mich zu bereichern. Ich verdiene daran keinen Penny. Ich möchte Sie vielmehr deshalb überzeugen, weil die beiden Grundpfeiler, auf denen Vanguard vor all den Jahren gegründet wurde – unsere wirklich wechselseitige anteilsinhabereigene Fondsstruktur und unsere Indexfondsstrategie – *Sie* auf lange Sicht reicher macht.

Wenn Sie mir nicht glauben ...

In der Frühzeit der Indexnachbildung war ich ein einsamer Rufer in der Wüste. Es gab aber ein paar weitere tiefsinnige, angesehene Anhänger dieser Methode, deren Ideen mich dazu inspirierten, an meiner Mission festzuhalten. Heute sprechen sich viele unserer klügsten und erfolgreichsten Investoren für das Indexfondskonzept aus, das in der Wissenschaft nahezu universell akzeptiert wird. *Doch mir müssen Sie das nicht glauben.* Hören Sie, was diese unabhängigen Fachleute zu sagen haben, denen es ausschließlich um die Wahrheit über die Kapitalanlage geht. Einer von ihnen kommt am Ende jedes Kapitels zu Wort.

Zuspruch äußerte beispielsweise der mittlerweile verstorbene Paul A. Samuelson, Wirtschaftsnobelpreisträger und Wirtschaftsprofessor am Massachusetts Institute of Technology, dessen Andenken dieses Buch gewidmet ist:

»Bogles wohlbegründete Regeln können es Millionen von uns Sparern ermöglichen, in 20 Jahren den Neid der Nachbarn in unserer Stadtrandsiedlung auf uns zu ziehen – während wir in dieser ereignisreichen Zeit immer ruhig schlafen können.«

Es wird lange dauern, unser Finanzsystem zu sanieren. Doch der quälend langsame Wandel sollte Sie nicht davon abhalten, Ihre eigenen Interessen wahrzunehmen. Sie müssen sich nicht am kostspieligen Irrsinn beteiligen. Wenn Sie sich für das gewinnbringende Spiel entscheiden, Aktien von Unternehmen zu halten, und sich aus dem verlustreichen Spiel heraushalten, den Markt zu schlagen, dann können Sie diese Aufgabe ganz einfach angehen, indem Sie Ihren gesunden Menschenverstand einschalten, das System durchschauen und im Wesentlichen alle überflüssigen Kosten eliminieren.

Dann ist Ihnen schließlich der Ihnen zustehende Anteil an den Erträgen sicher, die unsere Unternehmen in den kommenden Jahren so großzügig erwirtschaften und die sich jeweils in unseren Aktien- und Rentenmärkten widerspiegeln. (Doch seien Sie gewarnt: Sie werden zwischenzeitlich auch den Ihnen zustehenden Anteil an eintretenden Verlusten tragen müssen.) Wenn Sie das begriffen haben, werden Sie erkennen, dass es nur eine Frage der Vernunft ist.

Die zehnte Jubiläumsausgabe des *Kleinen Handbuchs des vernünftigen Investierens*

Als vor zehn Jahren die erste Auflage des *Kleinen Handbuchs des vernünftigen Investierens* erschien, hatte ich die Hoffnung, dass es die Anleger nützlich finden würden, um sich ihren Anteil an den – positiven wie negativen – Erträgen zu sichern, die unsere Finanzmärkte abwerfen.

Dieses erste *Kleine Handbuch* aus dem Jahr 2007 war ein direkter Nachfolger meines ersten Buches, *Bogle on Mutual Funds: New Perspectives for the Intelligent Investor*, das 1994 veröffentlicht wurde. Beide Bücher argumentierten für Indexnachbildung, und beide entwickelten sich zu den absoluten Bestsellern unter Büchern über Investmentfonds. Insgesamt kauften die Anleger davon über 500.000 Exemplare.

In den fast 25 Jahren seit dem Erscheinen meines ersten Buches haben sich Indexfonds freigeschwommen. Das in Aktienindexfonds investierte Vermögen hat sich ver-168-facht – von 28 Milliarden US-Dollar auf 4,6 Billionen US-Dollar Mitte 2017. Allein in den vergangenen zehn Jahren haben US-Anleger ihre Bestände in Aktienindexfonds um 2,1 Billionen US-Dollar aufgestockt und über 900 Milliarden US-Dollar aus Positionen in aktiv gemanagten Aktienfonds abgezogen. Eine solch gewaltige Verschiebung der Anlegerpräferenz in der Größenordnung von 3 Billionen US-Dollar darf sicherlich als revolutionär bezeichnet werden.

Rückblickend scheint klar, dass ich mit der Auflegung des ersten Indexfonds 1975 als Pionier den Funken ausgelöst habe, der die Index-Revolution entfachte. Ebenso liegt der Schluss nahe, dass meine Bücher, die von schätzungsweise 1,5 Millionen Menschen gelesen wurden, wesentlich zu der erstaunlichen Kraft der anschließenden Revolution beitrugen.

Die von Indexfonds herbeigeführte schöpferische Zerstörung hat den Anlegern im Großen und Ganzen gute Dienste geleistet. Wenn Sie diese zehnte Jubiläumsauflage des *Kleinen Handbuchs des vernünftigen Investierens* lesen, werden Sie feststellen, dass sie nach wie vor fest hinter den soliden Grundsätzen ihrer Vorläufer steht – mit neuen Kapiteln über Dividenden, Vermögensstruktur und Altersvorsorge mit Fokus auf der Umsetzung dieser Prinzipien.

Hoffentlich finden Sie es informativ und unterhaltsam und handeln dann entsprechend.

Valley Forge, Pennsylvania
September 2017

Wenn Sie mir nicht glauben ...

Charles T. Munger, Warren Buffetts Partner bei Berkshire Hathaway, hat es so formuliert:

»Die allgemeinen Systeme der Kapitalverwaltung verlangen [heute] von den Leuten, so zu tun, als könnten sie das Unmögliche leisten – und hätten auch noch Spaß dabei. [Das ist] ein seltsames Geschäft, denn per saldo schafft die gesamte Anlageverwaltungsindustrie für die Gesamtheit der Käufer keinen Mehrwert. *Das muss so sein*. Investmentfonds berechnen 2 Prozent pro Jahr und die Makler, die Umschichtungen vornehmen, kosten weitere drei bis vier Prozentpunkte. Dem breiten Anlegerpublikum leisten die Profis einen Bärendienst. Ich finde das verabscheuungswürdig. Es ist viel besser, Teil eines Systems zu sein, das den Menschen Wert liefert, die das Produkt kaufen.«

Der Anlageberater (und Neurologe) **William Bernstein**, Autor von *The Four Pillars of Investing,* meint darin: »Schlimm genug, dass man das Marktrisiko tragen muss. Nur ein Narr nimmt das zusätzliche Risiko auf sich, noch mehr Schaden zu erleiden, indem er sein Kapital nicht richtig streut. Vermeiden Sie diesen Fehler – kaufen Sie einen gut geführten Indexfonds, mit dem Sie auf den Gesamtmarkt setzen.«

Und das schreibt der Londoner *Economist:* »In Wirklichkeit haben die Fondsmanager größtenteils ein ausgesprochen schlechtes Preis-Leistungs-Verhältnis geboten. Auf erzielte Überrenditen folgen fast immer Phasen mit Ertragsrückständen. Langfristig hat kaum ein Fondsmanager jeden Marktdurchschnitt geschlagen. … Und die ganze Zeit über berechnen sie ihren Kunden hohe Gebühren für das Privileg, ihr Geld zu verspielen. … [Eine] konkrete Lehre … besteht in den Vorzügen der Indexnachbildung. … Einen Fondsmanager, der den Markt wiederholt schlagen kann, werden Sie kaum finden. Besser, Sie investieren in einen Indexfonds, der den Marktertrag verspricht – allerdings zu deutlich niedrigeren Gebühren.«

Wirklich erstaunlich, dass so viele führende Wissenschaftler und zahlreiche der größten Investoren der Welt, die den Markt bekanntermaßen geschlagen haben, die Vorteile der Indexnachbildung bestätigen und hervorheben. Möge ihre Vernunft – vielleicht mehr noch als meine – Sie alle zu klügeren Anlegern machen.

HINWEIS: Leser der *Little Book*-Reihe, die gerne die Quellen für die Zitate aus der ans Ende jedes Kapitels gestellten Rubrik »Wenn Sie mir nicht glauben« sowie andere Zitate aus dem Haupttext und die Quellen für die umfangreichen Daten überprüfen möchten, auf die ich verweise, finden diese auf meiner Website: www.johncbogle.com. Da ich ungern kostbare Seiten dieses kleinen Handbuchs für eine raumgreifende Bibliografie verschwenden möchte, bitte ich Sie, meine Website zu besuchen.

Erstes Kapitel

Die Parabel von der Familie Gotrocks

Bevor Sie über »Indexfonds« nachdenken – in ihrer Urform Investmentfonds, die einfach alle Aktien des US-Aktienmarkts kaufen und ewig halten –, müssen Sie wissen, wie der Aktienmarkt wirklich funktioniert. Vielleicht klärt ja diese volkstümliche Parabel – meine Version der lehrreichen Kurzgeschichte, die Warren Buffett als Chairman von Berkshire Hathaway, Inc. 2005 im Geschäftsbericht seines Unternehmens erzählte –, wie verrückt und kontraproduktiv unser riesiges, komplexes Finanzmarktsystem ist.

Es war einmal …

Die Gotrocks waren eine wohlhabende Familie, aus der über die Generationen Tausende von Brüdern, Schwestern, Tanten, Onkel, Cousins und Cousinen hervorgegangen waren. Ihnen gehörten 100 Prozent aller US-amerikanischen Aktien. Jedes Jahr ernteten sie die Früchte ihrer Anlagen: sämtliche Ertragssteigerungen, welche die vielen tausend Unternehmen erzielten, und sämtliche Dividenden, die sie ausschütteten.* Alle Familienmitglieder wurden im gleichen Tempo reicher, und es herrschte Harmonie. Ihre Anlagen kumulierten sich über die Jahrzehnte und es entstand ein riesiges Vermögen. Die Familie Gotrocks spielte ein Spiel für Gewinner.

Doch irgendwann erscheinen wortgewandte Helfer auf der Bildfläche und reden mehreren »besonders schlauen« Gotrocks-Cousins ein, sie könnten sich einen größeren Anteil sichern als ihre Verwandten. Diese Helfer überreden die Cousins, von ihnen gehaltene Aktien mancher Unternehmen an andere Familienmitglieder zu verkaufen und dafür deren Aktien anderer Unternehmen zu erwerben. Die Helfer führen die Geschäfte aus und erhalten als Makler eine Provision für ihre Dienste. Damit verändern sich die Eigentumsverhältnisse in der Familie. Diese stellt jedoch überrascht fest, dass das Familienvermögen plötzlich langsamer zunimmt. Wieso? Weil ein Teil des Anlageertrags nunmehr den Helfern zufließt und sich der Anteil der Familie an

---

* Um die Sache noch etwas komplizierter zu machen, kaufte die Familie Gotrocks auch noch jedes Jahr alle Aktien auf, die im Zuge von Börsengängen emittiert wurden.

dem großen Kuchen, den die US-Wirtschaft jedes Jahr backt – also alle gezahlten Dividenden und alle in die Unternehmen reinvestierten Gewinne – und der zu Anfang 100 Prozent betrug, verringert, und zwar einfach deshalb, weil ein Teil der Erträge jetzt auf die Helfer entfällt.

Schlimmer noch, neben den Steuern, die die Familie stets auf ihre Dividenden entrichten musste, zahlen manche Familienmitglieder nun auch Steuern auf Veräußerungsgewinne. Durch das Hin- und Herschieben von Aktien entstehen solche Veräußerungsgewinne, die das Gesamtvermögen der Familie weiter dezimieren.

Die cleveren Cousins merken schnell, dass ihr Vorhaben die Wachstumsrate des Familienvermögens in Wirklichkeit verringert. Sie erkennen, dass ihr Stock-Picking-Vorstoß gescheitert ist, und folgern daraus, dass sie fachkundige Unterstützung benötigen, um für sich die richtigen Aktien auszuwählen. Also beauftragen sie Experten mit der Auswahl der Aktien – noch mehr Helfer! –, um sich einen Vorteil zu verschaffen. Diese Kapitalverwalter verlangen ein Honorar für ihre Leistungen. Als die Familie ihr Vermögen ein Jahr später bewertet, stellt sie fest, dass ihr Anteil vom Kuchen weiter geschrumpft ist.

Doch damit nicht genug: Die neuen Verwalter fühlen sich berufen, ihr Geld damit zu verdienen, in hektischer Aktivität mit den Aktien der Familie zu handeln, was nicht nur die an die erste Helfercharge gezahlten Maklerprovisionen in die Höhe treibt, sondern auch die steuerliche Belastung. Dadurch verringert sich der zuvor 100-prozentige Anteil der Familie am Dividenden- und Ertragskuchen noch mehr.

»Tja, es ist uns selbst nicht gelungen, uns die besten Aktien auszusuchen, und als das nicht geklappt hat, haben wir es auch nicht geschafft, Verwalter auszuwählen, die das zuwege bringen konnten«, stellen die schlauen Cousins fest. »Was machen wir nun?« Unbeeindruckt von ihren bisherigen Fehlgriffen beschließen sie, weitere Helfer hinzuzuziehen. Sie lassen sich von den besten Anlageberatern und Finanzplanern, die sie auftreiben können, erklären, wie man die richtigen Verwalter auswählt, die dann sicherlich die richtigen Aktien aussuchen würden. Die Berater versprechen ihnen natürlich, dass sie das können. »Sie müssen lediglich unser Honorar zahlen«, versichern die neuen Helfer den Cousins. »Dann wird alles gut.« Bedauerlicherweise nagen diese Zusatzkosten erneut am Stück der Familie vom großen Kuchen.

Seht zu, dass ihr alle Helfer loswerdet – dann erhält eure Familie wieder 100 Prozent des Kuchens, den die amerikanischen Unternehmen für euch backen

Bei der Familie klingeln endlich die Alarmglocken. Sie setzt sich zusammen und rekapituliert, was passiert ist, seit ein paar wenige versucht haben, klüger zu sein als die anderen. »Wie kann es sein«, fragen sie, »das unsere ursprünglichen 100 Prozent vom Kuchen – die sich jedes Jahr aus allen Dividenden und Erträgen zusammensetzen – auf nur 60 Prozent abgeschmolzen sind?« Das klügste Familienmitglied, ein weiser alter Onkel, entgegnet darauf leise: »Das ganze Geld, das ihr den Helfern gezahlt habt, und die vielen unnötigen Steuern, die ihr entrichten müsst, gehen direkt von den gesamten Erträgen und Dividenden unserer Familie ab. *Geht zurück an den Start, und zwar gleich. Seht zu, dass ihr alle eure Makler loswerdet, alle eure Kapitalverwalter und alle eure Berater.* Dann fallen unserer Familie wieder jedes Jahr 100 Prozent des Kuchens zu, den Amerikas Unternehmen für uns backen – ganz gleich, wie groß er ist.«

Sie befolgten den weisen Rat des alten Onkels und besinnen sich wieder auf ihre ursprüngliche passive, aber produktive Strategie, alle Aktien der amerikanischen Unternehmen zu kaufen und zu halten.

Nichts anderes tut ein Indexfonds.

… und wenn sie nicht gestorben sind, dann leben die Gotrocks noch heute

Indem er Sir Isaac Newtons drei Bewegungsgesetzen ein viertes hinzufügt, formuliert der unvergleichliche Warren Buffett die Moral dieser Geschichte folgendermaßen: Für die Gesamtheit aller Anleger gilt, dass die Erträge abnehmen, wenn die Bewegung zunimmt.

So zutreffend diese kryptische Aussage ist, ich würde noch hinzufügen, dass diese Parabel den grundlegenden Interessenkonflikt zwischen den im Anlagegeschäft Tätigen und all jenen deutlich macht, die in Aktien und Anleihen investieren. Wer von der Geldanlage lebt, wird reich, wenn er seinen Kunden einredet: »Bleibt nicht untätig. Tut etwas.« Die Kunden in ihrer Gesamtheit profitieren aber, wenn sie sich nach dem gegenteiligen Grundsatz richten: »Tut nichts. Bleibt einfach untätig.« Denn nur so können sie sich aus dem verlustreichen Spiel heraushalten, zu versuchen, den Markt zu schlagen.

Wird ein Unternehmen so geführt, dass es in direktem Widerspruch zu den Interessen seiner Kunden steht, ist es nur eine Frage der Zeit, bis das die Kunden merken. Dann setzt der Umschwung ein – und genau dieser Umschwung steckt hinter der Revolution, die sich heute in unserem Finanzsystem vollzieht.

Die Moral der Geschichte von den Gotrocks: Bei erfolgreicher Kapitalanlage geht es darum, Eigentum an Unternehmen zu erwerben und den Gewinn einzustreichen, den die Dividenden und Ertragssteigerungen der Unternehmen unserer Nation – beziehungsweise der ganzen Welt – bringen. *Je größer die Anlageaktivität, desto größer die Kosten für Finanzvermittler und Steuern und desto geringer der Nettoertrag der Aktionäre – also als Gruppe der Eigentümer unserer Unternehmen.* Je geringer die Kosten, welche die Anleger als Gruppe tragen, desto höher der Gewinn, den sie verbuchen können. Ein intelligenter Anleger wird daher, um sich die Gewinne zu sichern, die Unternehmen langfristig erzielen, die Kosten für Finanzvermittler auf ein Minimum reduzieren. Ist doch logisch. Und genau darum geht es bei der Anlage in Indizes. Das ist die zentrale Botschaft dieses Buches.

Wenn Sie mir nicht glauben …

Hören Sie, was **Jack R. Meyer** dazu zu sagen hat, Ex-Vorsitzender der Harvard Management Company und sagenhaft erfolgreicher Finanzjongleur, der das Vermögen des Stiftungsfonds der Harvard University von 8 auf 28 Milliarden US-Dollar vergrößert hat. Er äußerte sich in einem Interview mit der *Business Week* 2004 folgendermaßen: »*Das Anlagegeschäft ist ein einziger großer Schwindel.* Die meisten Leute meinen, sie können Manager finden, die überdurchschnittliche Renditen erzielen, doch die Mehrheit liegt falsch. Ich würde sagen, 85 bis 90 Prozent der Manager verfehlen ihre Referenz-Indizes. Weil sie Honorare verlangen und Transaktionskosten verursachen, steht schon dran, dass sie unter dem Strich Wert vernichten.«

Auf die Frage, ob Privatanleger etwas von Harvard lernen können, entgegnete Meyer: »Allerdings. Erstens: breit streuen. Stellen Sie ein Portfolio zusammen, das viele Anlageklassen abdeckt. Zweitens: Kosten niedrig halten. Das bedeutet, die gefeierten, aber teuren Fonds meiden und stattdessen in kostengünstige Indexfonds investieren. Und schließlich: langfristig anlegen. [Anleger] sollten auf jeden Fall in Indexfonds investieren, um ihre Kosten und ihre steuerliche Belastung gering zu halten. *So viel steht fest.*«

Etwas weniger kontrovers klingen die Ansichten von Princeton-Professor **Burton G. Malkiel,** Autor von *Börsenerfolg ist (k)ein Zufall:* »Indexfonds werfen regelmäßig [jährliche] Renditen ab, die knapp 2 Prozent über denen aktiver Manager liegen. Insgesamt kann aktives Management keine Bruttoerträge erzielen, die den Gesamtmarkt schlagen. Sie müssen daher im Schnitt um den Betrag schlechter abschneiden als die Indizes, der auf solcherlei Aufwendungen und auf Transaktionskosten entfällt.

Erfahrungswerte zeigen schlüssig, dass die Käufer von Indexfonds aller Voraussicht nach bessere Ergebnisse erzielen als der typische Fondsmanager, dessen hohe Beratungsgebühren und erhebliche Portfolioumschläge die Anlagerenditen tendenziell drücken. … Der Indexfonds ist eine vernünftige, zweckdienliche Methode zur Erzielung der Marktrendite – ganz ohne Aufwand und zu minimalen Kosten.«

Zweites Kapitel

Rationaler Überschwang

Warum die Aktionäre so viel verdienen müssen wie die Unternehmen

Die herrliche Parabel über die Familie Gotrocks aus dem ersten Kapitel verdeutlicht die zentrale Realität der Kapitalanlage: »Von heute an bis zum jüngsten Tag können Eigentümer insgesamt nicht mehr verdienen, als was ihre Unternehmen insgesamt erwirtschaften«, so Warren Buffett. Das beste Beispiel dafür ist die Aktiengesellschaft Berkshire Hathaway, die er seit 46 Jahren leitet. Bitte nehmen Sie sich Buffetts Worte zu Herzen:

> »Entwickelt sich eine Aktie vorübergehend besser oder schlechter als das Unternehmen, so profitiert eine begrenzte Zahl von

Aktionären – entweder die Verkäufer oder die Käufer – unverhältnismäßig auf Kosten ihrer Handelspartner. ... Über längere Zeit müssen die Gewinne von Berkshire-Aktionären aber notgedrungen den Gewinnen des Unternehmens entsprechen.«

»Über längere Zeit müssen die Gewinne von ... Aktionären aber notgedrungen den Gewinnen des Unternehmens entsprechen«

Allzu oft lassen Anleger dieses unvergängliche Prinzip außer Acht! Doch die Bilanz spricht eine klare Sprache. Ein Blick auf die Geschichte, wenn wir uns denn die Mühe machen, enthüllt die erstaunliche, aber so wesentliche Verknüpfung zwischen dem kumulierten langfristigen Ertrag von US-Unternehmen – der jährlichen Dividendenrendite zuzüglich der jährlichen Gewinnwachstumsrate – und dem kumulierten Ertrag des Aktienmarkts. Machen Sie sich diesen Sachverhalt kurz bewusst. Erkennen Sie die bestechende Logik dahinter?

Sie brauchen noch Beweise? Werfen Sie einen Blick auf die Zahlen seit Anfang des 20. Jahrhunderts (Abbildung 2.1). Der durchschnittliche Gesamtertrag von Aktien belief sich auf 9,5 Prozent. Alleine der *Anlageertrag* betrug 9,0 Prozent – 4,4 Prozent aus der Dividendenrendite und 4,6 Prozent aus Ertragssteigerungen.

Die Differenz von 0,5 Prozentpunkten pro Jahr ergibt sich aus dem, was ich als *spekulativen* Ertrag bezeichne. Spekulativer Ertrag kann ein positives oder negatives Vorzeichen haben, je nach der Bereitschaft der Anleger, für jeden Dollar Gewinne am En-

ABBILDUNG 2.1 Anlageertrag und Marktertrag – eine Gegenüberstellung: Wachstum von 1 US-Dollar, 1900–2016

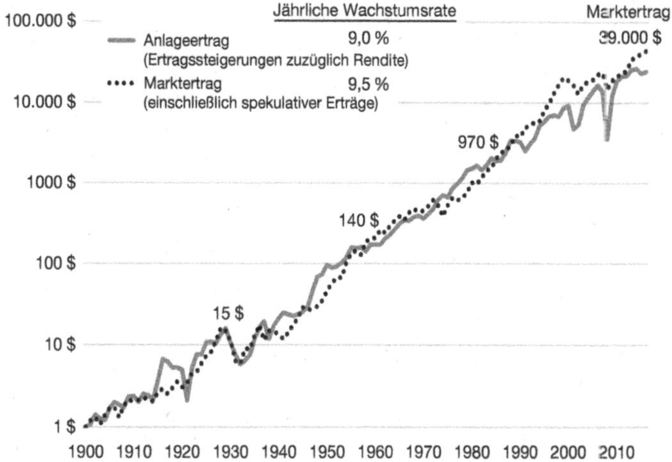

de eines beliebigen Zeitraums höhere oder niedrigere Preise zu zahlen als am Anfang.

Das Kurs-Gewinn-Verhältnis (KGV) misst, wie viele Dollars Anleger für jeden Dollar Gewinn zu zahlen bereit sind. Und mit dem Anlegervertrauen nimmt auch das KGV zu und ab.* Herrscht Hoffnung vor, ist das KGV moderat. Greift Angst um sich, ist es in aller Regel sehr niedrig. Stimmungsschwankungen der Anleger schlagen sich so oder so immer wieder im speku-

* Zinsänderungen wirken sich ebenfalls auf das KGV aus, wenn auch uneinheitlich. Vielleicht stelle ich das also etwas zu einfach dar.

lativen Ertrag nieder und werfen den stetigen langfristigen Aufwärtstrend in der Ökonomie der Kapitalanlage vorübergehend aus der Bahn.

Wie in Abbildung 2.1 dargestellt, deckt sich der Anlageertrag von Aktien – also die Dividendenrendite zuzüglich des Gewinnwachstums – auf lange Sicht stark mit dem Gesamtmarktertrag (einschließlich der Effekte spekulativer Erträge). Größere Abweichungen sind von kurzer Dauer.

Rechnet man diese Erträge über 116 Jahre auf, ist das Gesamtergebnis regelrecht atemberaubend. Aus einem im Jahr 1900 in Aktien investierten Dollar sind bei einer Rendite von 9,5 Prozent bis Ende 2015 43.650 Dollar geworden.* Schon klar, die wenigsten von uns haben 116 Jahre Zeit! Doch wie die Familie Gotrocks haben wir ja Nachfahren, denen das Wunder der stetigen Rendite zugutekommt. Und diese Rendite ist geradezu verblüffend – das ultimative Spiel für Gewinner also.

Wie Abbildung 2.1 zeigt, weist die Entwicklung der von unseren Unternehmen erwirtschafteten Anlageerträge Dellen auf, bisweilen – etwa während der Weltwirtschaftskrise Anfang der 1930er-Jahre – auch größere. Wir haben sie aber überstanden. Betrachtet man die Kurve mit ein bisschen Abstand und zusammengekniffenen Augen, wirkt der fundamentale Trend fast wie

---

* Wir wollen fair bleiben. Berechnen wir nicht zur *Nominalrendite* von 9,5 Prozent, sondern zur *Effektivrendite* von 6,3 Prozent, was aus dem ursprünglichen Dollar geworden ist (nach Abzug der für den Zeitraum vorliegenden 3,2 Prozent Inflation nämlich), ergeben sich 1.339 Dollar, also nur ein Bruchteil des nominalen Gesamtwerts. Doch auch eine reale Vergrößerung des Vermögens auf mehr als das 1.300-Fache ist nicht zu verachten.

eine kontinuierlich leicht ansteigende Linie. Die gelegentlichen Einbuchtungen fallen kaum ins Gewicht.

Rückkehr zum Mittelwert

Natürlich eilen die Aktienmarkterträge den Fundamentaldaten mitunter deutlich voraus (wie Ende der 1920er-, Anfang der 1970er- und Ende der 1990er-Jahre, und vielleicht auch heute). Doch es ist nur eine Frage der Zeit, bis sie, wie von einem Magneten angezogen, letztlich wieder zu ihrer langfristigen Norm zurückkehren, wenngleich oft auch erst, nachdem sie eine Zeitlang klar im Rückstand lagen, wie Mitte der 1940er- oder Ende der 1970er-Jahre und bei den Markttiefs von 2003. Das nennt sich Rückkehr (oder Regression) zum Mittelwert (Reversion to the Mean oder kurz RTM). Darauf wollen wir im elften Kapitel noch näher eingehen.

Durch unseren unklugen Fokus auf den momentanen kurzfristigen Ablenkungen des Aktienmarkts verlieren wir Anleger diese langfristige Historie häufig aus den Augen. Weichen die Aktienerträge wesentlich von der langfristigen Norm ab, ignorieren wir die Realität, dass es sich dabei kaum um Folgen der Ökonomie der Kapitalanlage handelt, nämlich der Gewinnsteigerungen und der Dividendenrenditen unserer Unternehmen. Der Grund für die Volatilität der jährlichen Aktienrenditen liegt vielmehr vor allem in der Anlegerstimmung, die sich in den KGV-Veränderungen niederschlägt.

»Es ist gefährlich ..., induktive Argumente auf der Grundlage früherer Erfahrungen auf die Zukunft zu übertragen«

Abbildung 2.1 zeigt, dass sich die für Aktien gezahlten Kurse zwar häufig von der Realität der Unternehmenswerte abkoppeln, *doch diese Realität auf lange Sicht die Strippen zieht*. Die Anleger gehen offenbar intuitiv davon aus, dass die Vergangenheit unweigerlich ein Prolog für die Zukunft ist. Frühere Aktienmarktrenditen, die eine hohe spekulative Aktienertragskomponente beinhalten, sind allerdings gar keine guten Indikatoren für künftige Entwicklungen. Um zu begreifen, warum in der Vergangenheit erzielte Erträge keinen prognostischen Wert haben, müssen wir nur die Worte des großen britischen Ökonomen John Maynard Keynes beherzigen. Er schrieb vor 81 Jahren:

> »Es ist gefährlich ... induktive Argumente auf der Grundlage früherer Erfahrungen auf die Zukunft zu übertragen, wenn man nicht in groben Zügen erkennen kann, warum frühere Erfahrungen so und nicht anders aussahen.«

Wenn wir jedoch erkennen können, warum die Vergangenheit so war, wie sie war, dann können wir begründete Zukunftserwartungen entwickeln. Keynes hat uns zu dieser Erkenntnis verholfen, indem er deutlich machte, dass langfristige Erwartungen für Aktien auf einer Kombination aus unternehmerischen Aspekten (»der Prognose der voraussichtlichen Rendite von Vermögenswerten über ihre gesamte Lebensdauer«) und spekulativen Elementen (»eine Prognose der Marktpsychologie«) beruhten.

Mir sind diese Worte sehr vertraut, denn ich habe sie vor 66 Jahren in meiner Abschlussarbeit an der Princeton University verwendet. Ihr Titel lautete: »The Economic Role of the Investment Company« (Die wirtschaftliche Rolle der Investmentgesellschaft). Wie eine glückliche Fügung legte das den Grundstein für meine lebenslange Karriere in der Investmentfondsbranche.

Der Doppelcharakter von Aktienmarkterträgen

Dieser Doppelcharakter der Aktienmarkterträge wird deutlich, wenn wir die Zahlen über die Jahrzehnte betrachten (Abbildung 2.2). Ich unterfütterte Keynes' Gedanken mit meinen Zahlen und unterteilte die Aktienmarkterträge in zwei Teile: (1) *die Anlageerträge* (die unternehmerische Komponente), die sich aus den ursprünglichen Dividendenrenditen der Aktien zuzüglich ihrer anschließenden Gewinnsteigerungen zusammensetzten (die in Kombination im Wesentlichen das bilden, was wir als »Substanzwert« bezeichnen) und (2) die *spekulativen Erträge*, also die Effekte der Veränderung von Kurs-Gewinn-Verhältnissen auf die Aktienkurse. Setzen wir zunächst bei den Anlageerträgen an.

Im oberen Abschnitt von Abbildung 2.2 sind die durchschnittlichen jährlichen Anlageerträge von Aktien für jedes Jahrzehnt seit 1900 ausgewiesen. Bitte beachten Sie zunächst den steten Beitrag der Dividendenrenditen zum Gesamtertrag in den einzelnen Zehnjahreszeiträumen: Er ist stets positiv, liegt nur zweimal außerhalb der Bandbreite von 3 bis 7 Prozent und beträgt im Schnitt 4 Prozent.

ABBILDUNG 2.2 Gesamtaktienerträge nach Jahrzehnt, 1900–2016 (in Prozent pro Jahr)

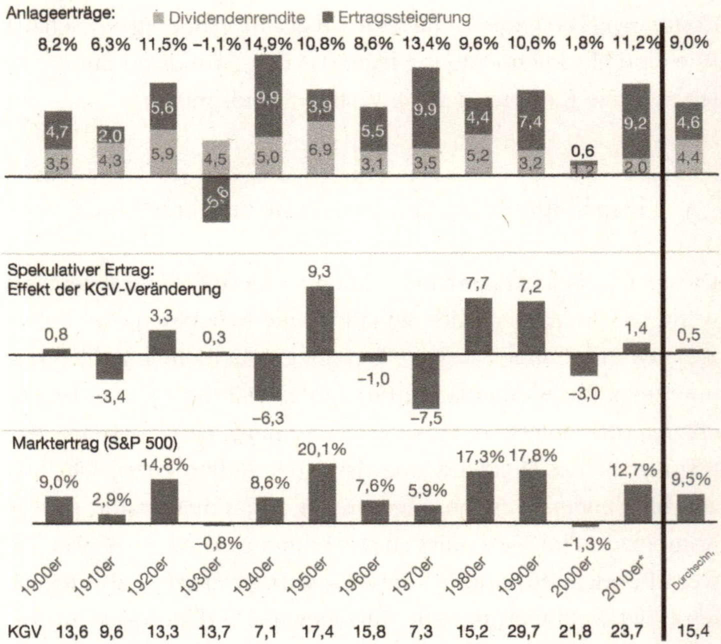

* Bis einschließlich 2016. KGVs zum Ende des jeweiligen Jahrzehnts sind oben angegeben. Das KGV für 1900 betrug 12,5.

Beachten Sie im Anschluss, dass der Beitrag der Ertragssteigerungen zum Anlageertrag, abgesehen von der Weltwirtschaftskrise in den 1930er-Jahren, in jedem Zehnjahreszeitraum positiv war und in mehreren Dekaden über 9 Prozent betrug, gewöhnlich allerdings zwischen 4 und 7 Prozent lag und pro Jahr im Schnitt bei 4,6 Prozent.

Ergebnis: Der Gesamtanlageertrag (der obere Abschnitt, in dem Dividendenrendite und Ertragssteigerungen zusammengefasst sind) fiel nur in einer einzigen Zehnjahresperiode negativ aus (wieder die 1930er-Jahre). Über die Jahrzehnte war der Gesamtanlageertrag – also die von den Unternehmen erwirtschafteten Gewinne – zwar unterschiedlich hoch, aber meines Erachtens erstaunlich stabil. Generell bewegte er sich in einem Band von 8 bis 13 Prozent pro Jahr und betrug im Schnitt 9 Prozent.

Ertrag unter Berücksichtigung der spekulativen Komponente

Die Berücksichtigung der spekulativen Ertragskomponente erfolgt im mittleren Abschnitt von Abbildung 2.2. Gegenüber der über die Jahrzehnte verhältnismäßig beständigen Entwicklung der Dividenden und Ertragssteigerungen weist die Grafik beim spekulativen Ertrag heftige Ausschläge aus. Die KGVs steigen und fallen, was sich häufig spürbar auf den Ertrag auswirkt. So entspräche ein Anstieg des KGV von 100 Prozent, von 10 auf 20, über ein Jahrzehnt einem jährlichen spekulativen Ertrag von 7,2 Prozent.

Wie Sie sehen, schließt sich an jedes Jahrzehnt mit eindeutig negativem spekulativem Ertrag unmittelbar eine Dekade an, in der der spekulative Ertrag entsprechend positiv ausfällt: Auf die negativen 1910er-Jahre folgten die rauschenden 1920er, auf die deprimierenden 1940er-Jahre dann die florierenden 1950er und auf die frustrierenden 1970er-Jahre die hochfliegenden 1980er.

Bei diesem Muster wird die Rückkehr zum Mittelwert großgeschrieben. RTM ist demnach als Tendenz der KGVs zu betrachten, längerfristig wieder zu ihrer Norm zurückzufinden. Auf Phasen mit unterdurchschnittlicher Entwicklung folgen Erholungsperioden, und umgekehrt. In den 1990er-Jahren setzte dann erstaunlicherweise ein beispielloser zweiter überschwänglicher Anstieg in Folge ein – ein bisher ungekanntes Muster.

Die Rückkehr zur Vernunft

Im April 1999 war das KGV auf nie dagewesene 34 angestiegen, was den Boden für die Rückkehr der Bewertungen auf vernünftigere Werte bereitete, die bald darauf einsetzte. Der Einbruch der Aktienkurse brachte uns unsere wohlverdiente Strafe. Bei weiter steigenden Gewinnen steht das KGV derzeit bei 23,7 gegenüber 15 zu Anfang des 20. Jahrhunderts. Infolgedessen trägt der spekulative Ertrag nur 0,5 Prozentpunkte zu den von unseren Unternehmen langfristig erwirtschafteten jährlichen Anlageerträgen bei.*

* Unser KGV-Maßstab zum Jahresende 2016 basiert auf dem Jahresschlussstand des S&P 500 von 2.247 im Verhältnis zu den *ausgewiesenen Gewinnen* für 2016 von 95 US-Dollar je Aktie – woraus sich ein KGV von 23,7 errechnet. Die Wall-Street-Analysten ziehen gewöhnlich das *Betriebsergebnis* (vor Abschreibungen und anderen Abzügen) heran, das für das kommende Jahr prognostiziert wird (118 US-Dollar je Aktie). Daraus ergäbe sich ein KGV von 17,4.

Kombination aus Anlageerträgen und spekulativen Erträgen – der Gesamtaktienmarktertrag

Legen wir diese beiden Treiber der Aktienerträge zusammen, erhalten wir den vom Aktienmarkt generierten Gesamtertrag (der untere Abschnitt von Abbildung 2.2). Trotz des enormen Einflusses des spekulativen Ertrags – in Auf- wie Abwärtsrichtung – in den meisten Einzeldekaden hat er langfristig praktisch *keinen* Effekt. Daraus folgt: Der durchschnittliche Jahresgesamtertrag aus Aktien von 9,5 Prozent entfällt fast ausschließlich auf die *unternehmerischen* Komponenten und lediglich zu 0,5 Prozentpunkten auf die *spekulativen*.

Die Aussage ist ganz klar: Langfristig richten sich die Aktienerträge nahezu komplett nach der Realität der von unseren Unternehmen erwirtschafteten Anlageerträge. Die Wahrnehmung der Anleger, die sich in der spekulativen Ertragskomponente niederschlägt, macht kaum etwas aus. Es ist die Ökonomie, welche die langfristigen Aktienerträge bestimmt. Der kurzfristig so dominante Einfluss der Emotionen verliert sich.

Es ist nicht möglich, kurzfristige Stimmungsschwankungen der Anleger zutreffend vorauszusagen. Doch die langfristige Ökonomie der Kapitalanlage zu prognostizieren, hat bislang beachtliche Erfolgschancen gebracht.

Selbst nach über 66 Jahren in diesem Geschäft habe ich im Grunde keine Ahnung, wie sich diese kurzfristigen Stimmungsschwankungen der Anleger vorhersehen lassen.* Doch vor allem aufgrund ihrer mathematischen Schlichtheit ist es mir sehr wohl gelungen, die langfristige Ökonomie der Kapitalanlage mit erstaunlich hoher Erfolgswahrscheinlichkeit zu prognostizieren.

Wieso? Ganz einfach: weil es langfristig die *Anlageerträge* sind – also die von amerikanischen Unternehmen erwirtschafteten Gewinne und Dividenden –, die nahezu gänzlich für den Ertrag verantwortlich zeichnen, den unser Aktienmarkt langfristig abwirft. Während die Illusion (die momentan für Aktien gezahlten Kurse) häufig den Kontakt zur Realität (dem Substanzwert unserer Unternehmen) verliert, setzt sich langfristig die Realität durch.

Der reale Markt und der Erwartungsmarkt

Das kann man sich gut verdeutlichen, indem man sich die Kapitalanlage als eine Kombination aus zwei verschiedenen Spielen vorstellt. Roger Martin, Dekan der Rotman School of Management der University of Toronto, beschreibt das folgendermaßen: Ein Spiel ist »der *reale* Markt, auf dem große Aktiengesellschaften im Wettbewerb stehen. Auf dem reale Unternehmen reales Geld zahlen, um reale Produkte und Dienstleistungen herzustellen und zu verkaufen, und dann, wenn sie geschickt spielen,

* Und da bin ich in guter Gesellschaft. Ich kenne keinen, dem das auf Dauer gelungen ist – ja, noch nicht einmal jemanden, der einen solchen Menschen kennt. Tatsächlich konnte in 70 Jahren Finanz-Research noch niemand ermittelt werden, der das geschafft hat.

reale Gewinne erzielen und reale Dividenden zahlen. Dieses Spiel erfordert aber auch reale Strategie, Entschlossenheit und Fachkenntnis, reale Innovation und reale Weitsicht.« In lockerem Zusammenhang mit diesem Spiel steht noch ein anderes, nämlich der *Erwartungsmarkt*. Auf diesem »werden die Preise nicht von realen Faktoren wie Umsätzen, Margen oder Gewinnen bestimmt. Kurzfristig ziehen die Aktienkurse nur an, wenn die Erwartungen der Anleger steigen – nicht unbedingt auch Umsätze, Margen oder Gewinne.«

Der Aktienmarkt ist eine einzige riesige Ablenkung für das Anlagegeschäft

Dieser wichtigen Unterscheidung würde ich noch hinzufügen, dass der Erwartungsmarkt größtenteils ein Produkt der Erwartungen von *Spekulanten* ist, die versuchen, zu erraten, was andere Anleger erwarten und wie sie auf jede neue Information reagieren werden, die ihren Weg auf den Markt findet. *Auf dem Erwartungsmarkt geht es um Spekulation. Auf dem realen Markt um Kapitalanlage. Der Aktienmarkt ist insofern eine einzige riesige Ablenkung für das Anlagegeschäft.*

Allzu oft sorgt der Markt dafür, dass sich die Anleger auf kurzfristige, volatile Erwartungen konzentrieren statt auf das, worauf es wirklich ankommt: nämlich die allmähliche Anhäufung der von Unternehmen erwirtschafteten Erträge.

Shakespeare schrieb:

»Ein Märchen ist's, erzählt
Von einem Dummkopf, voller Klang und Wut,
Das nichts bedeutet«

Treffender hätte er die unerklärlichen täglichen, monatlichen oder auch jährlichen Schwankungen der Aktienkurse kaum beschreiben können. Mein Rat an alle Anleger: Ignorieren Sie den kurzfristigen Klang- und Wutfaktor der Emotionen, die sich auf unseren Finanzmärkten niederschlagen, und konzentrieren Sie sich auf die produktive langfristige Ökonomie unserer Unternehmen. Der Weg zum Anlageerfolg führt nicht über den Erwartungsmarkt der Aktienkurse, sondern über den realen Markt der Wirtschaft.

Wenn Sie mir nicht glauben …

Beherzigen Sie doch einfach die zeitlose Unterscheidung, die der legendäre Investor **Benjamin Graham** vornahm, Autor von *Intelligent Investieren* und Mentor von Warren Buffett. Er hat den Nagel auf den Kopf getroffen mit seiner Darstellung der grundlegenden Realität des Investierens: Die Börse ist »*kurzfristig wie eine Abstimmungsmaschine, doch langfristig eine Waage*«.

Mit seinem großartigen Gleichnis von »Mr. Market« erzählte Graham: »Stellen Sie sich vor, dass Sie an einer kleinen Firma mit einem kleinen Anteil beteiligt sind, für den Sie 1.000 Dollar bezahlt haben. Einer Ihrer Partner, Mr. Market, ist sehr zuvorkommend: Jeden Tag sagt er Ihnen, was Ihr Anteil seiner Meinung nach wert ist, und außerdem bietet er Ihnen an, Ihren Anteil zu kaufen oder Ihnen weitere Anteile zu verkaufen. Manchmal scheinen Ihnen seine Bewertungen plausibel und gerechtfertigt zu sein, je nach der Geschäftsentwicklung und den Geschäftsaussichten, soweit Sie sie kennen. Oft aber gehen Optimismus und Ängste mit ihm durch, und der Wert, den er Ihnen vorschlägt, erscheint Ihnen ein wenig albern.

Wenn Sie ein umsichtiger Investor oder ein vernünftiger Geschäftsmann sind …: Werden Sie sich dann von den täglichen Mitteilungen von Mr. Market beeinflussen lassen? Sicherlich nur in dem Fall, in dem Sie mit ihm einer Meinung sind oder wenn Sie mit ihm handeln wollen. … Ansonsten ist es besser, ... sich ... eine eigene Vorstellung vom Wert Ihrer Beteiligung zu machen. ... für den wahren Investor ... ist es besser, *er vergisst die Kurse und achtet eher auf die Dividendenrendite und auf die operativen Ergebnisse der Unternehmen, an denen er beteiligt ist.* (Hervorhebung des Autors.) ...

Der Investor mit einem Portfolio aus vernünftigen Aktien muss auf der einen Seite damit rechnen, dass die Kurse schwanken, und er sollte sich keine Sorgen machen, wenn es zu größeren Verlusten kommt. Auf der anderen Seit sollte er sich auch nicht von der allgemeinen Begeisterung bei ansehnlichen Kurssteigerungen anstecken lassen. Er muss sich immer wieder eines bewusst machen: Die Notierungen dienen seiner Bequemlichkeit, entweder weil er sie zu seinem Vorteil nutzt oder weil er sie ganz einfach ignoriert.«

Drittes Kapitel

Setzen Sie auf die Wirtschaft

Konsequent einfach zum Gewinn – durch Ockhams Rasiermesser

Wie setzt man auf die Wirtschaft? Ganz einfach: Indem man ein Portfolio aus Aktien aller US-Unternehmen aufbaut und dann ewig hält. Dieses einfache Konzept garantiert, dass Sie das Spiel gewinnen, das die meisten anderen Anleger spielen, die – als Gruppe – garantiert Verluste erleiden.

Verwechseln Sie aber Einfachheit nicht mit Dummheit. Schon 1320 beschrieb Wilhelm von Ockham trefflich die Vorzüge der Einfachheit, indem er folgenden Grundsatz formulierte: Gibt es mehrere Lösungen für ein Problem, ist die einfachste allen anderen vorzuziehen.* So wurde *Ockhams Rasiermesser*, auch Prinzip der Parsimonie oder Sparsamkeitsprinzip genannt, zu einem Grundsatz wissenschaftlicher Forschung. Und mit Abstand die einfachste Möglichkeit, alle US-Unternehmen zu besitzen, ist, das gesamte Aktienmarktportfolio zu halten – oder seine Entsprechung.

Ockhams Rasiermesser – gibt es mehrere Lösungen für ein Problem, dann wähle die einfachste

In den vergangenen 90 Jahren war der Standard & Poor's 500 Index (S&P 500) die allgemein anerkannte Entsprechung des Aktienmarktportfolios. Er wurde 1926 als Composite Index eingeführt und umfasst heute 500 Titel.** Im Wesentlichen setzt er sich zusammen aus den 500 größten US-Unternehmen, gewichtet nach dem Wert ihrer Marktkapitalisierung. In den letzten Jahren entfielen auf diese 500 Aktien rund 85 Prozent des Marktwerts aller US-Aktien. Das Geniale an einem solchen *marktkapitalisierungsgewichteten* Index ist, dass er nie durch Kauf und Verkauf von Aktien aufgrund von Veränderungen der Aktienkurse neu gewichtet werden muss.

Angesichts des enormen Zuwachses an unternehmenseigenen Pensionsfonds von 1950 bis 1990 entwickelte sich der S&P 500 zum idealen Maßstab – zur Benchmark (oder *Mindestrendite*), an der sich die Leistung der professionellen Verwalter

* Wilhelm von Ockham hat das etwas eleganter ausgedrückt: »Wesenheiten dürfen nicht über das Notwendige hinaus vermehrt werden.« Was er damit sagen will, ist jedoch unmissverständlich.

** Bis 1957 enthielt der S&P Index nur 90 Unternehmen.

von Pensionsfonds messen lassen musste. Bis heute ist der S&P 500 ein valider Standard, dem die von den professionellen Verwaltern von Pensions- und Investmentfonds erzielten Erträge gegenübergestellt werden können.

Der Index für den gesamten Aktienmarkt

1970 wurde eine noch umfänglichere Messgröße für den US-Aktienmarkt entwickelt. Sie hieß ursprünglich Wilshire 5000 und wurde inzwischen in Dow Jones Wilshire Total Stock Market Index umbenannt.* Er erfasst heute ganze 3.599 Aktien, die 500 Titel des S&P 500 eingeschlossen. Weil auch seine Komponenten nach ihrer Marktkapitalisierung gewichtet sind, machen die verbleibenden 3.099 Aktien mit geringerer Marktkapitalisierung nur 15 Prozent seines Wertes aus. Dieser breiteste aller US-Aktien-Indizes ist die ideale Messlatte für den Gesamtwert aller Aktien und daher ein hervorragender Maßstab für die von US-Aktien für alle Anleger als Gruppe erwirtschafteten Erträge. Wie eben angesprochen, enthalten beide Indizes die gleichen Standardwerte. Abbildung 3.1 zeigt die zehn größten Titel und ihre Gewichtungen beim Aufbau des jeweiligen Index.

Angesichts der großen Ähnlichkeit der beiden Portfolios kann es kaum überraschen, dass sich die Erträge der beiden Indizes im Gleichschritt bewegen. Das Center for Research in Security

* Der Vollständigkeit halber: 1975 legte Vanguard seinen ersten Indexfonds auf, der den Standard & Poor's 500 Index nachbildete. 1992 legte das Unternehmen auch den ersten Indexfonds auf den gesamten Aktienmarkt auf.

Prices der University of Chicago hat die Erträge aller US-Aktien bis 1926 errechnet. Das Ergebnis des S&P 500 Index und des Dow Jones Wilshire Total Stock Market Index fiel nahezu deckungsgleich aus. Von 1926, als die Aufzeichnungen begannen, bis 2016 ist kaum ein Unterschied festzustellen (Abbildung 3.2).

ABBILDUNG 3.1 S&P 500 gegenüber Gesamtmarktindex: Portfoliovergleich, Dezember 2016

S&P 500		**Gesamtmarktindex**	
Position	Gewichtung	Position	Gewichtung
Apple Inc.	3,2 %	Apple Inc	2,5 %
Microsoft Corp.	2,5	Microsoft Corp.	2,0
Alphabet Inc.	2,4	Alphabet Inc.	2,0
Exxon Mobil Corp.	1,9	Exxon Mobil Corp.	1,6
Johnson & Johnson	1,6	Johnson & Johnson	1,3
Berkshire Hathaway Inc.	1,6	Berkshire Hathaway Inc.	1,3
JPMorgan Chase & Co.	1,6	JPMorgan Chase & Co.	1,3
Amazon.com Inc.	1,5	Amazon.com Inc.	1,3
General Electric Co.	1,4	General Electric Co.	1,2
Facebook Inc.	1,4	Facebook Inc.	1,1
Top 10	19,1 %	Top 10	15,6 %
Top 25	33,3	Top 25	27,3
Top 100	63,9	Top 100	52,9
Top 500	100	Top 500	84,1
Gesamtmarkt-kapitalisierung	19,3 Bio. USD		22,7 Bio. USD

ABBILDUNG 3.2 S&P 500 und Total Stock Market Index, 1926–2016

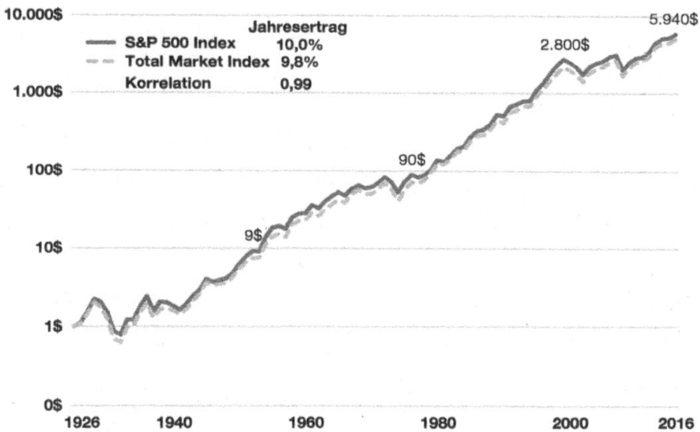

Für den gesamten Zeitraum betrug der durchschnittliche Jahresertrag des S&P 500 10,0 Prozent, der Total Stock Market Index verbuchte 9,8 Prozent. Dieser Vergleich ist *periodenabhängig* – das heißt, alles steht und fällt mit dem Ausgangs- und dem Enddatum. Hätten wir mit dem Vergleich Anfang 1930 eingesetzt statt 1926, hätten beide Indizes die gleiche Rendite erzielt: nämlich 9,6 Prozent pro Jahr.

Und ja, zwischenzeitlich gab es Abweichungen: Von 1982 bis 1990 schnitt der S&P 500 deutlich besser ab. Mit 15,6 Prozent Jahresertrag überrundete er den Total Stock Market Index, der 14,0 Prozent verzeichnete. Doch seither haben sich Aktien mit geringer und mittlerer Marktkapitalisierung (Small- und Mid-Caps) etwas stärker gezeigt. Der Total Stock Market Index erzielte mit 10,2 Prozent pro Jahr einen knappen Vorsprung vor den 9,9 Prozent des S&P 500. Doch angesichts einer langfristigen Korrelation der Erträge der beiden Indizes von 0,99 (1,00 wäre vollkommen) ist es nahezu unerheblich, für welchen Sie sich entscheiden.*

Die vom Aktienmarkt erzielten Erträge müssen den von allen Anlegern auf dem Markt erwirtschafteten Bruttoerträgen entsprechen

Welchen Maßstab wir auch anlegen, inzwischen sollte klar sein, dass die Gewinne der Aktiengesellschaften, aus denen sich der Aktienmarkt zusammensetzt, notgedrungen den gesamten von allen Anlegern auf diesem Markt als Gruppe vereinnahmten Erträgen entsprechen müssen. Genauso offensichtlich ist, wie im vierten Kapitel noch näher erläutert wird, dass die von diesen Anlegern erzielten Nettoerträge auf jeden Fall geringer ausfallen als die gesamten Bruttoerträge – und zwar um den Betrag der angefallenen Vermittlungskosten. Unser gesunder Menschenverstand erklärt uns das Offensichtliche, was wir bereits im ersten Kapitel erfahren haben: Langfristig den Aktienmarkt *zu halten*, ist eine gewinnbringende Strategie. Zu versuchen, den Aktienmarkt *zu schlagen*, bringt dagegen Verluste.

Ein preiswerter Gesamtmarktfonds wird daher über längere Zeit garantiert höhere Erträge abwerfen, als sie die Aktienanleger als Gruppe erzielen. Haben Sie das begriffen, dann wissen

* Vielleicht interessiert Sie ja, dass Warren Buffett bei der Errichtung eines Treuhandfonds als Nachlassregelung für seine Frau angewiesen hat, 90 Prozent seines Vermögens in einen kostengünstigen Indexfonds auf den S&P 500 zu investieren.

Sie auch, dass der Indexfonds nicht nur im Zeitverlauf garantiert Gewinne bringt, sondern jedes Jahr, jeden Monat, jede Woche, ja, sogar jede Minute des Tages. Gänzlich ungeachtet des Zeithorizonts entspricht der Bruttoertrag des Aktienmarkts abzüglich der Vermittlungskosten dem von den Anlegern als Gruppe erzielten Nettoertrag. Wenn die Daten nicht belegen, dass sich Indexnachbildung besser auszahlt – nun, dann stimmen die Daten nicht.

Wenn die Daten nicht belegen, dass sich Indexnachbildung besser auszahlt – nun, dann stimmen die Daten nicht

Kurzfristig sieht es aber nicht immer so aus, als lägen der S&P 500 (noch immer der meistverwendete Referenzindex für Investmentfonds und Pensionspläne) oder der Total Stock Market Index vorne. Das kommt daher, weil sich die von Millionen verschiedenen Marktteilnehmern, Amateuren ebenso wie Profis, US-Amerikanern und Ausländern, auf dem US-Aktienmarkt erzielten Erträge unmöglich exakt berechnen lassen.

Im Investmentfondssegment berechnen wir die Erträge verschiedener Fonds, indem wir jeden Fonds – ungeachtet seines Volumens – einzeln erfassen. Da es viele Small- und Mid-Cap-Fonds mit gewöhnlich eher moderatem Fondsvermögen gibt, können sich diese zeitweilig überproportional auf die Daten auswirken. Liegen Small- und Mid-Cap-Fonds auf dem Gesamtmarkt vorn, scheinen Gesamtmarktfonds in Rückstand zu geraten. Hinken Small- und Mid-Cap-Fonds hinter dem Markt her, wirken Indexfonds besonders erfolgreich.

Aktive Fonds und Referenz-Indizes im Vergleich

Die offensichtliche Lösung für das Problem, wie man aktive Aktienfonds aller Art mit dem S&P 500 Index vergleichen kann, ist eine Gegenüberstellung ihrer Wertentwicklung mit Indizes, die eher ihren jeweiligen Anlagestrategien entsprechen. Und genau das geschieht in dem sogenannten SPIVA-Bericht seit einigen Jahren. (SPIVA steht für S&P Indices versus Active). Dieser Bericht liefert umfassende Daten zum Vergleich aktiver Investmentfonds, die nach Strategie geordnet sind, mit einschlägigen Markt-Indizes. Mit dem SPIVA-Bericht zum Jahresende 2016 erweiterte sich dessen längster berücksichtigter Zeithorizont auf 15 Jahre (2001 bis 2016). Darin wurde der Prozentsatz aktiv gemanagter Fonds ausgewiesen, die hinter ihren jeweiligen Benchmark-Indizes zurückblieben. Das Ergebnis war beeindruckend (Abbildung 3.3). Im Schnitt hatten immerhin 90 Prozent der aktiv verwalteten Investmentfonds ihre Vergleichs-Indizes über die vorausgegangenen 15 Jahre verfehlt. Die Indizes zeigten sich beständig haushoch überlegen.

Der S&P 500 überrundete 97 Prozent der aktiv gemanagten Large-Cap-Core-Fonds. Der S&P 500 Growth bzw. Value Index wird als Referenz für Fonds aus den jeweiligen Large-Cap-Kategorien herangezogen. Ebenso wird in den drei Mid-Cap-Kategorien und den drei Small-Cap-Kategorien verfahren. Die pauschal auf breiter Front erzielten Überrenditen der Indizes lassen wenig Zweifel daran, dass Indexfonds eine Zukunft haben. 1951 schrieb ich in meiner Abschlussarbeit an der Princeton University, Investmentfonds »können nicht den Anspruch erheben, besser zu sein als die Marktdurchschnitte.« 66 Jahre später ist klar, dass das stark untertrieben war.

ABBILDUNG 3.3 Prozentsätze aktiv gemanagter Investmentfonds mit Rückstand auf vergleichbare S&P-Indizes, 2001–2016

Fondskategorie	Growth	Core	Value
Large-Cap	95 %	97 %	79 %
Mid-Cap	97	99	90
Small-Cap	99	95	81

Bilanz eines Investors in den ersten Indexfonds: 15.000 im Jahr 1976 investierte Dollars wären bis 2016 auf 913.340 Dollar angewachsen

In jüngster Zeit hat sich die Gesamtbilanz des ersten Indexfonds der Welt nicht nur nicht verschlechtert, sondern sogar deutlich verbessert. Dieser Fonds heißt inzwischen Vanguard 500 Index Fund. Er nahm seine Tätigkeit am 31. August 1976 auf. Lassen Sie mich ganz konkret werden: Bei einem Mittagessen am 20. September 2016 anlässlich des 40. Jubiläums des Börsengangs des Fonds erzählte der Rechtsberater des Emissionshauses des Fonds, er habe damals für 15 Dollar je Aktie 1.000 Aktien erworben – eine Investition von 15.000 US-Dollar. Er verkündete stolz, dass seine Position am Tag des Jubiläums (unter Berücksichtigung der durch Wiederanlage der Dividenden und Ausschüttungen des Fonds über die Jahre erworbenen zusätzlichen Aktien) 913.340 US-Dollar wert sei.* Diese Zahlen muss man nicht beschönigen. Ein Vorbehalt und ein Warnhinweis sind jedoch angezeigt.

* Und dabei zahlte der Investor jeweils die fälligen Steuern auf Dividenden und Ausschüttungen durch Veräußerungsgewinne.

Ein Vorbehalt und eine Warnung

Der Vorbehalt: Von den 360 Aktienfonds, die bei Auflegung des ersten Indexfonds 1976 auf dem Markt waren, gibt es nur noch 74. Aktiv gemanagte Fonds kommen und gehen, doch der Indexfonds läuft ewig. *Die Warnung:* In diesen 40 Jahren legte der S&P 500 Index jährlich 10,9 Prozent zu. Angesichts der inzwischen niedrigeren Dividendenrenditen, der Aussicht auf geringere Gewinnsteigerungen und der aggressiven Marktbewertungen ist nach vernünftigem Ermessen nicht davon auszugehen, dass in den nächsten vier Jahrzehnten ähnliche Erträge erzielt werden. Siehe neuntes Kapitel »Wenn die Party vorbei ist«.

Die bisherige Bilanz bestätigt, dass es nicht nur folgerichtig, sondern, gelinde gesagt, unglaublich produktiv ist, über einen breit gestreuten Indexfonds in amerikanische Unternehmen zu investieren. Nicht minder bedeutsam: Es entspricht auch dem überlieferten Grundsatz der Einfachheit, den Sir Wilhelm von Ockham formulierte. Statt sich der Masse der Anleger anzuschließen, die mit komplexen Algorithmen oder anderen Tricks versuchen, Einzeltitel auszuwählen oder Investmentfonds auf der Grundlage ihrer früheren Wertentwicklung aussuchen oder versuchen, klüger zu sein als der Aktienmarkt (für die Gesamtheit der Anleger drei unweigerlich fruchtlose Unterfangen), sollten Sie sich lieber für die einfachste aller Lösungen entscheiden – ein diversifiziertes, kostengünstiges Portfolio zu kaufen und zu halten, das den Aktienmarkt nachbildet.

Wenn Sie mir nicht glauben …

Hören Sie doch auf **David Swensen,** den hoch angesehenen Chief Investment Officer des Stiftungsfonds der Yale University. »[Über die 15 Jahre bis 1998] erzielten [nur kümmerliche 4 Prozent aller [Investment-]Fonds nach Steuern bessere Ergebnisse als der Markt und übertrafen ihn um magere 0,6 Prozent [pro Jahr]. Die 96 Prozent der Fonds, die hinter dem Vanguard 500 Index Fund zurückblieben, erlitten Verluste in vermögensvernichtendem Umfang von 4,8 Prozent pro Jahr.«

Die einfache Indexfondslösung wird nicht nur von Anlegern gewählt, die über durchschnittliche Mittel verfügen. Sie ist auch Eckpfeiler der Anlagestrategie vieler US-amerikanischer Pensionspläne, die von Großkonzernen, Staatsregierungen und Kommunen betrieben werden. Die Indexnachbildung ist auch die vorherrschende Strategie für die größte solche Organisation überhaupt zur Altersvorsorge für Angestellte der US-Bundesregierung, der Thrift Savings Plan (TSP).* Dessen Vermögen beläuft sich inzwischen auf rund 460 Milliarden US-Dollar, die unseren Staatsdienern und Angehörigen der Streitkräfte zufließen

* Der TSP bietet auch die Möglichkeit von Roth-Beiträgen, die steuerlich ähnlich behandelt werden wie Roth IRAs. Roth-Beiträge erfolgen vom versteuerten Einkommen, doch alle anschließenden Wertzuwächse sind komplett steuerfrei. Auf das Thema Altersvorsorge geht das neunzehnte Kapitel noch näher ein.

sollen. Sämtliche Beiträge und Erträge werden erst bei Entnahme besteuert – ähnlich wie bei einem betrieblichen Altersvorsorgeprogramm vom Typ 401(k).

Die Indexnachbildung wird auch auf der anderen Seite des »großen Teichs« gepriesen. **Jonathan Davis,** Kolumnist des Londoner Blattes *The Spectator,* schrieb darüber: »Nichts macht besser deutlich, wie sehr Rhetorik und Substanz im britischen Finanzdienstleistungssektor auseinanderklaffen, als die Tatsache, dass es die Anbieter hier nicht geschafft haben, den Erfolg von Jack Bogles Indexfonds in den Vereinigten Staaten nachzuvollziehen. Jeder Profi in der City weiß, dass Indexfonds das Grundgerüst jedes langfristigen Anlageportfolios bilden sollten. Seit 1976 erwirtschaftet der Vanguard-Indexfonds eine kumulierte Jahresrendite von 12 Prozent – besser als drei Viertel seiner Vergleichsgruppe. Doch auch 30 Jahre später verhindern die Ignoranz und die Omertà der Profis, dass mehr Anleger den Erfolg dieses unbesungenen Helden der Investmentwelt teilen dürfen.«

Viertes Kapitel

Wie die Kapitalanlage vom Spiel für Gewinner zum Spiel für Verlierer wird

»Die unerbittlichen Regeln einfacher Arithmetik«

Bevor wir uns dem Erfolg der Indexnachbildung als Anlagestrategie widmen, wollen wir etwas genauer ergründen, warum die Anleger als Gruppe eben nicht die Erträge einstreichen, die unsere Unternehmen durch ihre Dividenden und Gewinnsteigerungen erwirtschaften – welche sich letztlich in ihren Aktienkursen niederschlagen. Warum ist das so? Weil die Anleger als Gruppe notgedrungen genau den gleichen Ertrag erzielen wie der Markt, *von dem dann aber noch die Anlagekosten in Abzug gebracht werden.*

Wenn wir die Kosten für die Finanzvermittler abrechnen – also alle Verwaltungsgebühren, die Kosten für den Portfolioumschlag, die Maklerprovisionen und sämtliche Emissionsgebühren, Werbungs- und Betriebskosten und Anwaltshonorare –, dann müssen die Erträge genau um den Gesamtbetrag dieser Kosten hinter der Marktrendite zurückbleiben. Und das tun sie auch. *Das ist schlicht und ergreifend die unwiderlegbare Grundwahrheit der Kapitalanlage.*

Auf einem Markt, der in einem bestimmten Jahr 7 Prozent Rendite erzielt, erhalten wir Anleger einen Bruttoertrag von 7 Prozent. (Ganz ordentlich.) Doch in unsere Taschen fließt nur, was übrig bleibt, nachdem wir unsere Finanzvermittler bezahlt haben. (Und die bezahlen wir in jedem Fall, ob unsere Erträge nun positiv oder negativ ausfallen!)

Vor Kosten ist es ein Nullsummenspiel, den Markt zu schlagen. Nach Kosten ist es ein Spiel für Verlierer.

Zwei Dinge stehen folglich fest: (1) *Den Markt zu schlagen, ist vor Abzug der Kosten ein Nullsummenspiel.* (2) *Den Markt nach Abzug der Kosten zu schlagen, ist ein Spiel für Verlierer.* Die Erträge, die alle Anleger zusammen erzielen, sind unweigerlich deutlich geringer als die Erträge, die auf unseren Finanzmärkten realisiert werden. Wie hoch sind eigentlich die Kosten? Für den Privatanleger, der direkt in einzelne Aktien investiert, können sich die Handelskosten auf durchschnittlich 1,5 Prozent oder mehr pro Jahr belaufen. Sie fallen geringer aus (und liegen dann vielleicht bei 1 Prozent), wenn nicht so viel gehandelt wird, aber wesentlich höher (für Anleger mit einer Portfolioumschlagsrate von über 200 Prozent pro Jahr betragen sie beispielsweise 3 Prozent), wenn Anleger eifrig handeln.

Bei aktiv gemanagten Aktienfonds belaufen sich die Verwaltungsgebühren und Betriebskosten – also das, was wir zusammen als *Kostenquote* eines Fonds bezeichnen – im Schnitt auf rund 1,3 Prozent pro Jahr und, nach Fondsvermögen gewichtet, auf rund 0,8 Prozent. Hinzu kommen noch, sagen wir, 0,5 Prozent Ausgabeaufschlag, wenn wir davon ausgehen, dass die ursprünglichen Emissionsgebühren von 5 Prozent auf eine Haltefrist von 10 Jahren umgelegt werden. Werden die Anteile nur fünf Jahre lang gehalten, betrügen diese Kosten das Doppelte von 0,5 Prozent – also 1 Prozent pro Jahr. (Viele Fonds werden heute mit Emissionsgebühren beaufschlagt, die oft über zehn Jahre oder mehr gestreckt werden. Rund 60 Prozent aller Fonds haben keinen Ausgabeaufschlag.)

Obendrauf kommen noch enorme zusätzliche Kosten, die intransparent und daher umso nachteiliger sind. Damit meine ich die versteckten Kosten des Portfolioumschlags, die ich im Schnitt auf ein ganzes Prozent pro Jahr schätze. Aktiv gemanagte Fonds schichten ihre Portfolios angeblich mit einer Rate von rund 80 Prozent pro Jahr um. Das bedeutet beispielsweise, dass ein Fonds mit einem Volumen von 5 Milliarden US-Dollar jedes Jahr Aktien für 2 Milliarden US-Dollar kauft und Aktien für weitere 2 Milliarden US-Dollar verkauft – also insgesamt 4 Milliarden US-Dollar umsetzt. In dieser Größenordnung belaufen sich Maklerprovisionen, Geld-Brief-Spannen und Markteinflusskosten als zusätzlicher Kostenfaktor, der von den Fondsanlegern zu tragen ist, vielleicht auf 0,5 bis 1,0 Prozent.

Wir Anleger als Gruppe erhalten genau das, wofür wir *nicht* bezahlen – wenn wir nichts zahlen, kriegen wir alles

Ergebnis: Alles in allem kann es bis zu 2 oder 3 Prozent pro Jahr kosten, Anteile an einem Aktienfonds zu halten.* Also ja, *die Kosten spielen eine Rolle.* Die grausame Ironie der Kapitalanlage ist folglich, dass wir Anleger als Gruppe nicht nur nicht bekommen, wofür wir zahlen, sondern genau das bekommen, wofür wir *nicht* zahlen. *Wenn wir nichts zahlen, kriegen wir alles* – logisch, oder?

Vor ein paar Jahren habe ich zum wiederholten Mal *Other People's Money* von Louis C. Brandeis gelesen (das 1914 erstveröffentlicht wurde). Ich stieß dabei auf eine herrliche Passage, die diese einfache Lektion veranschaulicht. Brandeis, der später einer der einflussreichsten Juristen am obersten US-Gerichtshof werden sollte, wetterte gegen die Oligarchen, die hundert Jahre

* Die versteckten Opportunitätskosten, die Fondsanleger zahlen, habe ich dabei nicht berücksichtigt. Die meisten Aktienfonds halten Barreserven von rund 5 Prozent. Wenn Aktien 7 Prozent abwerfen, diese Barmittel aber nur 2 Prozent, ergeben sich daraus jährlich Zusatzkosten in Höhe von weiteren 0,25 Prozentpunkten (5 Prozent des Vermögens, multipliziert mit den 5 Prozent Renditegefälle).

zuvor die amerikanische Investmentlandschaft kontrollierten – und die Wirtschaft gleich mit.

Die unerbittlichen Regeln einfacher Arithmetik

Brandeis beschrieb die eigennützige Kapitalverwaltung und ihre verzahnten Interessen als »*ungestraftes Herumtrampeln auf menschlichen wie göttlichen Gesetzen, besessen von der Wahnvorstellung, dass zwei plus zwei fünf ergibt*«. Er prophezeite (zu Recht, wie sich weisen sollte), dass die in jener Zeit verbreitete Spekulation zum Zusammenbruch führen würde als »*Opfer der unerbittlichen Regeln einfacher Arithmetik*«. Das Ganze verbrämte er mit folgender niemandem zugeschriebener Warnung (die von Sophokles stammt, wie ich meine): »*Vergiss nicht, Fremder. Die Arithmetik ist die erste der Wissenschaften und die Mutter der Sicherheit.*«

Brandeis' Worte schlugen bei mir ein wie der sprichwörtliche Blitz. Warum? Weil die unerbittlichen Regeln der Anlagearithmetik so offensichtlich sind. (Böse Stimmen sagen mir nach, ich verfüge lediglich über die »unheimliche Fähigkeit, das Offensichtliche zu erkennen«.)

Das Seltsame ist: Die meisten Anleger haben damit offenbar Probleme. Oder vielleicht wollen sie ja die Wahrheit einfach nicht sehen, weil sie in so starkem Widerspruch zu ihren tief verwurzelten Überzeugungen, ihren Vorurteilen, ihrer Vermessenheit und ihrer unkritischen Akzeptanz der scheinbar ewigen Funktionsweise der Finanzmärkte steht.

Erstaunlich, wie schwer etwas für einen Menschen zu verstehen ist, wenn man ihm ein kleines Vermögen dafür zahlt, es *nicht* zu verstehen

Hinzu kommt, dass es kaum im Interesse unserer Finanzvermittler liegt, ihre Anleger/Kunden auf die offensichtliche Wahrheit hinzuweisen. In Wirklichkeit zwingt der Eigennutz die einflussreichsten Persönlichkeiten in unserem Finanzsystem förmlich dazu, diese unerbittlichen Regeln zu ignorieren. Um mit Upton Sinclair zu sprechen: *Erstaunlich, wie schwer etwas für einen Menschen zu verstehen ist, wenn man ihm ein kleines Vermögen dafür zahlt, es* nicht *zu verstehen.*

Unser System der Finanzintermediation hat all jene enorm reich gemacht, die das Kapital anderer verwalten. Ihre Interessen dürften sich in absehbarer Zeit kaum verändern. Doch als Anleger müssen Sie sich um *Ihre eigenen* Belange kümmern. Und ein kluger Anleger kann nur dann Erfolg haben, wenn er sich den offensichtlichen Realitäten der Kapitalanlage stellt.

Wie sehr die Kosten der Finanzintermediation ins Gewicht fallen? Ganz gewaltig. Die hohen Kosten von Aktienfonds sind sogar eine ganz entscheidende Erklärung dafür, warum die Fondsmanager schon so lange beständig hinter den Erträgen des Aktienmarkts herhinken. Wenn man darüber nachdenkt, ist das vollkommen logisch.

Im Großen und Ganzen sind diese Manager intelligent, gebildet, erfahren, kenntnisreich und ehrlich. *Doch sie stehen im Wettbewerb miteinander.* Wenn einer eine Aktie kauft, verkauft sie ein anderer. Für die Aktionäre als Gruppe ist da per saldo kein Gewinn drin. Vielmehr fallen ihnen Verluste in der Höhe der Transaktionskosten an, die sie diesen »Helfern« zahlen, vor denen uns Warren Buffett im ersten Kapitel gewarnt hat.

Anleger achten viel zu wenig auf die mit der Kapitalanlage verbundenen Kosten. Ihre Bedeutung ist vor allem unter den heute herrschenden drei Voraussetzungen leicht zu unterschätzen: (1) wenn die Aktienmarkterträge hoch sind (seit 1980 brachten Aktien im Schnitt 11,5 Prozent pro Jahr und der durchschnittliche Fonds erkleckliche – aber eben eindeutig unzulängliche – 10,1 Prozent); (2) wenn sich Anleger auf kurzfristige Renditen ausrichten und die de facto vorliegenden Enteignungseffekte der Kosten über die gesamte Laufzeit einer Anlage ignorieren; und (3) wenn so viele Kosten intransparent sind (wie Portfoliotransaktionskosten, der weitgehend unerkannte Effekt von Ausgabeaufschlägen und die auf Ausschüttungen eines Fonds aus häufig ohne Not realisierten Veräußerungsgewinnen anfallenden Steuern).

Ein Beispiel macht das vielleicht besser deutlich. Nehmen wir an, der Aktienmarkt wirft über 50 Jahre im Schnitt insgesamt 7 Prozent pro Jahr ab. Eine Anlage kann heute jedoch sogar noch länger gehalten werden – 65 oder 70 Jahre, wenn der Anleger mit 22 anfängt zu arbeiten, sofort zu investieren beginnt, sagen wir, mit 65 in den Ruhestand eintritt und dann noch die 20 oder mehr Jahre weiter anlegt, die seiner versicherungsmathematischen Lebenserwartung entsprechen. Gehen wir davon aus, dass dem durchschnittlichen Investmentfonds Betriebskosten von mindestens geschätzten 2 Prozent pro Jahr entstehen. Ergebnis: Der jährliche *Nettoertrag* des Durchschnittsfonds liegt nur bei 5 Prozent.

Aus 10.000 Dollar werden 294.600 ... oder nur 114.700. Was ist aus den übrigen 179.900 Dollar geworden?

Betrachten wir auf der Grundlage dieser Annahmen die mit 10.000 US-Dollar über 50 Jahre erwirtschafteten Erträge (Abbildung 4.1). Legen wir dabei eine nominale Jahresrendite von 7 Prozent zugrunde, wächst die einfache Anlage auf dem Aktienmarkt auf 294.600 Dollar an. Wieso? Dahinter steckt der magische Effekt kumulierender *Erträge* über die gesamte Lebensdauer der Anlage. In den ersten Jahren unterscheidet sich die Linie, die das Wachstum mit einer Jahresrate von 5 Prozent abbildet, noch nicht so sehr vom Wachstum des Aktienmarktes als solchem.

ABBILDUNG 4.1 Die Magie der kumulierten Erträge, die Tyrannei der kumulierten Kosten: Wachstum von 10.000 US-Dollar über 50 Jahre

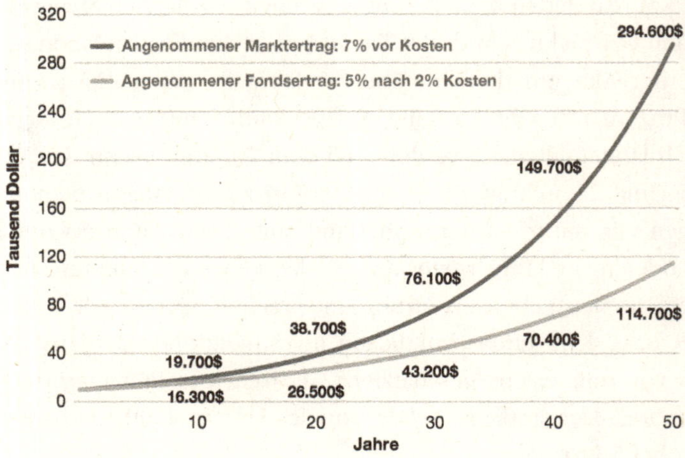

Doch nach und nach weichen die Linien immer stärker voneinander ab, woraus sich am Ende eine wirklich drastische Lücke ergibt. Am Ende des 50-Jahres-Zeitraums beläuft sich der vom Fonds insgesamt erwirtschaftete Wert auf nur 114.700 US-Dollar. Das sind empfindliche 179.900 US-Dollar weniger als der auf dem Markt selbst erzielte kumulative Ertrag. Warum? Aufgrund der Tyrannei der kumulierten *Kosten* über die gesamte Laufzeit. In der Investmentwelt heilt die Zeit nicht alle Wunden, sie verschlimmert sie sogar. *Wenn es um Erträge geht, ist die Zeit Ihr Freund. Bei den Kosten ist sie Ihr Feind.* Dieser Punkt wird sonnenklar, wenn wir uns anschauen, wie viel Wert der Anlage von 10.000 US-Dollar mit jedem vergehenden Jahr vernichtet wird (Abbildung 4.2).

ABBILDUNG 4.2 Die Tyrannei der Kumulation: Langfristiger Effekt eines Rückstands von 2 Prozent auf den Markt

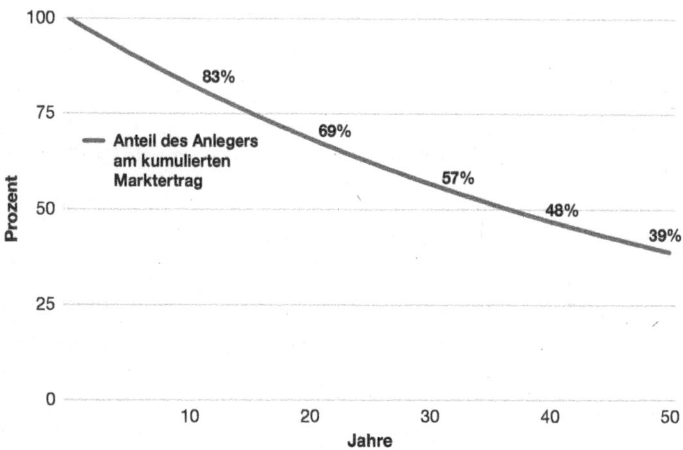

Am Ende des ersten Jahres sind nur rund 2 Prozent des potenziellen Werts Ihres Kapitals verschwunden (10.500 statt 10.700 Dollar). Nach dem zehnten Jahr sind es bereits 17 Prozent (16.300 statt 19.700 Dollar). Nach dem dreißigsten Jahr sind es schon 43 Prozent (43.200 statt 76.100 Dollar). Und am Ende der 50-jährigen Anlagefrist haben die Kosten ganze 61 Prozent der durch einfaches Halten eines Marktportfolios potenziell möglichen Kumulation aufgezehrt. Dem Anleger bleiben dann nur noch 39 Prozent.

Sie bringen 100 Prozent des Kapitals auf und tragen 100 Prozent des Risikos. Dennoch erhalten Sie weniger als 40 Prozent des potenziellen Ertrags.

In diesem Beispiel erhielt der Anleger, der 100 Prozent des Kapitals bereitstellte und 100 Prozent des Risikos übernahm, nicht einmal 40 Prozent des potenziellen Marktertrags. Unser Finanzvermittlerapparat, der null Prozent des Kapitals einbrachte und null Prozent des Risikos übernahm, griff im Grunde 60 Prozent des Ertrags ab.

Noch einmal: Dieses Beispiel zeigt – und vergessen Sie das bitte nicht! –, dass das Wunder kumulierter *Erträge* auf lange Sicht von der Tyrannei kumulierter *Kosten* zunichtegemacht wird. Diese mathematische Gewissheit können Sie getrost den zuvor beschriebenen unerbittlichen Regeln einfacher Arithmetik hinzufügen.

Schlicht gesagt haben sich unsere Fondsmanager, die an der Spitze der Investment-Nahrungskette sitzen, einen unverhältnismäßig großen Anteil an den Erträgen angeeignet, die unsere Finanzmärkte abwerfen. Fondsanlegern, die unweigerlich ganz unten in der Nahrungskette angesiedelt sind, bleibt nur ein ernüchternd geringer Anteil. Dabei hätten sich die Anleger diese Verluste ersparen können, denn sie hätten ohne Weiteres in einen einfachen, äußerst kostengünstigen Indexfonds investieren können, der den S&P 500 nachbildet.

Die Kosten entscheiden über Erfolg oder Misserfolg der Kapitalanlage

Kurz, die einfache Arithmetik der Kapitalanlage – die logische, unvermeidliche und unerbittliche Strafe, die durch die mit der Kapitalanlage verbundenen Kosten auferlegt wird – hat die Erträge von Investmentfondsanlegern drastisch zusammengestrichen. Um mit Richter Brandeis zu sprechen: Unsere Investmentfondsvertreiber scheinen *»besessen von der Wahnvorstellung«*, dass Anleger zu 100 Prozent vom Aktienmarktertrag profitieren – und versuchen, den Anlegern diese Irrmeinung unterzujubeln.

Indem sie den in der Vergangenheit seit 1900 erzielten Jahresertrag von 9,5 Prozent hernehmen und die 2 Prozent Fondskosten und die 3 Prozent Inflation ignorieren, erwecken sie den Eindruck, die Anleger könnten effektiv nach Kosten mit 9,5 Prozent Ertrag rechnen. Tja, offenkundig sollten sie das besser nicht. Rechnen Sie einfach selbst. In Wahrheit beläuft sich der effektiv von Anlegern erzielte Ertrag (Sie ahnen es schon) lediglich auf 4,5 Prozent.

Fondsanleger verdienen einen fairen Anteil

Wenn die Fondsindustrie die Anleger nicht fair behandelt und den Inhabern von Fondsanteilen keine höheren Nettoerträge zahlt, dann wird sie Probleme bekommen und am Ende scheitern – richtig, als Opfer der unerbittlichen Regeln einfacher Arithmetik. Könnte Ihnen Richter Brandeis beim Lesen dieser Zeilen über die Schulter schauen, würde er Ihnen sicher zu bedenken geben: »*Vergessen Sie nicht, werter Leser: Arithmetik ist die erste der Wissenschaften und die Mutter der Sicherheit.*«

Die Kosten entscheiden über Erfolg und Misserfolg der Kapitalanlage. Also spitzen Sie Ihren Bleistift und rechnen Sie selbst. Erkennen Sie, dass Sie das hyperaktive Spielchen der Fondsmanager nicht mitspielen müssen, auf das sich die große Mehrheit der Privat- und Investmentfondsanleger einlässt. Es gibt ihn, den kostengünstigen Indexfonds, der Ihnen Ihren gerechten Anteil an den Gewinnen (oder auch Verlusten) sichert, die unsere Unternehmen erzielen, und an eventuellen Zuwächsen bei Aktienkursen und Dividenden.

Wenn Sie mir nicht glauben …

Die naturgegebene Überlegenheit des Indexfonds wird (mitunter widerstrebend) von zahlreichen Insidern der Investmentfondsbranche bestätigt. **Peter Lynch**, der legendäre Manager, der dem Fidelity Magellan Fund während seiner Amtszeit von 1977 bis 1990 so großen Erfolg bescherte, sagte bei seinem Rücktritt gegenüber *Barron's*: »Der S&P hat in zehn Jahren 343,8 Prozent zugelegt. Das sind vier Strikes in Folge. Aktienfonds haben pauschal 283 Prozent gewonnen. Der abträgliche Effekt der Profis verschlimmert sich also. Das Anlegerpublikum wäre mit einem Indexfonds besser dran.«

Branchenführer **Jon Fossel**, Ex-Chef des Investment Company Institute und der Oppenheimer Funds, äußerte im *Wall Street Journal:* »Die Leute sollten erkennen, dass der durchschnittliche Fonds den Gesamtmarkt *nie* schlagen kann«. (Hervorhebung vom Autor.)

Selbst hyperaktive Investoren glauben offenbar an Indexstrategien. Der Kapitalverwalter und Moderator von *Mad Money* auf CNBC **James J. Cramer** formulierte das so: »Nach einem ganzen Leben als Stockpicker muss ich zugeben, dass ich aufgrund von Bogles Argumenten für Indexfonds eher dazu tendiere, mich auf seine Seite zu schlagen, als gegen ihn anzutreten. Bogles Logik und Vernunft [sind] unverzichtbar … für jeden, der wissen will, wie er sich auf diesem verrückten Aktienmarkt engagieren soll.« (Bisher hat sich Herr Cramer allem Anschein nach aber nicht an seinen Rat gehalten.)

Selbst die Manager alternativer Anlagen stimmen in den Chor ein. Mit **Clifford S. Asness** steuert einer der ganz Großen der Kapitalverwaltung, geschäftsführender Gesellschafter und Gründer von AQR Capital Management, seine Erkenntnisse, Erfahrungen und Integrität bei: »Die marktkapitalisierungsbasierte Indexnachbildung wird nie von ihrem verdienten Thron als zentrale, rechtmäßige Königin der Investmentwelt gestoßen werden. Diese Lehre, die einer großen Zahl von Anlegern zu kostengünstigen Aktienerträgen verholfen hat, sollten wir alle beherzigen … *als absolutes Erfolgsmodell für jetzt und alle Zeit.*«

Fünftes Kapitel

Die kostengünstigsten Fonds im Fokus

Je mehr die Manager abgreifen, desto weniger bleibt den Anlegern

So gut wie alle Fondsexperten und Anlageberater, die Finanzmedien und die Anleger selbst stützen sich bei der Fondsauswahl stark – ja, nahezu als einzige Informationsquelle – auf die frühere Wertentwicklung. Wie sich ein Fonds in der Vergangenheit entwickelt hat, verrät uns aber nur, was bisher gewesen ist, und kann nichts darüber aussagen, was *künftig* passiert. Die Fokussierung auf die Wertentwicklung eines Fonds ist, wie Sie noch erfahren werden, in Wirklichkeit nicht nur *un-*, sondern sogar *kontraproduktiv*. Tief in uns sagt uns unser gesunder Menschenverstand: *Performance kommt und geht*.

Es gibt jedoch einen häufig ignorierten, aber ausschlaggebenden Faktor für den Fondsertrag, den Sie unbedingt kennen sollten. Sie können Ihren Erfolg bei der Auswahl gewinnbringender Fonds steigern, indem Sie sich nicht auf die unvermeidbare Flüchtigkeit der früheren Wertentwicklung konzentrieren, sondern auf etwas scheinbar Bleibendes – besser gesagt, auf einen Faktor, der sich in der langen Geschichte der Fondsindustrie beständig als prägend für den Fondsertrag erwiesen hat. Dieser Faktor sind die *Kosten* des Engagements in Investmentfonds, denn *Kosten fallen immer an*.

Die Performance eines Fonds kommt und geht – Kosten fallen immer an

Um welche Kosten geht es hier? Der erste und bekannteste Posten ist die Kostenquote des Fonds, die sich über längere Zeiträume gewöhnlich nur wenig verändert. Bei manchen Fonds sinken zwar die Gebührensätze mit steigendem Vermögen, doch gewöhnlich in so moderatem Umfang, dass kostenintensive Fonds (die durchschnittliche Kostenquote der Fonds aus dem teuersten Dezil liegt bei 2,40 Prozent) tendenziell teuer bleiben, günstigere Fonds günstiger (die durchschnittliche Kostenquote im vierten Dezil liegt bei 0,98 Prozent) und die wenigen Fonds mit ausgesprochen geringen Kosten ebenfalls die billigsten (mit einer Kostenquote im untersten Dezil von durchschnittlich 0,32 Prozent).

Auch die Fonds mit durchschnittlichen Kosten aus dem fünften und sechsten Dezil (mit 1,10 Prozent beziehungsweise 1,24 Prozent) bleiben im Regelfall ebenfalls in der betreffenden Kategorie.

Der zweitgrößte Kostenpunkt für den Erwerb von Anteilen an Aktienfonds ist der bei jeder Zeichnung fällige Ausgabeaufschlag. Die Belastung durch diese Emissionskosten wird in den veröffentlichten Daten in den allermeisten Fällen unterschlagen, obwohl auch sie in aller Regel bestehen bleibt.* (Ich kenne keine große Fondsgesellschaft, die unmittelbar von einem Vertriebssystem mit auf eines ohne Aufschläge umgestellt hat, seit Vanguard 1977 diesen beispiellosen Schritt unternahm.)

Der dritte maßgebliche Kostenfaktor für Fondsanleger besteht in den für den Kauf und Verkauf von Portfoliowertpapieren anfallenden Kosten. Solche Transaktionen kosten Geld. Wir schätzen die Umschlagskosten auf rund 0,5 Prozent für jeden Kauf und jeden Verkauf. Das bedeutet, dass ein Fonds mit einem Portfolioumschlag von 100 Prozent für Anteilsinhaber Jahr für Jahr mit Kosten von rund 1 Prozent des Vermögens verbunden ist. Entsprechend würde ein Umschlag von 50 Prozent den Fondsertrag um 0,50 Prozent pro Jahr verringern. Bei einem Umschlag von 10 Prozent würde die Belastung nur noch 0,10 Prozent betragen, und so weiter.

---

* In den letzten Jahren werden immer seltener Ausgabeaufschläge verlangt. Diese Kosten werden stattdessen verteilt, wodurch sich die Kostenquoten der Fonds kräftig erhöhen. So galt für die Anlageklasse A eines der größten Investmentfondsanbieter beispielsweise 2016 noch ein Ausgabeaufschlag von 5,75 Prozent bei einer Kostenquote von 0,58 Prozent. Heute bietet derselbe Anbieter eine neue Anteilsklasse T für seine Fonds an, die bei Emission nur noch mit 2,5 Prozent beaufschlagt wird. Dafür fallen jedoch zusätzliche Marketingkosten von 0,25 Prozent pro Jahr an, die für den gesamten Zeitraum zahlbar sind, über den der Anleger die Anteile hält. Diese Jahresgebühr erhöht die Kostenquote des Fonds auf schätzungsweise 0,83 Prozent.

Faustregel: Gehen wir davon aus, dass die Umschlagskosten eines Fonds 1 Prozent der Umschlagsrate entsprechen. 2016 beliefen sich die Käufe und Verkäufe von Portfoliowertpapieren bei Aktienfonds insgesamt auf 6,6 Billionen US-Dollar, was 78 Prozent des durchschnittlichen Aktienfondsvermögens von 8,4 Billionen US-Dollar entspricht. Die Kosten all dieser Handelsgeschäfte, die oft unter Mitbewerbern ablaufen, betrugen etwa 66 Milliarden US-Dollar – was jährlichen Gesamtaufwendungen in Höhe von 0,8 Prozent des Fondsvermögens entspricht.

Die Kosten sind hoch und bleiben allzu oft unbeachtet

Bei einem Kostenvergleich für Fonds wird meist ausschließlich auf die ausgewiesenen Kostenquoten geachtet. Daraus ergibt sich immer wieder, dass höhere Kosten mit niedrigeren Erträgen einhergehen. Dieses Muster ist aber nicht nur bei Aktienfonds als Gruppe festzustellen, sondern in jeder der neun Stilkategorien von Morningstar (Large-, Mid- und Small-Cap-Fonds, jeweils nach Zielsetzung den drei Fondsgruppen Growth, Value oder Blended zugeordnet).

Unabhängige Vergleiche berücksichtigen die zusätzlich vom Portfolioumschlag eines Fonds verursachten Kosten nur selten, doch für diese gilt eine ähnliche Beziehung: Die Fonds aus dem Quartil mit dem niedrigsten Umschlag haben für alle Aktienfonds als Gruppe und jeweils in den neun Stilkategorien kontinuierlich besser abgeschnitten als die aus dem Quartil mit dem höchsten Umschlag.

Durch den Aufschlag dieser geschätzten Umschlagskosten auf die Kostenquote des jeweiligen Fonds erhält die Beziehung zwischen Fondskosten und Fondsertrag enorme Brisanz. Berücksichtigt man beide Kosten, so liegen die jährlichen Kosten aktiv gemanagter Aktienfonds nach unseren Feststellungen in einer Bandbreite von 0,9 Prozent des Vermögens im kostengünstigsten Quartil bis 2,3 Prozent im teuersten Quartil, wie aus Abbildung 5.1 ersichtlich. (In dieser Rechnung sind Ausgabeaufschläge unberücksichtigt, sodass der Nettoertrag der Fonds in jedem Quartil *zu hoch* angesetzt ist.)

Kosten spielen eine Rolle – und zwar eine gewaltige

Kosten spielen eine Rolle! Abbildung 5.1 weist einen Unterschied von 1,4 Prozent zwischen der durchschnittlichen Kostenquote von Fonds im obersten Kostenquartil und den kostengünstigsten Fonds aus. Dieses Kostengefälle ist eine maßgebliche Erklärung für den Ertragsvorsprung kostengünstiger Fonds vor den besonders kostspieligen Fonds. Für die vergangenen 25 Jahre lag der durchschnittliche Nettojahresertrag der kostengünstigsten Fonds bei 9,4 Prozent, der Jahresnettoertrag der kostenintensivsten Fonds bei nur 8,3 Prozent. Allein durch Kostenminimierung lässt sich also bereits eine Ertragssteigerung erreichen. Beachten Sie bitte auch, dass der jährliche Bruttoertrag der einzelnen Kategorien nach Beaufschlagung des ausgewiesenen Nettoertrags der Fonds mit den Fondskosten praktisch identisch ist. Dieser Bruttoertrag (vor Abzug der Kosten) liegt erwartungsgemäß in einer engen Spanne zwi-

ABBILDUNG 5.1 Aktienfonds: Erträge und Kosten in der Gegenüberstellung, 1991–2016

Jahressatz								
Kosten								
Kostenquartil	Brutto-ertrag	Kosten-quote	Umschlag (geschätzt)	Gesamt-kosten	Netto-ertrag*	Kumulier-ter Ertrag	Risiko**	Risikobe-reinigter Ertrag
Eins (niedrigste Kosten)	10,3 %	0,71 %	0,21 %	0,91 %	9,4 %	855 %	16,2 %	8,9 %
Zwei	10,6	0,99	0,31	1,30	9,3	818	17,0	8,4
Drei	10,5	1,01	0,61	1,62	8,9	740	17,5	7,8
Vier (höchste Kosten)	10,6	1,44	0,90	2,34	8,3	632	17,4	7,4
500 Index Fund	9,2 %	0,04 %	0,04 %	0,08 %	9,1 %	783 %	15,3 %	9,1 %

* In dieser Analyse sind nur Fonds berücksichtigt, die über den gesamten 25-Jahres-Zeitraum bestanden. Die Daten setzen die von Aktienfonds erzielten Ergebnisse daher aufgrund des »Survivorship Bias« (Verzerrung infolge des Umstands, dass nicht alle Fonds diesen Zeitraum überdauert haben) deutlich zu hoch an.

** Jährliche Standardabweichung des Ertrags.

schen 10,6 Prozent für das kostenintensivste Quartil und 10,3 Prozent für das kostengünstigste Quartil. *Die Kosten sind in jedem Quartil im Wesentlichen für alle Unterschiede bei den jährlich von den Fonds verbuchten Nettoerträgen verantwortlich.*

Es gibt aber noch einen weiteren maßgeblichen Unterschied: Mit den Kosten steigen auch die Risiken. Legt man die Volatilität der Jahreserträge als Risikomaßstab zugrunde, waren die Risiken bei den kostengünstigsten Fonds deutlich geringer (mit einer durchschnittlichen Volatilität von 16,2 Prozent) als bei den besonders kostenintensiven (17,4 Prozent). Berücksichtigen wir diese Risikominderung, so beläuft sich der risikoadjustierte Jahresertrag für das kostengünstigste Quartil auf 8,9 Prozent und damit auf ganze 1,5 Prozentpunkte mehr als für das Quartil mit den höchsten Kosten (nämlich 7,4 Prozent).

Und wieder: das Wunder der Kumulation

Der jährliche Vorsprung um 1,5 Prozent beim risikobereinigten Ertrag mag gering erscheinen. Über längere Zeit kumuliert, nimmt er aber gewaltige Ausmaße an. Die kumulierte Rendite für den Zeitraum liegt bei den kostengünstigsten Fonds bei 855 Prozent und bei den kostenintensivsten bei 632 Prozent – eine Differenz von mehr als 35 Prozent, die sich fast ausschließlich aus dem Kostengefälle ergibt. Das bewirken die gnadenlosen Regeln einfacher Arithmetik.

Anders formuliert: Der Endwert bei den kostengünstigsten Fonds entspricht mehr als dem Achtfachen der ursprünglichen

Anlage, während die Erträge im kostenintensivsten Quartil lediglich in etwa eine Versechsfachung bewirkten. Zweifellos verbessern sich Ihre Erträge also, wenn sie »im billigen Teich fischen« – und zwar ganz enorm. Um es noch einmal zu sagen: Die Kosten spielen eine Rolle.

Stellen wir die Bedeutung der Fondskosten hier überzogen dar? Ich glaube nicht. Die folgenden Zeilen eines namhaften Morningstar-Analysten bestätigen meine Schlussfolgerungen – und mehr als das:

> *Wenn Sie sich in der Welt der Investmentfonds auf irgendetwas verlassen können, dann darauf, dass Ihnen die Kostenquoten zu besseren Entscheidungen verhelfen. In jedem überprüften Zeitraum und an jedem getesteten Datenpunkt schnitten kostengünstige Fonds besser ab als hochpreisige.*
>
> *Die Kostenquoten sind aussagekräftige Indikatoren für die Performance. In jeder Anlageklasse und in jedem Zeitraum warf das billigste Quintil höhere Gesamterträge ab als das teuerste.*
>
> *Für Anleger sollten die Kostenquoten das wichtigste Kriterium bei der Fondsauswahl sein. Sie haben nach wie vor die verlässlichste Prognosekraft für die Performance. Wenn Sie sich auf Fonds aus dem billigsten oder den untersten beiden Quintilen konzentrieren, sind Sie auf dem richtigen Weg zum Erfolg.*

Niedrige Kosten und Indexfonds

Wenn Sie diese überzeugende Bestätigung zu der Auffassung bringt, dass die Kosten tatsächlich eine Rolle spielen, und Sie sich folglich auf die kostengünstigsten Fondsgruppen fokussieren wollen – warum sollten Sie sich dabei dann auf aktiv gemanagte Fonds beschränken? Am allergünstigsten sind nun einmal traditionelle Indexfonds: Deren Kosten beliefen sich im betreffenden Zeitraum auf nur 0,1 Prozent. Ohne messbare Umschlagskosten betrugen die Gesamtkosten inklusive allem lediglich 0,1 Prozent. Der Bruttoertrag des S&P 500 Indexfonds lag bei 9,2 Prozent pro Jahr, der Nettoertrag bei 9,1 Prozent. Mit geringeren Risiken als für alle vier Kostenquartile (mit einer Volatilität von 15,3 Prozent) lag auch der risikobereinigte Jahresertrag bei 9,1 Prozent – ein kumulativer Gewinn, mit dem sich der Indexfonds mit 0,2 Prozent Vorsprung pro Jahr an die Spitze des kostengünstigsten Fondsquartils katapultierte.

Wenn die Manager nichts davon abschöpfen, bleibt er komplett den Anlegern: der Marktertrag

Achtung: Der risikobereinigte Jahresertrag des Indexfonds von 9,1 Prozent für die zurückliegenden 25 Jahre ist umso beeindruckender, als die Erträge aktiver Aktienfonds häufig zu hoch angesetzt werden, und zwar (wie immer) aufgrund der Tatsache, dass nur die Fonds in den Daten berücksichtigt wurden, die so gut waren, dass sie das gesamte Jahrzehnt hindurch Bestand hatten. Um diese Verzerrung bereinigt, würde der Ertrag des durchschnittlichen Aktienfonds von 9,0 Prozent auf schätzungsweise 7,5 Prozent zurückgehen.

Doch das ist noch nicht alles: Wer sich für den Indexfonds entscheidet, entzieht sich damit der Notwendigkeit, nach den seltenen Nadeln im Marktheuhafen zu suchen – die wenigen aktiven Fonds nämlich, die besser abgeschnitten haben als der besagte Heuhaufen –, in der oft vergeblichen Hoffnung, dass ihre Gewinnstrategie auch in künftigen Jahrzehnten noch funktioniert.

Wie Morningstar sagt: Müssten sich Anleger bei der Auswahl der Fonds, die künftig bessere Erträge erzielen als andere, und der Vermeidung anderer, die sich in Zukunft schwächer entwickeln werden, auf nur einen Faktor stützen, sollten das die Fondskosten sein. Die Statistik könnte nicht deutlicher sein: *Je mehr Manager und Makler verdienen, desto weniger bleibt den Anlegern.* Noch einmal: Wenn Manager und Makler *gar nichts* abgreifen, bekommen die Anleger *alles* (also den gesamten Ertrag, den der Aktienmarkt abwirft).

Wenn Sie mir nicht glauben ...

Tyler Mathisen, mittlerweile Chefredakteur von CNBC Business News, verdient Anerkennung, weil er bereits 1995 zu den ersten Journalisten gehörte – und womöglich sogar der allererste war –, die einräumten, was für eine wichtige Rolle die Kosten eines Investmentfonds (Kostenquoten, Umschlagskosten und vermeidbare Steuern) bei der Erosion der Erträge spielen, die für die Inhaber von Fondsanteilen abfallen. Mathisen, damals Redaktionsleiter bei *Money*, gestand dem kostengünstigen, steuereffizienten Indexfonds mit dem niedrigen Portfolioumschlag Überlegenheit zu:

»Seit über 20 Jahren propagiert der scharfzüngige Chef der Vanguard Group John Bogle nun schon die Vorzüge der Indexfonds – jener langweiligen Portfolios, die darauf abzielen, die Performance eines Marktbarometers nachzubilden. Und in dieser Zeit haben ihn Millionen von Fondsanlegern (von Dutzenden von Finanzjournalisten, den Autor eingeschlossen) mehr oder minder ignoriert.

Sicher, wir kannten die ureigenen Werte von Indexfonds, wie niedrige jährliche Aufwendungen und verschwindend geringe Transaktionskosten, weil die Fonds den Portfolioumschlag auf ein Minimum begrenzten. Hinzu kam, dass die Anteilsinhaber weniger Steuern ans Finanzamt abführen mussten, weil die Manager der Indexfonds Gewinne, die auf dem Papier bestehen, seltener realisieren als die

Verwalter aktiv gemanagter Fonds. Und diese drei Vorteile geben ohne jeden Zweifel ein ähnlich beeindruckendes Trio ab wie Domingo, Pavarotti und Carreras.

Also gut, Jack, wir lagen falsch. Du hast gewonnen. Sich mit dem Durchschnitt zu begnügen ist – zumindest für einen erheblichen Teil der Aktien- und Anleihenportfolios der meisten Anleger – gut genug. Tatsächlich können sich Anleger, indem sie versuchen, über Indexfonds Benchmark-neutrale Ergebnisse zu erzielen, in den meisten Fällen eine überdurchschnittliche Chance auf einen Vorsprung vor dem typischen gemanagten Aktien- oder Anleihenportfolio sichern. Das Paradoxe an der Fondsanlage von heute: Wer den Durchschnitt anvisiert, hat bessere Aussichten auf eine überdurchschnittliche Trefferquote.

Wir sehen es ein und stimmen ihm zu, dem mitunter kratzbürstigen, stets provokativen Fondsmagnaten, den seine Bewunderer und seine Kritiker gern als den heiligen Jack bezeichnen: Indexnachbildung sollte zentraler Bestandteil der meisten Fondsportfolios von Anlegern sein. Ein Hoch auf dich, Jack. Du sprichst, wie unlängst als Buchautor, mit Fug und Recht vom *Triumph des Indexing*.«

(Vielen Dank, Tyler!)

Sechstes Kapitel

Dividenden: des Anlegers (bester?) Freund

Nur, dass Investmentfonds zu viel davon für sich behalten

Die Dividendenrenditen sind eine wesentliche Komponente des langfristig vom Aktienmarkt erwirtschafteten Ertrags. Seit 1926 (dem ersten Jahr, für das uns umfassende Daten zum S&P 500 Index vorliegen) haben Dividenden sogar durchschnittlich 4,2 Prozent Jahresrendite beigetragen, was ganzen 42 Prozent des vom Aktienmarkt in diesem Zeitraum erzielten Jahresertrags von 10,0 Prozent entspricht.

Eine erstaunliche Erkenntnis

Kumuliert man die Dividenden über diesen langen Zeitraum, ist ihr Beitrag zur Wertsteigerung des Marktes geradezu unglaublich. Ohne Dividendenerträge wären aus einer ursprünglichen Anlage von 10.000 US-Dollar in den S&P 500 vom 1. Januar 1926 Anfang 2017 über 1,7 Millionen US-Dollar geworden. Doch mit wiederangelegten Dividenden wäre diese Anlage auf rund 59,1 Millionen Dollar angewachsen! Diese unfassbare Lücke von 57,4 Millionen US-Dollar zwischen (1) der Kurssteigerung an sich und (2) dem Gesamtertrag mit wiederangelegten Dividenden macht schlicht (wieder einmal) »die Magie der kostenlosen Kumulation« deutlich (Abbildung 6.1).

ABBILDUNG 6.1 Kursertrag und Gesamtertrag des S&P in der Gegenüberstellung

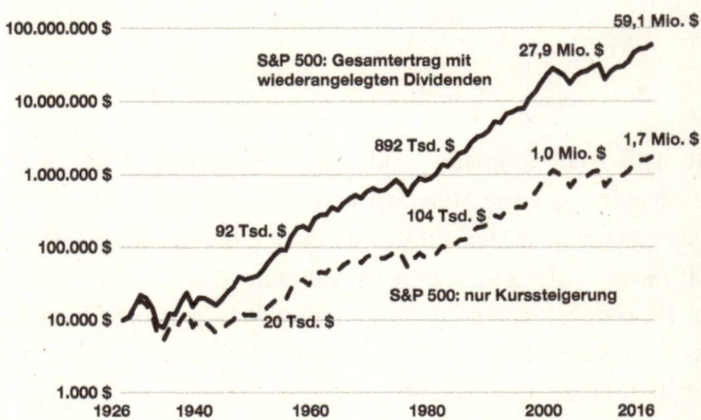

Die Stabilität der jährlichen Dividenden je Aktie des S&P 500 ist wirklich bemerkenswert (Abbildung 6.2). Über die 90 Jahre ab 1926 gab es nur drei deutliche Einbrüche: (1) ein Rückgang um 55 Prozent in den ersten Jahren der Weltwirtschaftskrise (1929–1933); (2) ein Rückgang um 36 Prozent 1938 im Nachgang zur Depression; und (3) ein Rückgang um 21 Prozent während der globalen Finanzkrise von 2008/2009. Zu diesem letzten Rückgang kam es in erster Linie, weil die Banken gezwungen waren, Dividenden zu streichen. Die Dividenden je Aktie im S&P fielen von 28,39 US-Dollar im Jahr 2008 auf 22,41 US-Dollar im Jahr 2009, erreichten 2016 aber ein neues Hoch von 45,70 US-Dollar – 60 Prozent mehr als der vorausgegangene Höchstwert von 2008.

ABBILDUNG 6.2 S&P 500 – Dividenden je Aktie

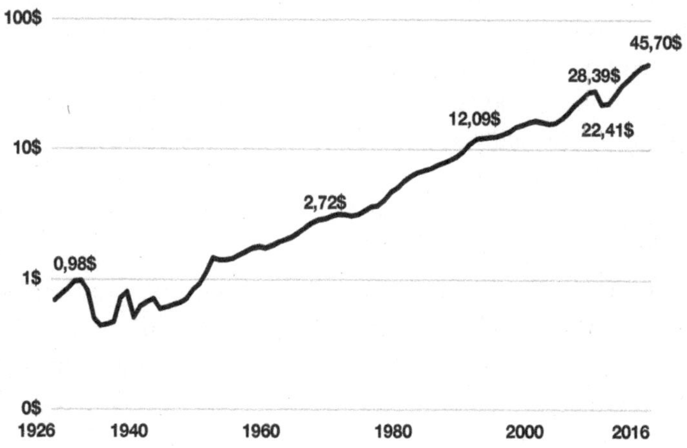

Für Investmentfondsmanager haben Dividendenerträge geringe Priorität

Angesichts der offensichtlichen langfristigen Wirkung kumulierter Dividenden und der relativen Stabilität der Dividendenausschüttungen durch die Unternehmen müssen gemanagte Investmentfonds den Dividendenerträgen doch sicher hohe Priorität einräumen, oder?

Falsch! Denn die Fondsverwaltungsverträge sehen stets Beratungsgebühren vor, die auf dem *Nettovermögen* eines Fonds basieren – nicht auf seinen *Dividendenerträgen*. Sind die Dividendenrenditen auf dem Aktienmarkt niedrig (wie in den letzten Jahren), zehren die Fondskosten einen gewaltigen Anteil der gesamten Dividendenerträge auf, die Fonds erzielen.

Das Ergebnis: Ein schwindelerregender Anteil an den Dividendenerträgen von Aktienfonds geht für die Aufwendungen drauf. Und »schwindelerregend« ist hier keine Übertreibung. Bei aktiv gemanagten Growth-Fonds werden sage und schreibe 100 Prozent der Dividendenerträge für die Aufwendungen verbraucht. Bei aktiv gemanagten Value-Fonds sind es immerhin noch 58 Prozent.

Der Kontrast zwischen aktiv gemanagten Fonds und vergleichbaren Indexfonds könnte kaum größer sein. Bei einem vergleichbaren Value-Indexfonds entfielen 2016 2 Prozent der Fondserträge auf die Aufwendungen. Bei einem kostengünstigen Growth-Indexfonds waren es nur 4 Prozent (Abbildung 6.3).

ABBILDUNG 6.3 Dividendenrenditen und Fondsaufwendungen, 2016

Aktiv gemanagte Fonds	Bruttorendite	Kostenquote	Nettorendite	Anteil der von den Aufwendungen aufgezehrten Bruttorendite
Growth-Fonds	1,3 %	1,3 %	0,0 %	100 %
Value-Fonds	2,1	1,2	0,9	58
Kostengünstige Indexfonds				
Growth-Fonds	1,4 %	0,1 %	1,3 %	4 %
Value-Fonds	2,5	0,1	2,4	2

Quelle: Morningstar

Aktiv gemanagte Aktienfonds zehren ihre Dividendenerträge auf

Trotz des großen Einflusses der Dividenden auf den langfristigen Ertrag sind Sie sich wie nahezu alle Anleger vermutlich dieses unfassbaren Entzugs von Dividendenerträgen nicht bewusst. Wie sollten Sie auch? Möglicherweise kann man diese Daten zwar aus dem Abschluss eines Fonds errechnen, doch solche Abschlüsse sind eher keine leuchtenden Beispiele für vollständige, klare und offene Angaben.

Warum ziehen Sie also nicht einen kostengünstigen Indexfonds in Betracht, der ohne aktiven Portfoliomanager auskommt. Seine jährliche Kostenquote liegt bei nur 0,04 Prozent, wodurch Sie den Anteil an den Dividendenerträgen des Fonds erhalten, der Ihnen zusteht. Außerdem werden die Aktien so gut wie nicht von den eingangs erwähnten Helfern hin- und hergeschoben. Warum also nicht? Darüber sprechen wir im dreizehnten Kapitel noch ausführlicher.

Wenn Sie mir nicht glauben …

Ein Blogger namens »**Dividend Growth Investor**« reagierte auf meine Auslassungen zur Bedeutung von Dividenden und schrieb einen Artikel, der meine Dividendenphilosophie widerspiegelt.

»John Bogle ist eine Investmentlegende. … Ich habe mehrere seiner Bücher gelesen und finde seine klaren Ansagen richtig gut. Bogles Rat, die Kosten und den Umschlag gering zu halten, langfristig am Ball zu bleiben und auf Einfachheit zu achten, sagte mir zu. Er hat mich beim Lesen sofort angesprochen. … Ganz besonders überzeugend fand ich, was Bogle über Dividenden zu sagen hatte.

Er spricht sich dafür aus, sich auf Dividendenzahlungen zu fokussieren und die Schwankungen der Aktienkurse zu ignorieren. Er bezeichnet den Aktienmarkt als ein einziges großes Ablenkungsmanöver und empfiehlt dem Anleger, ein Auge auf die Dividenden zu haben. …

Zu Recht weist er darauf hin, dass sich die Dividenden im Zeitverlauf kontinuierlich steigern. Damit sind sie die ideale verlässliche Ertragsquelle im Ruhestand. … Bogle spricht auch an, dass Dividenden zwar nicht garantiert sind, aber in der Vergangenheit nur wenige Male deutlich nachgegeben haben. …

Richtiggehend begeistert hat mich das Gesamtpaket, das er uns mit auf den Weg gibt: bei der Stange bleiben, sich auf die Dividenden konzentrieren, die Anlagekosten niedrig halten und die Aktienkurse ignorieren. Er plädiert auch dafür, auf Einfachheit zu achten. Bogle ist gegen die heutzutage verbreitete Praxis, Portfolios aufzubauen, die aus 10 bis 15 Anlageklassen bestehen und nur dem Zweck dienen, für Komplexität zu sorgen, um Gebühren für gierige Anlageverwalter zu generieren. Das heißt auch, dass wir uns Extravaganzen verkneifen und uns nicht dazu hinreißen lassen sollten, in neumodische Anlagekategorien zu investieren, deren Vorzüge auf den Rückvergleichen von Computermodellen beruhen.«

Siebtes Kapitel

Die große Illusion

Überraschung! Die von Investmentfonds ausgewiesenen Erträge fallen nur selten den Anteilsinhabern zu

Es tut mir gut, wenn mir Brancheninsider, wie Peter Lynch von Fidelity, der Ex-Chef des Investment Company Institute (ICI) Jon Fossel, James Cramer von *Mad Money* oder Clifford Asness von AQR, zustimmen, wie Sie vielleicht aus dem vierten Kapitel noch wissen. Im Regelfall sind die von einem Aktienfonds vereinnahmten Erträge im Vergleich zu den Erträgen, die es bringt, über einen Indexfonds auf der Grundlage des S&P 500 einfach den gesamten Aktienmarkt zu halten, unweigerlich unzulänglich.

Doch auch die Vorstellung, dass die Fondsanleger *selbst* tatsächlich 100 Prozent dieser unzulänglichen Investmentfondserträge erhalten, erweist sich als große Illusion. Und als großzügig berechnete obendrein. Die Wahrheit sieht nämlich viel schlimmer aus. Die Anteilsinhaber tragen nicht nur die hohen Kosten, die die Fondsmanager für ihre Dienste in Abzug bringen, sondern auch noch weitere Aufwendungen, die weit schwerer ins Gewicht fallen. Warum das so ist, soll das vorliegende Kapitel erklären.

Gewöhnlich weisen Fondsmanager die traditionellen *zeitgewichteten* Erträge aus, die von ihren Fonds berechnet werden – also die Veränderung des Nettoinventarwerts jedes Fondsanteils, angepasst um die Wiederanlage aller Dividenden und ausgeschütteten Veräußerungsgewinne. In den vergangenen 25 Jahren erzielte der durchschnittliche Investmentfonds einen Ertrag von 7,8 Prozent pro Jahr – 1,3 Prozentpunkte weniger als der S&P 500 mit 9,1 Prozent. Dieser *Fondsertrag* verrät aber nicht, welchen Ertrag der durchschnittliche *Fondsanleger* vereinnahmte. Und dieser ist weit geringer, wie sich zeigt.

Kleiner Hinweis: In die meisten Fonds fließt Kapital, *nachdem* sie sich gut entwickelt haben. Abflüsse erfolgen, wenn sich die Wertentwicklung dann verschlechtert.

Um zu bestimmen, welchen Ertrag der durchschnittliche Fondsanleger erhält, müssen wir den *dollargewichteten* Ertrag in Betracht ziehen, der die Effekte des Zu- und Abflusses von Fondskapital berücksichtigt.* (Kleiner Tipp: Zu Kapitalzuflüssen in Fonds kommt es meist nach guter Wertentwicklung, Abflüsse setzen ein, wenn sich die Performance im Anschluss verschlechtert.)

Stellen wir den nach der klassischen Methode berechneten Fondsertrag den Erträgen gegenüber, welche die Anleger im letzten Vierteljahrhundert tatsächlich vereinnahmen konnten, so zeigt sich, dass der durchschnittliche Fondsanleger nicht etwa die vom Durchschnittsfonds ausgewiesenen 7,8 Prozent erhielt, sondern stattdessen 6,3 Prozent – einen Jahresertrag, der 1,5 Prozentpunkte pro Jahr unter dem Ertrag des Fonds liegt.

Auch der Indexfondsanleger ließ sich vom steigenden Markt zur Anlage verleiten, erhielt aber einen Ertrag von 8,8 Prozent – nur 0,2 Prozent weniger als der eigentliche Fondsertrag. Tatsächlich: In den vergangenen 25 Jahren, in denen der S&P-500-Index jährlich 9,1 Prozent Ertrag abwarf und der durchschnittliche *Aktienfonds* eine Jahresrendite von 7,8 Prozent erzielte, blieben dem durchschnittlichen *Fondsanleger* nur 6,3 Prozent pro Jahr.

Gleich doppelt bestraft: durch Kosten und Anlegerverhalten

Über den gesamten Zeitraum hochgerechnet war die dem durchschnittlichen Fonds jedes Jahr auferlegte »Strafe« von 1,5 Prozent

* Ein Extrembeispiel: Erzielt ein Fonds mit einem Vermögen von 100 Millionen US-Dollar in einem beliebigen Jahr einen zeitgewichteten Ertrag von 30 Prozent auf seinen Nettoinventarwert und die Anleger honorieren diese gute Entwicklung, indem sie am letzten Tag des Jahres Anteile im Wert von 1 Milliarde US-Dollar kaufen, dann läge der durchschnittliche dollargewichtete Ertrag für die Anleger bei nur 4,9 Prozent.

aufgrund der Kosten enorm. Doch durch schlechtes Timing und ungünstige Auswahl fiel die Bestrafung gleich noch drastischer aus.

Abbildung 7.1 zeigt, dass 10.000 im Jahr 1991 in einen kostengünstigen S&P-500-Indexfonds investierte US-Dollar nominal einen Gewinn von 77.000 US-Dollar gebracht hätten (vor Berücksichtigung der Inflation). Der durchschnittliche Aktienfonds erzielte nur 55.500 US-Dollar – also 72 Prozent des Möglichen. Der vom durchschnittlichen Fondsanleger vereinnahmte kumulierte Ertrag betrug nur 36.100 US-Dollar – weniger als 50 Prozent der von den Anlegern eines einfachen Indexfonds erzielten 73.100 US-Dollar. In der Summe werden die Anleger also empfindlich abgestraft!

ABBILDUNG 7.1 S&P-Indexfonds und durchschnittlicher Large-Cap-Fonds in der Gegenüberstellung: Gewinn auf Erstanlage von 10.000 US-Dollar, 1991–2016

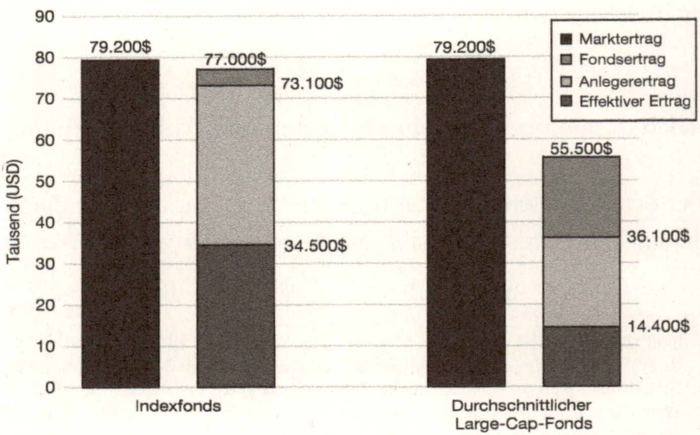

Unter Berücksichtigung der Inflation dezimiert sich der Wert all dieser Dollars. Bei einer Inflation von durchschnittlich 2,7 Prozent pro Jahr fällt der *effektive* Ertrag des Indexfonds auf 6,2 Prozent pro Jahr, der effektive Ertrag des durchschnittlichen Fondsanlegers aber auf nur 3,6 Prozent. Das entspricht einem kumulierten effektiven Wert von 34.500 US-Dollar für den Indexfonds gegenüber lediglich 14.400 US-Dollar für den Fondsanleger. Eine solche Differenz ist wahrhaftig unvorstellbar – doch Fakten sind Fakten.

Die Daten belegen eindeutig, dass die Erträge der Fondsanleger weit unter dem Fondsertrag liegen. Wie hoch der Fehlbetrag genau ist, lässt sich jedoch nicht sagen.* Doch diese Untersuchung der vom Aktienmarkt, vom Durchschnittsfonds und vom durchschnittlichen Anteilseigner erzielten Erträge soll lediglich *richtungweisend* sein, nicht *auf den Cent genau*.

Wie die genauen Daten auch aussehen, sie weisen überzeugend nach, dass (1) die langfristigen Erträge von Aktienfonds erheblich unter dem vom Aktienmarkt erzielten Ergebnis herhinken und (2) die Erträge der Fondsanleger noch einmal *um mehr als das Doppelte* dieses ohnehin beträchtlichen Gefälles hinter dem Markt zurückbleiben.

* Das Gefälle wurde geschätzt auf der Grundlage der Differenz der von Morningstar für den durchschnittlichen Large-Cap-Fonds ausgewiesenen zeitgewichteten Erträge und der tatsächlichen dollargewichteten Erträge über den gesamten 25-Jahres-Zeitraum.

Vom berauschenden Optimismus und der Gier angesteckt und durch die Tricks der Investmentfondsanbieter animiert, steckten die Anleger ihre Ersparnisse auf dem Höhepunkt der Hausse in Aktienfonds

Wie ist diese schockierende Lücke zu erklären? Schlicht gesagt durch kontraproduktive Ein- und Ausstiegszeitpunkte und unglückliche Fondsauswahl. Erstens zahlten Aktienfondsanleger eine empfindliche Zeitstrafe. In den Jahren, in denen Aktien preiswert waren – den 1980er- und frühen 1990er-Jahren – investierten die Anleger zu wenig ihrer Ersparnisse in Aktienfonds. Später, angesteckt vom berauschenden Optimismus und der Gier der Zeit und animiert durch die Tricks der Investmentfondsanbieter, investierten sie gerade dann einen zu großen Teil ihrer Ersparnisse in Aktienfonds, als sich der Bullenmarkt seinem Höhepunkt näherte.

Zweitens zahlten sie auch noch eine Strafe für missglückte Auswahl, denn sie legten ihr Geld nicht nur zur falschen Zeit auf dem Markt an, sondern auch noch in den falschen Fonds – Fonds, die in der Vergangenheit herausragende Ergebnisse erzielt hatten, doch, wie wir gleich sehen werden, danach abgestürzt sind.

Wieso? Nun, ganz einfach: Weil hohe Fondserträge dazu tendieren, auf oder unter den Mittelwert des Durchschnittsertrags zurückzufallen. (Über die Rückkehr zum Mittelwert – RTM – sprechen wir im elften Kapitel noch.) Durch kontraproduktives Timing und missglückte Fondsauswahl richteten sich die Anleger schlicht nicht nach der Stimme der Vernunft.

Wird eine kontraproduktive Anlegerstimmung noch verstärkt durch kontraproduktive Werbung der Fondsindustrie, kann daraus nichts Gutes werden

Dieser Differenzeffekt war erstaunlich weit verbreitet. So erwirtschafteten 186 der 200 größten Aktienfonds von 2008 bis 2016 für ihre Anleger niedrigere Erträge, als sie denselben Anlegern auswiesen!

Besonders deutlich zeigte sich der Abstand während des »New Economy«-Wahns Ende der 1990er-Jahre. Damals legte die Fondsindustrie immer mehr Fonds auf, die gewöhnlich mit höheren Risiken verbunden waren als der Aktienmarkt als solcher. Noch verschärft wurde das Problem durch die intensive Werbung mit ansprechenden bisherigen Erträgen, die die heißesten Fonds eingefahren hatten.

Als die Märkte in die Höhe schossen, steckten die Anleger noch größere Summen in Aktienfonds. 1990, als Aktien billig waren, investierten sie netto insgesamt nur 18 Milliarden US-Dollar, 1999 und 2000, als Aktien erheblich überbewertet waren, dagegen 420 Milliarden US-Dollar (Abbildung 7.2).

Hinzu kam, dass sich die überwiegende Mehrheit der Anleger für »New Economy«-Fonds, Technologiefonds und die ertragsstärksten Wachstumsfonds interessierte, und praktisch überhaupt nicht für eher konservative, substanzwertorientierte Fonds. Während 1990 nur 20 Prozent ihres Kapitals in aggressiven Wachstumsfonds steckten, waren ganze 95 Prozent in solche Fonds geflossen, als deren Erträge 1999 und Anfang 2000 Höchststände erreichten. Nachdem die Blase geplatzt war – also, als es zu spät

ABBILDUNG 7.2 Die negativen Konsequenzen von Timing und Auswahl: Nettozuflüsse in US-amerikanische Aktienfonds

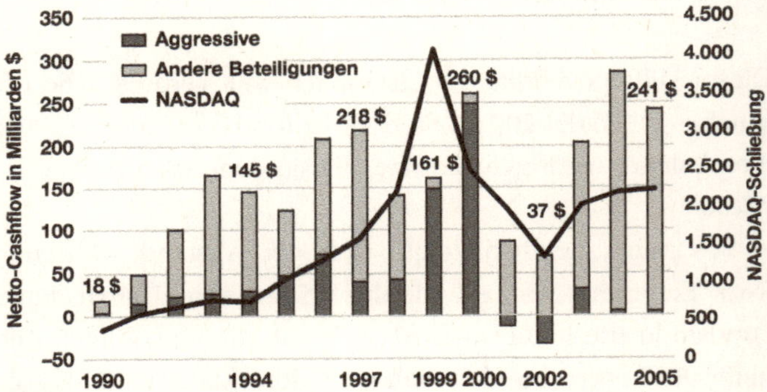

	1990	1994	1997	1999	2000	2002	2005
NASDAQ Level	374	752	1570	4069	2471	1336	2205
Aggressive Aktien	20 %	20 %	18 %	92 %	96 %	neg.	2 %

war –, schrumpften die Anlegerkäufe auf nur mehr 36 Milliarden US-Dollar zusammen, kurz bevor der Markt einen Boden bildete. Auch aus Wachstumsfonds wurde Geld abgezogen und – ebenfalls zu spät – in wertorientierte Fonds umgeschichtet.

Die enttäuschende Vorstellung der Fondsinvestoren wiederholte sich in der Finanzkrise von 2008/2009 und während der anschließenden Erholung. Seit jeher jagen Fondsanleger früheren Erträgen nach und lassen zu, dass ihre Gefühle – vielleicht auch ihre Gier – ihren Verstand vernebeln. Viele Anleger reagierten heftig – und letztlich kontraproduktiv – auf den Einbruch der Märkte während der Finanzkrise, indem sie auf dem Tiefpunkt aus Aktien ausstiegen. Viele dieser Anleger verpassten die nachfolgende Erholung ganz oder zumindest teilweise – einen Anstieg um insgesamt rund 250 Prozent vom Tief bis Ende 2016.

Anlegerstimmung plus Werbung der Fondsindustrie ist gleich Ärger

Die Fondsindustrie selbst hat die Problematik noch verschärft, indem sie die Anlegerstimmung ausnutzte und immer neue (häufig kostenintensive und spekulative) Fonds herausbrachte, um den jeweils aktuellen Launen und Moden zu entsprechen, und diese dann aggressiv bewarb und vermarktete. Man kann durchaus sagen: Wenn kontraproduktive Anlegerstimmung von kontraproduktiver Werbung der Fondsindustrie ausgenutzt wird, ist davon nichts Gutes zu erwarten.

Die Fondsindustrie wird ihre neuen Produkte und ihre Werbeaktionen nicht so schnell aufgeben, und es wird dauern (und persönliche Erfahrungen erfordern), bis Anleger aus kontraproduktivem kurzfristigem Verhalten lernen. Intelligente Anleger sind gut beraten, wenn sie nicht nur die Botschaft des vierten Kapitels zur Kostenminimierung beherzigen, sondern auch die Aussage dieses Kapitels zur Streichung der Emotionen aus der Gleichung – also zur Verbesserung ihres kurzfristigen, marktorientierten Verhaltens.

Das Schöne am Indexfonds ist nicht nur, dass er so billig ist, sondern auch, dass all die verführerischen Auswahlmöglichkeiten wegfallen, die so viel versprechen und so wenig halten. Der Indexfonds mit seiner langfristigen Ausrichtung, der die kurzfristigen Störgeräusche des Aktienmarkts möglichst ignoriert und die heißen Fonds des Tages außen vor lässt, kann ein ganzes Anlegerleben lang durch dick und dünn gehalten werden. Emotionen spielen dabei grundsätzlich keine Rolle. Die Erfolgsformel für Anlagegewinne ist es, über einen Indexfonds den gesamten Aktienmarkt zu halten und dann einfach gar nichts mehr zu tun. Nur dabei zu bleiben.

Wenn Sie mir nicht glauben …

Der weise Warren Buffett ist da ganz meiner Meinung. Er formulierte das so: »Die größten Feinde des Aktieninvestors sind Kosten und Emotionen.« Diese Auffassung teilt auch MIT-Professor **Andrew Lo**, Autor von *Adaptive Markets* (2017), der selbst »investiert, indem er Indexfonds kauft und hält«.

Noch überraschender ist aber vielleicht, dass der Gründer und Chef des größten Investmentfonds-Supermarkts zwar eifrig für Aktienhandel und aktiv gemanagte Fonds wirbt, aber persönlich ebenfalls den traditionellen Indexfonds vorzieht. Auf die Frage, warum Anleger in gemanagte Fonds investieren, entgegnete **Charles Schwab**: »Es macht Spaß, herumzuspielen … es entspricht dem Wesen des Menschen, zu versuchen, auf das richtige Pferd zu setzen … [Doch] für den Durchschnittsbürger tendiere ich eher zur Indexnachbildung. … Das ist so vorhersagbar. … Über 10, 15, 20 Jahre liegen Sie damit im 85. Performance-Perzentil. Warum sollten Sie sich das vermasseln?« (Der Großteil von Schwabs privatem Portfolio steckt in Indexfonds.)

Mark Hulbert, Herausgeber des hochangesehenen *Hulbert Financial Digest,* stimmt ebenfalls zu. »Wenn wir davon ausgehen, dass die Zukunft ähnlich wird wie die Vergangenheit, können Sie über die nächsten Jahrzehnte besser abschneiden als 80 Prozent Ihrer Mitanleger, wenn Sie in einen Indexfonds investieren – und nur das. …[E]ignen Sie sich die Disziplin an, es besser zu machen [als zu versuchen, den Markt zu schlagen]: Werden Sie zum langfristigen Indexfondsanleger.«

Sein Artikel in der *New York Times* erschien unter der Überschrift: »Kaufen und halten? Aber sicher, nur vergessen Sie das Halten nicht.«

Achtes Kapitel

Auch Steuern sind Kosten

Zahlen Sie nicht zu viel ans Finanzamt

Damit sind wir mit den unerbittlichen Regeln der einfachen Arithmetik aber noch nicht durch. Und ebenso wenig mit den logischen, unvermeidlichen und gnadenlosen langfristigen Strafen, die Aktienmarktteilnehmer in Form von Anlagekosten, durch den mächtigen Einfluss der Inflation, durch kontraproduktives Anlegerverhalten und durch die Werbung der Fondsindustrie für nicht bewährte, »heiße« Investmentfonds auf sich ziehen. Solche Praktiken dezimieren das von Fondsanlegern aufgebaute Kapital. Der Indexfonds bietet hervorragenden Schutz vor fast allen dieser versteckten Kosten und ihren unliebsamen Folgen. (Nicht geschützt sind die realen Indexerträge natürlich vor den verheerenden Folgen der Inflation, die sich auf alle Anlagen gleichermaßen auswirkt.)

Es gibt aber noch einen – gern vernachlässigten – Kostenfaktor, der den tatsächlich vom Anleger vereinnahmten Nettoertrag noch weiter dezimiert. Ich meine damit die Steuern, die Bund, Bundesstaaten und Kommunen auf das Einkommen erheben.* Auch diesbezüglich verfügt der Indexfonds über enorme Vorzüge. De facto sind die meisten gemanagten Investmentfonds steuerlich erstaunlich ineffizient. Warum? Weil die Portfoliomanager kurzfristig orientiert sind und allzu oft eifrig mit den Aktien aus den Portfolios handeln, die ihrer Aufsicht unterstehen.

Gemanagte Fonds sind steuerlich erstaunlich ineffizient

Der Portfolioumschlag des durchschnittlichen gemanagten Aktienfonds unter Berücksichtigung von Käufen und Verkäufen liegt mittlerweile bei 78 Prozent pro Jahr. (Der »klassische« Umschlag – der nur Käufe oder Verkäufe berücksichtigt, wobei jeweils der geringere Wert herangezogen wird – liegt bei 39 Prozent.) Branchenübergreifend hält ein durchschnittlicher aktiver Fonds eine Aktie im Schnitt nur 19 Monate. (Basierend auf dem

* Etwa die Hälfte aller Aktienfondsanteile wird von Privatanlegern auf voll steuerpflichtigen Anlagedepots gehalten. Die andere Hälfte liegt auf Depots mit nachgelagerter Besteuerung, etwa zur privaten Altersvorsorge (Individual Retirement Accounts oder kurz IRAs) oder im Rahmen von unternehmensinternen oder anderen Sparplänen oder Mitarbeiterbeteiligungsprogrammen. Sollten Ihre Anteilsbestände ausschließlich in die letztgenannten Kategorien fallen, sind die Ausführungen in diesem Kapitel für Sie nicht von Belang.

Gesamtvermögen beträgt die durchschnittliche Haltefrist 31 Monate.) Kaum zu glauben, dass der jährliche Portfolioumschlag von Aktienfonds im Zeitraum von 1945 bis 1965 im Schnitt nur 16 Prozent betrug und die durchschnittliche Haltefrist der durchschnittlichen Aktie in einem Fondsportfolio sechs Jahre. Dieser gewaltige Anstieg des Umschlags und die damit einhergehenden Transaktionskosten leisten den Anlegern einen Bärendienst. Dass für die Fonds unnötige Steuern anfallen, die an die Anleger durchgereicht werden, kommt erschwerend hinzu.

Dieses Muster der steuerlichen Ineffizienz bei aktiven Managern dürfte sich wohl so lange fortsetzen, wie (1) die Aktienkurse steigen und (2) die Fondsmanager weiterhin ihr hyperaktives Handelsverhalten an den Tag legen. Im Klartext heißt das: Früher einmal fokussierten sich die meisten Fondsmanager auf die langfristige Kapitalanlage. Heute geht es ihnen allzu oft um kurzfristige Spekulation.

Der traditionelle Indexfonds verfolgt genau die entgegengesetzte Politik – er kauft und hält »für alle Zeit«. Sein jährlicher Portfolioumschlag bewegt sich bei 3 Prozent, und die Transaktionskosten dementsprechend zwischen verschwindend gering und null.

Wo bleiben die Daten?

Setzen wir dort ein, wo wir ein paar Kapitel zuvor aufgehört haben. Sie wissen ja: Der jährliche Nettoertrag des durchschnittlichen Aktienfonds für die vergangenen 25 Jahre betrug

7,8 Prozent, der Ertrag des S&P-500-Indexfonds 9,0 Prozent. Angesichts des hohen Portfolioumschlags aktiv gemanagter Fonds unterlagen ihre steuerpflichtigen Anleger einer geschätzten effektiven jährlichen Bundessteuer von 1,2 Prozentpunkten pro Jahr beziehungsweise rund 15 Prozent ihres gesamten Vorsteuerertrags. (Von Bundesstaaten und Kommunen erhobene Steuern sollten diese Zahl noch weiter aufblähen.) Ergebnis: Der jährliche Nachsteuerertrag fiel auf 6,6 Prozent.

Trotz der höheren Erträge, die sie erhielten, mussten die Anleger des Indexfonds de facto weniger Steuern entrichten, die hauptsächlich für Dividendenerträge anfielen. Die extrem niedrigen Kosten von Indexfonds nagen im Vergleich zu aktiv gemanagten Fonds nicht so sehr an den Dividendeneinnahmen, was zu höheren Dividendenrenditen führt und somit zu höheren Steuern auf Dividenden.

Mitte 2017 belief sich die Dividendenrendite eines kostengünstigen Standard-&-Poor's-500-Indexfonds insgesamt auf 2,0 Prozent, *das Doppelte* der Rendite des durchschnittlichen aktiv gemanagten Aktienfonds. Steuerpflichtige Indexfondsanleger mussten pro Jahr rund 0,45 Prozent an Bundessteuern berappen – nur etwa ein Drittel der jährlichen Steuerlast von 1,5 Prozent, die Anleger aktiv gemanagter Fonds zu tragen hatten.

Da aktive Fonds häufig größere kurzfristige Veräußerungsgewinne an Anteilsinhaber ausschütten – die mit dem höheren konventionellen Einkommensteuersatz besteuert werden, nicht mit dem niedrigeren Satz für langfristige Kapitalerträge –, sind Anleger aktiver Fonds steuerlich deutlich stärker belastet als Indexfondsanleger.

Fazit: Der durchschnittliche aktiv gemanagte Aktienfonds erzielte einen jährlichen Nachsteuertrag von 6,6 Prozent, der Indexanleger 9,6 Prozent. Kumuliert brachte eine Anlage von ursprünglich 10.000 US-Dollar im Jahr 1991 bei aktiven Fonds einen Nachsteuergewinn von 39.700 US-Dollar. Das sind 60 Prozent weniger als der kumulierte Zuwachs von 68.300 US-Dollar für den Indexfonds. Der Rückstand der aktiven Fonds brachte ihren Anlegern unter dem Strich einen Verlust von 28.600 US-Dollar.*

Die Fondserträge werden durch Kosten, schlechte Fondsauswahl, ungünstige Ein- und Ausstiegszeitpunkte, Steuern und Inflation enorm verringert

Ich zögere, einen dieser negativen Faktoren als den Tropfen zu bezeichnen, der bei den Aktienfondserträgen »das Fass zum Überlaufen bringt«. Doch die folgenden Faktoren tragen sicherlich dazu bei: (1) hohe Kosten (viertes, fünftes und sechstes Kapitel), (2) Fehlentscheidungen von Anlegern und kontraproduktive zeitliche Gestaltung (siebtes Kapitel) und (3) Steuern (achtes Kapitel). Wie man es auch betrachtet, übergelaufen ist das Fass auf jeden Fall. Der allerletzte Tropfen ist aber, wie sich herausstellt, die Inflation.

* Der Indexfondsanleger unterläge dabei einer Steuer auf jeden durch eine Veräußerung von Anteilen erzielten Gewinn. Hinterlässt ein Anleger seine Anteile aber seinen Erben, so werden die Kosten am Sterbedatum auf ihren Marktwert »aufgestockt«. Dann würden keine Veräußerungsgewinne verbucht oder besteuert.

Nominale und reale Renditen im Vergleich

Solange wir unsere Fondskosten Jahr um Jahr in *aktuellen* Dollars zahlen – und genau das gilt für Fondsaufwendungen und Steuern auf Veräußerungsgewinne (die obendrein oft noch kurzfristig realisiert werden) –, unser Vermögen aber nur in *realen* Dollars aufbauen, die vom unerbittlichen Anstieg der Lebenshaltungskosten angeknabbert werden, der unserer Wirtschaft innewohnt, sind die Folgen verheerend.

Dass diese Katastrophe in den Informationen, die Investmentfonds ihren Anlegern erteilen, so oft ausgeklammert wird, ist wirklich erstaunlich – und wenig löblich.

Es ist paradox: Während der Indexfonds beim Management von Kapitalerträgen bemerkenswert steuereffizient ist, erweist sich, dass er bei der Ausschüttung von Dividendenerträgen im Vergleich steuerlich ineffizient ist. Wieso? Weil seine minimalen Kosten bedeuten, dass die auf Aktien, die von kostengünstigen Indexfonds gehalten werden, gezahlten Dividenden direkt an die Inhaber der Anteile des Indexfonds fließen.

Wenn Sie mir nicht glauben …

John B. Shoven von der Stanford University und dem National Bureau of Economic Research und **Joel M. Dickson**, damals noch bei der US-Notenbank (heute geschäftsführender Gesellschafter von Vanguard) haben dazu Folgendes zu sagen: »Es ist den Investmentfonds nicht gelungen, ihre realisierten Veräußerungsgewinne so zu steuern, dass sie nachgelagert besteuert werden, was die Steuerlast der Anleger erheblich [erhöht]. … Hätte der Vanguard 500 Index Fund alle seine realisierten Veräußerungsgewinne aufgeschoben, läge er für Anleger mit hohem Steuersatz im 91,8 Perzentil« (und hätte damit besser abgeschnitten als alle gemanagten Aktienfonds).

Anlageberater **William Bernstein**, Autor von *The Four Pillars of Investing*, ist folgender Auffassung: »Es ist überhaupt keine so gute Idee, aktiv gemanagte Investmentfonds zu halten. Eine *ausgesprochen schlechte Idee* ist aber, sie auf steuerpflichtigen Depots zu halten. … [Die Steuern] mindern die Wertentwicklung jedes Jahr um bis zu 4 Prozentpunkte … viele Indexfonds sehen vor, dass Ihre Veräußerungsgewinne weitgehend unbehelligt anwachsen, bis Sie verkaufen. … *Für den steuerpflichtigen Anleger bedeutet die Anlage in Indizes, dass es nie etwas zu bereuen gibt.*«

Auch **Burton G. Malkiel** setzt auf den Indexfonds: »Indexfonds sind … steuerfreundlich, erlauben es dem Anleger, die Realisierung von Veräußerungsgewinnen hinauszuschieben oder gänzlich zu vermeiden, wenn er die Anteile später vererbt. Solange der langfristige Aufwärtstrend der Aktienkurse anhält, bedeutet die Umschichtung von einer Aktie in eine andere, dass Veräußerungsgewinne realisiert werden, die steuerpflichtig sind. Steuern sind ein entscheidendes Kriterium in Finanzfragen, weil eine vorzeitige Realisierung von Veräußerungsgewinnen den Nettoertrag erheblich verringert. Indexfonds springen nicht von Aktie zu Aktie und gehen Kapitalertragsteuern so tendenziell aus dem Weg.«

Neuntes Kapitel

Wenn die Party vorbei ist

Wer klug ist, rechnet künftig mit niedrigeren Erträgen auf Aktien- und Rentenmärkten

Erinnern Sie sich noch an den unfehlbaren Grundsatz aus dem zweiten Kapitel? Langfristig ist es die Realwirtschaft – also die Dividendenrenditen und die Gewinnsteigerungen der Unternehmen –, die beeinflusst, welchen Ertrag der Aktienmarkt abwirft. Betrachten wir jedoch einfach nur die 43 Jahre, seit ich am 24. September 1974 Vanguard gegründet habe, dann ist paradoxerweise Folgendes festzustellen: Die Erträge, die der Aktienmarkt lieferte, überstiegen die von den Unternehmen erwirtschafteten Gewinne über einen so langen Zeitraum stärker denn je in der gesamten US-Börsengeschichte.

Konkret sorgten die Dividendenrenditen und Ertragssteigerungen der Aktiengesellschaften, aus denen sich der Standard & Poor's 500 Index zusammensetzt, für einen *Anlageertrag* von nur 8,8 Prozent für den Zeitraum (Dividendenrendite von 3,3 Prozent, Ertragssteigerungen von 5,5 Prozent), während der Jahresgesamtertrag bei 11,7 Prozent lag. (Siehe Abbildung 9.1.)

Ganze 2,9 Prozentpunkte des Marktertrags – insgesamt also immerhin 25 Prozent – entfielen auf spekulative Erträge. Darin schlägt sich die Höherbewertung von Aktien durch Anleger nieder, da sich das Kurs-Gewinn-Verhältnis mehr als verdreifachte, von 7,5 auf 23,7. (Der durchschnittliche jahrzehntelange Beitrag des spekulativen Ertrags zum jährlichen Gesamtertrag des Marktes seit 1900 belief sich lediglich auf 0,5 Prozentpunkte, also nur ein Fünftel der großzügigen Zuflüsse, in deren Genuss wir Anleger seit 1974 gekommen sind.)

Der Gesamteffekt dieser kumulierten Erträge ist enorm (Abbildung 9.1). Über den besagten 43-Jahres-Zeitraum wären aus einem ursprünglichen Anlagebetrag von 10.000 US-Dollar knapp 1.090.000 US-Dollar geworden. Von diesem Vermögen von mehr als einer Million lassen sich rund 270.000 US-Dollar spekulativen Erträgen zuschreiben, die restlichen 820.000 US-Dollar entfielen auf Dividenden und Ertragssteigerungen.

Es stimmt schon, das extrem niedrige KGV von 7,5 im September 1974 war auf dem Tiefpunkt eines Aktienmarkteinbruchs um 50 Prozent zu verzeichnen. Darin spiegelten sich ausgeprägter Pessimismus, überzogene Ängste und verbreitete Besorgnis unter den Anlegern. Anfang 2017 bleibt abzuwarten, ob die ak-

ABBILDUNG 9.1 Kumulierter Anlageertrag und spekulativer Ertrag, 1900–2016

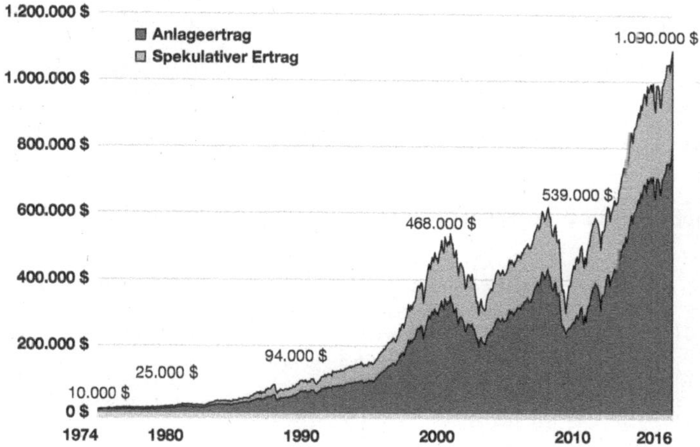

tuellen Bewertungen mit einem KGV von 23,7 eine Mischung aus ungezügeltem Optimismus, übermäßigem Vertrauen, Überschwang und Hoffnung darstellen oder eine neue Realität.

Vernunft und einfache Arithmetik sagen uns, dass wir vor einer Ära mit gedämpften Aktienmarkterträgen stehen

Per saldo haben Aktienanleger mehr als vier Jahrzehnte lang außergewöhnliche Erträge erzielt. Doch da der jährliche Marktertrag in diesem Zeitraum zu immerhin 25 Prozent auf spekulative

Erträge entfiel, ist es unrealistisch, davon auszugehen, dass sich das KGV erneut so entwickelt oder dass der KGV-Anstieg den von Aktien im anstehenden Jahrzehnt erzielten Erträgen größere Dynamik verleiht – wenn überhaupt. Unser Verstand sagt uns, dass wir im Vergleich zur langfristigen jährlichen Nominalrendite von 9,5 Prozent seit 1900 wieder vor einer Ära mit verhaltenen Aktienmarkterträgen stehen (Abbildung 9.2).

ABBILDUNG 9.2 Gesamtertrag von Aktien, Vergangenheit und Zukunft

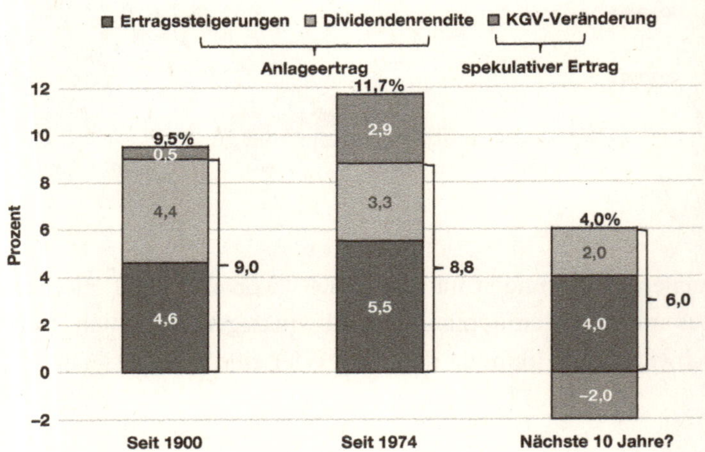

Ich sage bewusst *wieder*, denn in der ersten Ausgabe dieses Buches (von 2007) verwendete ich denselben Titel für dieses Kapitel: »Wenn die Party vorbei ist.« Damals ging ich von realistischen Erwartungen für die Aktienerträge in den zehn Jahren von 2006 bis 2016 von 7 Prozent pro Jahr aus. Tatsächlich warf der

S&P 500 fast exakt so viel ab: 6,9 Prozent. (Bitte keinen Beifall. Ich habe nämlich den spekulativen Ertrag um so viel zu tief angesetzt wie den Anlageertrag zu hoch.)

Die Arithmetik hinter der Vorsicht: die Treiber der Aktienerträge

Wieso also die erneute Zurückhaltung? Schlicht deshalb, weil uns die Treiber der Aktienerträge zur Vorsicht mahnen. Erinnern Sie sich an Lord Keynes' Warnung aus dem zweiten Kapitel: »Es ist gefährlich ..., induktive Argumente auf der Grundlage früherer Erfahrungen auf die Zukunft zu übertragen, wenn man nicht in großen Zügen erkennt, warum frühere Erfahrungen so und nicht anders aussahen.« In jenem Kapitel habe ich drei Quellen von Aktienerträgen beschrieben: die ursprüngliche Dividendenrendite und die Ertragssteigerungen (zusammen der »Anlageertrag«) und die Veränderungen des KGV (der »spekulative Ertrag«).

Künftiger jährlicher Anlageertrag: 6 Prozent?

Betrachten wir die Ertragstreiber, wie sie sich heute darstellen. Zum Ersten beträgt die Dividendenrendite von Aktien nicht 4,4 Prozent (wie früher), sondern nur 2 Prozent. Wir dürfen also mit einem Mitnahmeeffekt von 2,4 Prozentpunkten pro Jahr beim Beitrag der Dividendenerträge zum Anlageertrag rechnen.

Gehen wir davon aus, dass die Unternehmensgewinne weiter steigen (wie es im Zeitverlauf gewöhnlich der Fall war), und in etwa im selben Tempo wie die erwartete *nominale* Wachstumsrate unserer Wirtschaft von 4 bis 5 Prozent pro Jahr beim Bruttoinlandsprodukt (BIP) in den kommenden zehn Jahren – also langsamer als die langfristige nominale US-Wachstumsrate von 6 Prozent und mehr.

Sollte sich diese Erwartung als einigermaßen zutreffend erweisen, dann dürften sich die Anlageerträge von Aktien höchstwahrscheinlich zwischen 6 und 7 Prozent bewegen. Ich bin lieber vorsichtig und prognostiziere einen jährlichen *Anlageertrag* von durchschnittlich 6 Prozent.

Künftiger jährlicher spekulativer Ertrag – *minus* 2 Prozent?

Nehmen wir nun den *spekulativen* Ertrag. Anfang 2017 lag das KGV von Aktien bei 23,7. Diese Zahl basiert auf den *ausgewiesenen Vorjahreserträgen* des S&P 500. Hielte sich das KGV für die nächsten zehn Jahre auf diesem Niveau, würde der *spekulative* Ertrag weder etwas zu dem potenziellen Anlageertrag von 6 Prozent beitragen noch diesen verringern.

Wall-Street-Strategen berechnen das KGV im Allgemeinen lieber anhand der *prognostizierten operativen Gewinne für das kommende Jahr* statt auf der Grundlage der *ausgewiesenen Gewinne der letzten zwölf Monate*. Diese operativen Gewinne berücksichtigen keine Abschreibungen für die Einstellung der Geschäftstätigkeit und andere Misslichkeiten sowie Projektionen künftiger Gewinne, die möglicherweise realisiert werden, möglicherweise aber auch nicht. Anhand der prognostizierten operativen Gewinne berechnet, liegt das KGV der Wall Street nur bei 17. Ich würde diese Projektion außen vor lassen.

Nach meiner Schätzung – die zwar fundiert ist, aber trotzdem nur eine Schätzung – dürfte das KGV am Ende des Jahrzehnts vielleicht auf, sagen wir, 20 oder sogar stärker zurückgegangen sein. Eine solche Neubewertung würde den Marktertrag um rund 2 Prozentpunkte pro Jahr drücken, was in einer jährlichen Rendite des US-Aktienmarkts von 4 Prozent resultieren würde.

Wenn Sie meiner 4-Prozent-Erwartung nicht zustimmen, können Sie gern eigene Berechnungen anstellen

Sie müssen sich meiner Ansicht nicht anschließen. Wenn Sie meinen, dass das KGV auch in zehn Jahren noch wie heute 23,7 beträgt, dann läge der spekulative Ertrag bei null, und der gesamte Marktertrag bestünde nur aus dem Anlageertrag. Wenn Sie (anders als ich!) davon ausgehen, dass die Bewertungen auf 30 steigen, dann *addieren* Sie 1,5 Prozentpunkte, was den Jahresertrag von Aktien auf 7,5 Prozent erhöht. Glauben Sie, das KGV fällt auf 12, *subtrahieren* Sie 7 Prozentpunkte, was den gesamten Nominalertrag von Aktien auf *minus* 1 Prozent verringert.

Damit will ich Folgendes sagen: Sie müssen mein vorsichtiges Szenario nicht übernehmen. Sie können gern anderer Meinung sein. Rechnen Sie die Werte für das kommende Jahrzehnt ruhig selbst hoch, indem Sie die aktuelle Dividendenrendite zugrunde legen (daran führt kein Weg vorbei!), Ihre eigenen rationalen Erwartungen für die Ertragssteigerungen sowie Ihre Ansicht zum KGV von 2027. Der Gesamtbetrag entspricht dann Ihrer eigenen realistischen Erwartung für die Aktienerträge in den kommenden zehn Jahren.

Der Treiber der Anleiherenditen: die aktuelle Zinsrendite Die Aufstellung realistischer Erwartungen zu den künftigen Erträgen von Anleihen ist einfacher als bei Aktien. Wieso? Weil für Aktien die drei zuvor ermittelten Ertragstreiber vorliegen, bei Anleihen aber nur eine Hauptrenditequelle: der beim Kauf der Anleihe geltende Zinssatz.

Jawohl: Die Umlaufrendite einer Anleihe (oder eines Anleiheportfolios) stellt die erwartete Rendite dar, wenn die Anleihe langfristig gehalten wird. In der Vergangenheit hat sich die ursprüngliche Rendite als verlässlicher Indikator für künftige Erträge erwiesen. De facto sind über die Jahrzehnte seit 1900 ganze 95 Prozent der Anleiheerträge durch die ursprüngliche Rendite zu erklären (Abbildung 9.3). Logisch!

Warum das so ist? Nun, weil sich der Emittent einer zehnjährigen Anleihe verpflichtet, das ursprüngliche Kapital am Ende des Jahrzehnts auf den Cent genau vollständig zurückzuzahlen. Bei Anleihen mit Anlagequalität (Investment Grade) wurde diese Zusage in aller Regel auch eingehalten. Praktisch der gesamte Ertrag stammt also aus den Zinszahlungen. Sicher, zwischendurch kann der Marktwert der Anleihe schwanken, wenn sich die Zinssätze verändern. Wird die Anleihe aber bis zur Fälligkeit gehalten, wirken sich diese Schwankungen nicht aus.

ABBILDUNG 9.3 Ursprüngliche Anleiherenditen und anschließende Erträge

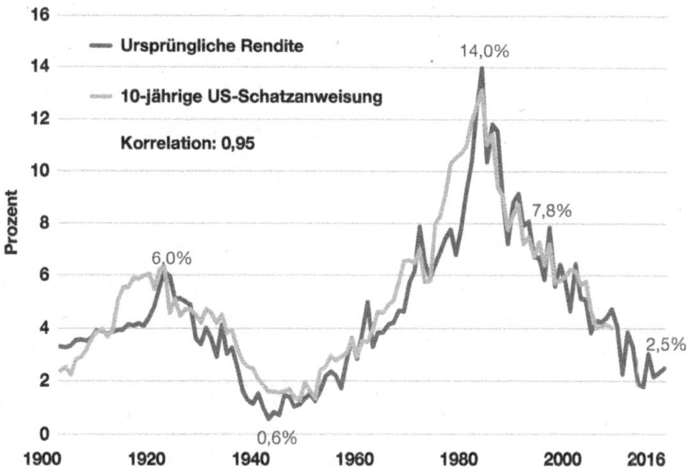

Abbildung 9.3 zeigt die erstaunlich enge Beziehung zwischen der ursprünglichen Rendite der zehnjährigen US-Schatzanweisung und ihrer anschließenden Zehnjahresrendite. Beachten Sie dabei den langen Zyklus bei Renditen (und anschließenden Erträgen) von einem Tief bei 0,6 Prozent 1940 bis zu einem Hoch von (beachtlichen!) 14,0 Prozent 1981. Danach fielen die Renditen bis 2012 auf 1,8 Prozent zurück und erholten sich dann leicht auf 2,2 Prozent Mitte 2017.

Die US-Schatzanweisung ist mit einem minimalen (oder noch geringeren) Rückzahlungsrisiko verbunden – will heißen, dem Risiko, dass der Kapitalbetrag bei Fälligkeit der Anleihe nicht zurückgezahlt wird. Die Umlaufrendite von 2,2 Prozent setzt also die künftigen Erträge des breiten Anleihenmarktes deutlich zu niedrig an, weil das Rückzahlungsrisiko bei Unternehmensanleihen höher ist. Ich stütze mich bei meinen Erwartungen zum künftigen Ertrag von Anleihen daher auf ein Portfolio, das sich zu 50 Prozent aus US-Schatzanweisungen mit einer aktuellen Rendite von 2,2 Prozent und zu 50 Prozent aus langfristigen Unternehmensanleihen mit Investment Grade zusammensetzt, die derzeit 3,9 Prozent abwerfen. Aus dieser Mischung ergibt sich eine Rendite von 3,1 Prozent für ein breit gestreutes Bondportfolio. Realistisch wäre daher, für die nächsten zehn Jahre von einem Jahresertrag von 3,1 Prozent für Anleihen auszugehen.

ABBILDUNG 9.4 Gesamtertrag von Anleihen, Vergangenheit und Zukunft

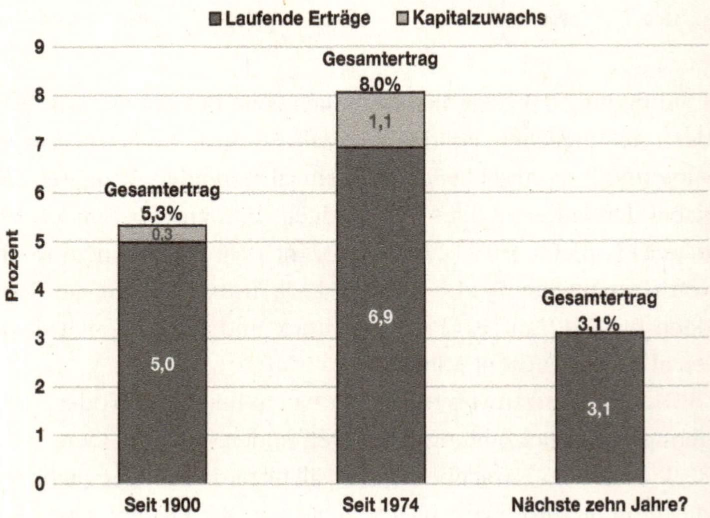

In den kommenden zehn Jahren dürften die Erträge von Anleihen wie bei Aktien deutlich unter ihrer historischen Norm bleiben (Abbildung 9.4). Über den langen Abschnitt seit 1900 betrug die jährliche Rendite von Anleihen im Schnitt 5,3 Prozent. In neuerer Zeit seit 1974 brachten Anleihen deutlich höhere Renditen – im Durchschnitt 8,0 Prozent pro Jahr. Dem lag in erster Linie der lange, kontinuierliche Bullenmarkt zugrunde, der 1982 einsetzte, als die Zinsen purzelten und die Kurse anzogen.

Angesichts der niedrigeren Erträge, die für Aktien und Anleihen in Aussicht stehen, gilt dasselbe auch für Mischportfolios aus Aktien und Anleihen

Im Zusammenspiel dieser realistischen Erwartungen für die künftigen Erträge von Aktien und Anleihen in einem Mischportfolio aus 60 Prozent Aktien und 40 Prozent Anleihen ergibt sich ein erwarteter jährlicher Bruttonominalertrag von 3,6 Prozent für die nächsten zehn Jahre – vor Abzug von Anlagekosten. Natürlich könnte sich diese Erwartung als zu niedrig oder zu hoch erweisen. Aber vielleicht verhilft sie uns zu einer realistischen Grundlage für unsere Finanzplanung.

So oder so, ein erwarteter jährlicher Ertrag von 3,6 Prozent läge deutlich unter dem langfristigen Durchschnitt eines solchen Mischportfolios von 7,8 Prozent und unter den denkwürdigen seit 1974 erzielten 10,2 Prozent (Abbildung 9.5).

Rechnen wir diese nominalen Jahreserträge in reale (inflationsbereinigte) Renditen um, so erkennen wir eine kleinere,

ABBILDUNG 9.5 Gesamtertrag eines Mischportfolios aus 60 Prozent Aktien/40 Prozent Anleihen, Vergangenheit und Zukunft

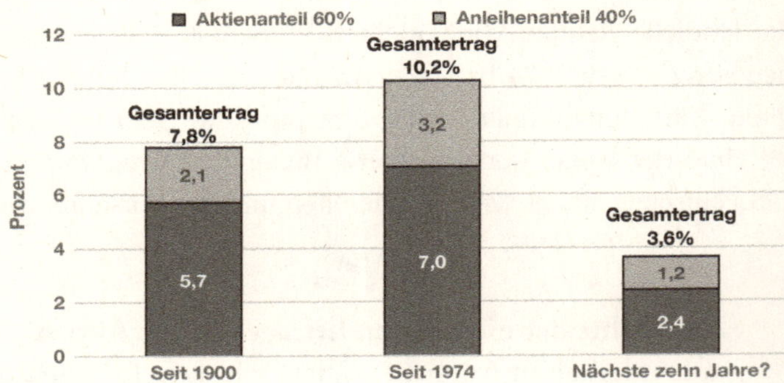

	Seit 1900	Seit 1974	Nächste zehn Jahre?
Nominale Rendite	**7,8%**	**10,2%**	**3,6%**
Inflation	**3,0**	**3,9**	**2,0**
Reale Rendite	**4,8%**	**6,3%**	**1,6%**

doch immer noch erhebliche Lücke: historisch 4,8 Prozent, seit 1974 6,3 Prozent und für die kommenden zehn Jahre vielleicht 1,6 Prozent. (Siehe die Tabelle am Ende von Abbildung 9.5.)

Wenn realistische Erwartungen von einem künftigen jährlichen Bruttoertrag von 3,6 Prozent für einen Mischfonds ausgehen, was bedeutet das für den Nettoertrag der Anteilsinhaber des Mischfonds?

Gehen wir davon aus, dass die 3,6 Prozent Ertrag Mitte 2017 eine realistische Erwartung (*keine* Prognose!) für den Jahresertrag eines Mischportfolios in den kommenden zehn Jahren sind. Bedenken

Sie dabei bitte, dass die Anleger als Gruppe nicht den gesamten Marktertrag für sich beanspruchen können (und auch nicht erhalten). Warum? Ganz einfach: Weil die Anlage auf den Aktien- und Rentenmärkten über aktiv gemanagte Fonds mit geschätzten jährlichen Kosten von mindestens 1,5 Prozent verbunden ist.

Um den voraussichtlichen Ertrag eines durchschnittlichen aktiv gemanagten Mischfonds in einem solchen Umfeld zu berechnen, müssen Sie sich schlicht auf die einfache Arithmetik der Fondsanlage besinnen: nominaler Marktertrag abzüglich Anlagekosten abzüglich einer angenommenen Inflationsrate von 2 Prozent (und damit etwas mehr, als von den Finanzmärkten derzeit für das kommende Jahrzehnt erwartet wird) ist gleich nur 0,1 Prozent pro Jahr. Hier die Rechnung:

Nominaler Bruttoertrag	3,6 %
Anlagekosten	–1,5
Nominaler Nettoertrag	2,1 %
Inflation	–2,0
Reale Jahresrendite	0,1 %

Es mag absurd erscheinen, für den typischen Mischfonds von einer Rendite nahe null auszugehen. Doch wenn Sie sich an die Lektion aus dem siebten Kapitel erinnern, dann erhält der durchschnittliche *Anleger* eines Mischfonds sogar noch weniger. Die Zahlen lügen nicht.

Im Vergleich dazu könnte ein kostengünstiger Misch-Indexfonds mit jährlichen Kosten von nur 0,1 Prozent eine reale Jahresrendite von, sagen wir, 1,5 Prozent abwerfen, wenn die Renditen sinken – deutlich mehr als ein aktiv gemanagter Fonds. Nicht berauschend, aber doch wenigstens nicht negativ, und damit unendlich viel besser.

Solange sich die Fondsindustrie nicht verändert, ist der typische aktiv gemanagte Fonds offenbar eine beispiellos unglückliche Wahl für den Anleger

Es ist leider eine Tatsache, dass niedrigere Renditen die unbarmherzige Arithmetik überhöhter Investmentfondskosten drastisch verstärken. Wieso? Aktienfondskosten von 2 Prozent in Kombination mit 2 Prozent Inflation würden »nur« rund 25 Prozent des Nominalertrags auf Aktien von 15 Prozent aufzehren – und »nur« 40 Prozent von 10 Prozent Ertrag. Doch Kosten und Inflation (ich hoffe, Sie sitzen gut!) würden ganze 100 Prozent der 4 Prozent Nominalrendite auf Aktien vernichten, die nach vernünftigem Ermessen zu erwarten sind.

Wenn sich die Fondsindustrie nicht allmählich verändert – indem sie die Managementkosten, die Betriebsaufwendungen, die Ausgabeaufschläge und den Portfolioumschlag (und die Begleitkosten) spürbar senkt – sind kostenintensive aktiv gemanagte Fonds offensichtlich eine selten schlechte Wahl für Anleger.

Die vom durchschnittlichen aktiven Aktienfonds erzielte Realrendite von null sollte eigentlich inakzeptabel sein. Was können Aktienfondsanleger tun, um nicht in die Falle dieser gnadenlosen Regeln einfacher Arithmetik zu tappen? Wie können Sie die finanziellen Verheerungen vermeiden, die automatisch erfolgen, wenn hohe Anlagekosten auf künftige Erträge anfallen, die voraussichtlich deutlich unter der langfristigen Norm liegen?

Fünf Möglichkeiten, die schlimmen finanziellen Folgen zu vermeiden – von denen nur zwei funktionieren

Hier fünf verführerische Optionen zur Aufbesserung Ihrer Anlageerträge:

1. Wählen Sie einen ausgesprochen kostengünstigen Indexfonds, der schlicht das Aktienmarktportfolio hält.
2. Wählen Sie Fonds mit minimalen Kosten, minimalem Portfolioumschlag und ohne Ausgabeaufschläge.
3. Wählen Sie gewinnbringende Fonds auf der Grundlage ihrer langfristigen bisherigen Erfolgsbilanz.
4. Wählen Sie gewinnbringende Fonds auf der Grundlage ihrer jüngsten kurzfristigen Wertentwicklung.
5. Lassen Sie sich bei der Fondsauswahl professionell beraten, um Fonds zu finden, die den Markt schlagen dürften.

Für welche Option entscheiden Sie sich? Kleiner Tipp: Die Wahrscheinlichkeit ist groß, dass Sie sich mit den ersten beiden Optionen insofern Anlageerfolg sichern, als Sie denselben Ertrag erzielen, den unsere Finanzmärkte liefern. Die Erfolgswahrscheinlichkeit der drei anderen Optionen ist erbärmlich. Ihre jeweiligen Grenzen werden in den folgenden drei Kapiteln aufgezeigt.

Wenn Sie mir nicht glauben …

So gut wie jeder Ökonom, Wissenschaftler und Aktienmarktstratege, der sich ernsthaft mit den Finanzmärkten auseinandersetzt, pflichtet mir bei, dass uns die guten Zeiten, die uns die Aktienmärkte nach den im Herbst 1974 erreichten Tiefs beschert haben, auf längere Sicht nicht erhalten bleiben.

Berücksichtigen Sie dazu die folgenden Hochrechnungen von **AQR Capital Management**, einem der größten und erfolgreichsten Verwalter alternativer Anlagen: »Die zu erwartenden Anlageerträge sind gering. Wir rechnen mit einer realen Rendite von 4,0 Prozent auf Aktien und 0,5 Prozent auf Anleihen, was für ein Mischportfolio aus 60 Prozent Aktien und 40 Prozent Anleihen [vor Anlagekosten] einen realen Ertrag von 2,6 Prozent ergibt.«

Diese Hochrechnungen von AQR wirken eindeutig absolut optimistisch neben denen von **Jeremy Grantham**, dem langjährigen Chef des Beratungsunternehmens GMO, das große Stiftungen betreut. Für die kommenden sieben Jahre rechnet GMO mit einer realen Jahresrendite von minus 2,7 Prozent für Aktien und einer Rendite von minus 2,2 Prozent für Anleihen – was für ein Mischportfolio im Verhältnis 60/40 aus Aktien und Anleihen einen realen Ertrag von minus 2,5 Prozent bedeuten würde.

Gary P. Brinson, CFA, Ex-Präsident von UBS Investment Management, ist ebenfalls meiner Meinung. »Für die Märkte muss sich die Wertschöpfung beziehungsweise Alpha insgesamt auf null summieren. Das positive Alpha des einen ist das negative Alpha des anderen. Zusammen genommen dürfte sich der Alphaertrag für die Bereiche institutionelle Anlage, Investmentfonds und Privatkundengeschäft nach Transaktionskosten bei oder unter null bewegen.

Die Gesamtgebühren für aktive Manager sollten daher maximal so hoch sein wie die mit passivem Management verbundenen Gebühren. Doch diese Gebühren machen das Mehrfache der für passives Management anfallenden Kosten aus. Das ist unlogisch und muss endlich ein Ende haben.«

Oder hören Sie, was **Richard M. Ennis, CFA,** von Ennis Knupp + Associates, Herausgeber des *Financial Analyst Journal,* schon 2006 zu sagen hatte: »Angesichts der Zinssätze von heute um die 4 Prozent [inzwischen liegen sie noch niedriger, eher bei 3 Prozent] und Aktien, die keine 2 Prozent abwerfen, können die wenigsten in absehbarer Zukunft für längere Zeit mit zweistelligen Anlageerträgen rechnen. Doch wir leben mit einem Vermächtnis dieser Ära: mit historisch hohen Gebührenstrukturen, die herbeigeführt wurden durch die vielen Billionen Dollar, die während des Booms auf Wachstum aus waren, und danach auf Sicherheit. Zweitens werden die Anleger ihr Kapital angesichts der doppelten Herausforderung der Markteffizienz und der hohen Kosten weiterhin von aktive auf passive

Verwalter umschichten. … Impulse dafür gibt die wachsende Erkenntnis, dass hohe Gebühren das Wertentwicklungspotenzial selbst der kompetentesten Manager zunichtemachen.«

Zehntes Kapitel

Langfristige Gewinner auswählen

Suchen Sie nicht nach der Stecknadel – kaufen Sie lieber gleich den ganzen Heuhaufen

Die meisten Anleger schauen auf die enttäuschenden bisherigen Erträge von Investmentfonds als Gruppe und denken sich: »Schon klar – aber ich suche mir ja nur Produkte aus, die besonders hohe Erträge bringen!« Leichter gesagt als getan: Im Voraus gewinnbringende Fonds auszuwählen, ist gar nicht so einfach. Es gibt zwar immer ein paar erfolgreiche Fonds, die 25 Jahre und länger überleben, doch nicht sehr viele. Nimmt man sich die Aufzeichnungen zur früheren Wertentwicklung vor, sind sie leicht zu erkennen.

Am meisten hört man von Investmentfonds, die mit dem Glanz vergangener Erfolge den Himmel erleuchten. Von solchen, die länger – vielleicht sogar sehr lange – im Höhenflug waren und dann abgeschmiert sind, hören wir wenig. Wenn so ein Fonds ins Trudeln gerät, dann ist er oft nicht mehr lange im Geschäft. Er wird aufgelöst oder mit anderen Fonds verschmolzen. So oder so, er verschwindet von der Bildfläche und wird dem Papierkorb der Investmentfondsgeschichte überantwortet.

Doch so leicht es ist, die Gewinner der Vergangenheit zu erkennen, so wenig sagt es darüber aus, ob sie ihre Performance auch in Zukunft fortsetzen können. Betrachten wir zunächst die historischen Daten von Fonds, die sehr lange Zeit erfolgreich waren. Abbildung 10.1 geht zurück bis 1970 und zeigt die 46-jährige Erfolgsbilanz der 355 Aktienfonds, die bereits zu Beginn dieses Zeitraums auf dem Markt waren. Und schon ereilt Sie die erste und offensichtlichste Überraschung: *Ganze 281 die-*

ABBILDUNG 10.1 Gewinner, Verlierer und Gescheiterte: langfristige Investmentfondsrenditen, 1970–2016

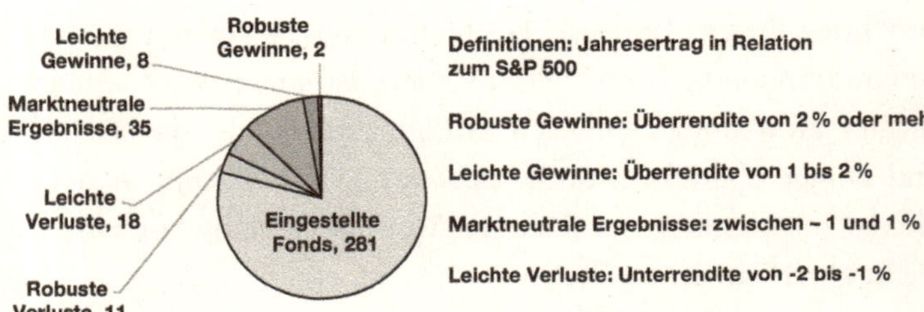

ser Fonds – also fast 80 Prozent – sind nicht mehr im Geschäft. Wenn aber Ihr Fonds nicht auf lange Sicht besteht, wie können Sie dann langfristig investieren?

Fast 80 Prozent aller Fonds sind aus dem Geschäft

Sie dürfen davon ausgehen, dass es nicht die ertragsstärksten Fonds waren, deren Betrieb verdientermaßen eingestellt wurde. Es waren die Verlustbringer, die das Feld geräumt haben. Nicht in jedem Fall übrigens auch ihre Manager. (Die durchschnittliche »Amtszeit« von Portfoliomanagern aktiver Aktienfonds liegt bei knapp neun Jahren.) Manchmal wurden die Verwaltungsgesellschaften solcher Fonds auch von großen Finanzkonzernen aufgekauft und die neuen Eigentümer haben »die Produktlinie bereinigt«. (Solchen Konzernen geht es in Wirklichkeit vor allem darum, *ihr* Kapital als Eigentümer der Verwaltungsgesellschaft des Fonds zu mehren – nicht *Ihr* Kapital als Anteilseigner.) Oft haben auch die Anleger ihr Kapital aus unterdurchschnittlichen Fonds abgezogen. Dadurch schmolz deren Vermögen ab und sie wurden zur Belastung für die Gewinne ihrer Manager. Es gibt viele Gründe für die Auflösung eines Fonds – und wenige davon sind gut für die Anleger.

Mitunter stellen auch Fonds mit robuster langfristiger Bilanz ihre Geschäftstätigkeit ein. Oft werden ihre Verwaltungsgesellschaften von Vermarktungsunternehmen übernommen, deren ehrgeizige Führungsriege beschließt, dass sich die Fonds zwar bislang nicht schlecht entwickelt haben, aber auch nicht so berauschend, dass damit größere Mengen an frischem Kapital von neuen Anlegern einzuwerben sind. Die Fonds erfüllen damit schlicht ihren Zweck nicht mehr. Bei anderen Fonds führen ein paar Jahre mit stockender Wertentwicklung zum selben Resultat.

Ein Todesfall in der Familie

Tragischerweise fiel vor reichlich zehn Jahren der zweitälteste Fonds der gesamten Investmentfondsindustrie dieser Einstellung zum Opfer. Er wurde vom neuen Eigentümer seiner Verwaltungsgesellschaft aus dem Verkehr gezogen. Obwohl er die Marktturbulenzen der vorausgegangenen 80 Jahre überstanden hatte, schied er dahin: der *State Street Investment Trust, 1925–2005. Er ruhe in Frieden.* Als einer der Dinosaurier der Fondsbranche, der sich noch sehr genau an die glanzvolle Bilanz dieses Fonds über so viele Jahre erinnert, ist der Verlust des State Street Investment Trust für mich fast wie ein Todesfall in der Familie.

Erbärmliche Erfolgschancen: Nur zwei von 355 Fonds haben tatsächlich eine herausragende Wertentwicklung vorzuweisen.

So oder so, von den im Jahr 1970 bestehenden Aktienfonds haben 281 nicht überlebt, allen voran die ertragsschwächsten. Nur 29 existieren noch, obwohl sie deutlich – nämlich um mehr als einen Prozentpunkt pro Jahr – hinter dem S&P 500 zurücklagen. Insgesamt ist es folglich 310 Fonds – 87 Prozent der ursprünglichen 355 Fonds – nicht gelungen, sich auf die eine oder andere Weise zu profilieren. Weitere 35 Fonds lieferten Renditen, die sich um einen Prozentpunkt unter oder über dem Ergebnis des S&P 500 bewegten – und damit auf Marktniveau.

Bleiben lediglich zehn Investmentfonds – *also einer von 35* –, die den Markt um mehr als einen Prozentpunkt pro Jahr übertrafen. Machen wir uns nichts vor: *Das sind verheerende Aussichten*. Hinzu kommt, dass der Vorsprung vor dem S&P 500 bei acht dieser zehn Fonds keine zwei Prozentpunkte pro Jahr betrug und damit genauso gut einem glücklichen Zufall zuzurechnen sein könnte wie besonderer Kompetenz.

Die Geschichte des Magellan Fund

Damit sind immerhin zwei Fonds mit robusten langfristigen Gewinnen übrig, die den S&P 500 seit 1970 um mehr als 2 Prozentpunkte pro Jahr überrunden konnten. Erlauben Sie mir, meinen Hut zu ziehen … und zwar vor dem Fidelity Magellan (+2,6 Prozent pro Jahr gegenüber dem S&P 500) und dem Fidelity Contrafund (+2,1 Prozent). Kein Zweifel, es ist eine gewaltige Leistung, den Jahresertrag des Marktes über fast 50 Jahre um mehr als 2 Prozentpunkte zu übertreffen. Dennoch liegt hier ein seltsamer – möglicherweise offensichtlicher – Umstand vor. Schauen wir uns die Bilanzen dieser beiden Fonds doch etwas genauer an und sehen, was wir daraus lernen können.

Abbildung 10.2 zeichnet das Wachstum des Magellan-Vermögens nach (schattierter Bereich) sowie seinen Ertrag im Verhältnis zum S&P 500 (schwarze Linie). Steigt die Linie an, schneidet der Magellan-Fonds besser ab als der Index. Fällt sie, liegt der Index vorne. In seiner Glanzzeit (von 1977 bis einschließlich 1990) stand der Magellan-Fonds unter der Leitung von Starfondsmanager Peter Lynch. Seither haben fünf verschiedene Manager den Fonds nicht minder erfolgreich geführt.* Doch dabei war mehr im Spiel als nur die Kompetenz (oder die glückliche Hand) des Managers. Auch das enorme Wachstum des Fondsvermögens ist zu berücksichtigen.

ABBILDUNG 10.2 Fidelity Magellan: Langfristige Bilanz im Vergleich zum S&P 500, 1970–2016

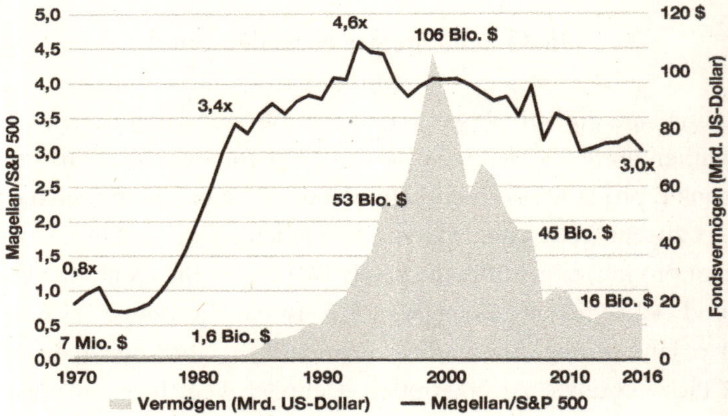

* Wie das *Wall Street Journal* am 28. Mai 2004 schrieb, äußerte der damalige Manager des Magellan-Fonds Bob Stansky, dass »er damit rechnet, den Markt längerfristig um 2 bis 5 Prozentpunkte pro Jahr zu schlagen. ›Ich will gewinnen.‹« Unter Stansky verfehlte der Magellan-Fonds den S&P 500 um 1,2 Prozent pro Jahr. Er wurde 2005 abgelöst. Es ist ein hartes Geschäft.

Die größten Gewinne verbuchte der Magellan-Fonds kurz nach seiner Auflegung mit einem Vermögen von nur 7 Millionen US-Dollar. Damals überrundete der Fonds den S&P 500 um umwerfende 10 Prozent pro Jahr (Magellan: 18,9 Prozent, S&P 500: 8,9 Prozent). Als das Fondsvermögen 1983 die 1-Milliarde-Dollar-Marke knackte, entwickelte sich der Fonds zwar weiterhin besser als der Markt, allerdings mit einem geringeren, wenn auch immer noch eindrucksvollen Vorsprung von 3,5 Prozent pro Jahr (Magellan: 18,4 Prozent, S&P 500: 14,9 Prozent), bis das Fondsvermögen dann 1993 über 30 Milliarden US-Dollar anstieg.

Der Fonds wuchs noch weiter, bis zu einem Höchstvolumen von 105 Milliarden US-Dollar am Jahresende 1999, erzielte jedoch keine Überrenditen mehr über den S&P 500: Vielmehr blieb er im Zeitraum von 1994 bis einschließlich 1999 um 2,5 Prozent pro Jahr hinter dem Index zurück (Magellan: 21,1 Prozent, S&P 500: 23,6 Prozent). Auch nach der Jahrtausendwende blieb der Fonds im Rückstand und verfehlte den S&P 500 um 1,8 Prozent pro Jahr (Magellan: 2,7 Prozent, S&P 500: 4,5 Prozent), obwohl sein Vermögen drastisch abschmolz – von 105 Milliarden US-Dollar im Jahr 1999 auf 16 Milliarden US-Dollar Ende 2016, ein Schwund um 85 Prozent. Dass das Geld in den Magellan-Fonds strömte, als er »heiß« war, und abfloss, als er »abkühlte«, könnte ein ganz klassischer Fall kontraproduktiven Anlegerverhaltens sein.

Die Contrafund-Story

Bislang ist die Contrafund-Story der Geschichte vom Magellan-Fonds in seinen ersten 30 Jahren nicht so unähnlich – großer

Erfolg, gefolgt von … der Rückkehr zum Mittelwert. Seit 1990 ist Will Danoff leitender Portfoliomanager. Seine bemerkenswerten Leistungen beim Contrafund sind unwiderlegbar.

Bevor Danoff die Zügel übernahm, übertraf der Fonds den S&P 500 um 1 Prozent pro Jahr (Contrafund: 12,6 Prozent, S&P 500: 11,6 Prozent). Danoff hat den jährlichen Vorsprung während seiner Amtszeit bis einschließlich 2016 beinahe verdreifacht (Contrafund: 12,2 Prozent, S&P 500: 9,4 Prozent). (Siehe Abbildung 10.3.) Früher oder später setzt aber stets die Rückkehr zum Mittelwert ein. In den vergangenen fünf Jahren blieb der Contrafund um 1,2 Prozent hinter dem S&P 500 zurück (Contrafund: 13,5 Prozent, S&P 500: 14,7 Prozent).

ABBILDUNG 10.3 Fidelity Contrafund: Langfristige Bilanz im Vergleich zum S&P 500, 1970–2016

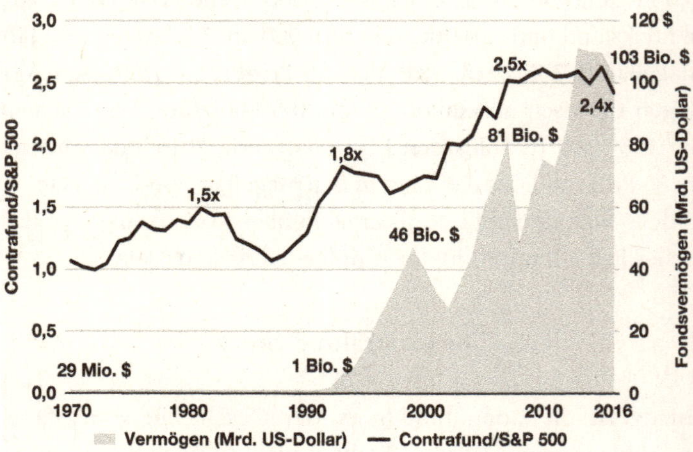

Doch der Erfolg hat seine Tücken. Als Danoff 1990 die Leitung übernahm, belief sich das Fondsvermögens auf insgesamt 300 Millionen US-Dollar. 2013 überschritt es die 100-Milliarden-US-Dollar-Schwelle. In den drei Jahren danach verflüchtigte sich die Überlegenheit des Contrafund. Pro Jahr verbuchte er 1,5 Prozent Rückstand auf den Index (Contrafund: 12,8 Prozent, S&P 500: 14,3 Prozent). Die Zeit wird weisen, was die Zukunft bringt.

Als das Anlegerpublikum spitz bekam, was Magellan und Contrafund für Anlageerträge erzielten, floss das Geld in Strömen, und das Fondsvermögen schwoll gewaltig an. Doch, wie uns Warren Buffett erklärt: »Eine dicke Brieftasche ist der Feind der Überrendite.« Und so kam es. Mit zunehmender Größe der beiden populären Fonds verloren ihre Bilanzen an Glanz. Zwar werden nur wenige aktiv gemanagte Fonds in absehbarer Zeit die Mammutgröße eines Magellan – oder auch eines Contrafund – erreichen, doch viele, vermutlich sogar die meisten Fondsmanager werden in guten Zeiten Kapitalzuflüsse verzeichnen und in schlechten Kapitalschwund. Das ist ein grundlegendes Problem der Sensibilität der Branche auf Schwankungen bei den Fondserträgen.

Wer zum Schwert greift, soll durch das Schwert umkommen

Nicht alle Fidelity-Fonds bewährten sich langfristig so wie der Magellan und der Contrafund. Ein gegenteiliges Beispiel war der 1957 gegründete Fidelity Capital Fund – einer der Stars der Go-Go-Ära (Ende der 1960er-, Anfang der 1970er-Jahre, A.d.Ü.).

Von 1965 bis 1972 belief sich seine kumulierte Rendite auf insgesamt 195 Prozent gegenüber 80 Prozent für den S&P 500. Doch im nachfolgenden Bärenmarkt verlor der Fonds 49 Prozent (während der S&P 37 Prozent einbüßte). Ein paar Jahre später war sein Vermögen von 727 Millionen US-Dollar im Jahr 1967 auf 185 Millionen US-Dollar im Jahr 1978 zusammengeschrumpft und er wurde mit einem anderen Fidelity-Fonds verschmolzen. »Wer zum Schwert greift, der kommt durch das Schwert um.«

Erst wägen, dann wagen

Doch genug von der Vergangenheit. Sprechen wir lieber über die Zukunft. Bevor Sie losrennen, um Ihr Geld in den Magellan oder den Contrafund zu investieren, weil sie langfristig eine so eindrucksvolle Erfolgsbilanz vorweisen können – mit zweieinhalb- bis dreimal so hohen Renditen wie der S&P 500, wenngleich ihre Vorstellung in späteren Jahren nicht mehr ganz so glanzvoll war –, sollten Sie an die nächsten zehn oder mehr Jahre denken. Sie sollten sich überlegen, wie groß die Wahrscheinlichkeit ist, dass ein gewinnbringender Fonds auch weiterhin Überrenditen erzielt. Denken Sie dabei ruhig auch an das derzeitige Volumen des Fonds. An die Tatsache, dass ein Fonds seine Manager im Regelfall in 25 Jahren dreimal austauscht. Daran, wie unwahrscheinlich es ist, dass auch nur ein einziger Anleger sein ganzes Leben lang Anteile an diesen Fonds gehalten hat. Und nicht zuletzt auch daran, wie groß die

Aussicht ist, dass ein bestimmter Fonds in 25 Jahren überhaupt noch existiert.

So skeptisch sollten Sie jeden Investmentfonds betrachten, der in der Vergangenheit über zehn oder mehr Jahre überdurchschnittliche relative Renditen erzielt hat. Die Investmentfondslandschaft da draußen verändert sich und ist von Wettbewerb geprägt. Niemand weiß, was die Zukunft bringt. Ich wünsche den Generationen von Portfoliomanagern, die auf den derzeitigen Manager folgen werden, auf jeden Fall alles erdenklich Gute – und ebenso den Anteilsinhabern der Fonds, die sie leiten. Wofür Sie sich auch entscheiden, bitte ignorieren Sie dabei auf keinen Fall einen Faktor, den die wenigsten durchschauen, der aber prägenden Einfluss auf die Wertentwicklung von Investmentfonds hat: die Rückkehr zum Mittelwert. (Wie groß dieser Einfluss wirklich ist, wird im Folgekapitel noch genauer erläutert.)

Suchen Sie nicht nach der Stecknadel, kaufen Sie den ganzen Heuhaufen

Die Wahrscheinlichkeit, dass gerade Sie einen der beiden einzigen Investmentfonds (von 355) erwischen würden, der langfristig wirklich überdurchschnittlich rentiert, lag lediglich bei einem halben Prozent. Wie man sich die Daten auch zurechtlegt, es besteht kein Zweifel, dass Fonds mit langgedienten Portfoliomanagern und beständig herausragenden Erfolgsbilanzen selbst über kürzere Zeiträume in der Investmentfondsbranche eine seltene Ausnahme darstellen, und nicht die Regel.

Es ist schlicht eine Tatsache: Wer versucht, einen Investmentfonds auszuwählen, der den Aktienmarkt langfristig schlägt, der sucht, um mit Cervantes zu sprechen, nach der Nadel im Heuhaufen. Ich kann Ihnen nur raten: »*Suchen Sie nicht nach der Stecknadel, kaufen Sie gleich den ganzen Heuhaufen.*«

Der Heuhaufen ist natürlich das gesamte Aktienmarktportfolio, das in Form eines kostengünstigen Indexfonds jederzeit zur Verfügung steht. Die Erträge eines solchen Fonds hätten die Ergebnisse von 345 der 355 Fonds, die sich dem in diesem Kapitel bereits beschriebenen 46-jährigen Wettbewerb stellten, mehr oder minder erreicht oder sogar übertroffen – also von 64 der 74 Fonds, die es nach Ablauf dieses langen Zeitraums noch gab, zuzüglich der 281 Fonds, die inzwischen abgetreten sind. Ich kann keinen Grund erkennen, weshalb ein solcher breiter Marktfonds, der den Standard & Poor's 500 Index nachbildet, in den kommenden Jahren keine entsprechende Entwicklung verzeichnen sollte – nicht durch irgendwelche Zaubertricks, sondern einfach durch die unerbittlichen Regeln der Arithmetik, die Ihnen vertraut sein dürften.

Indexing ist eine Entscheidung fürs Leben. Wollen Sie in 30 oder 40 aktive Fonds und Manager oder in einen Indexfonds mit keinem Manager investieren?

Sehen Sie es doch mal so: Wenn Sie fürs Leben investieren, haben Sie im Grunde zwei Möglichkeiten. Entweder Sie wählen (wie so viele) drei oder vier aktiv gemanagte Fonds aus und hoffen, die richtigen zu erwischen – in dem Bewusstsein, dass deren Portfoliomanager im Schnitt voraussichtlich nur rund neun Jahre Dienst tun und dass sich die Lebenserwartung solcher Fonds in aller Regel bei kaum mehr als zehn Jahren bewegt.

Ergebnis: Bis zu Ihrem Lebensende werden Sie vielleicht 30 oder 40 Fonds besessen haben, jeweils mit Gebührenlasten und Umschlagskosten beaufschlagt. Oder (Überraschung!) Sie können in einen kostengünstigen breiten Marktindexfonds mit minimalen Transaktionskosten investieren, bei dem Sie sicher sein können, dass derselbe nicht vorhandene Manager den Index bis ans Ende Ihrer Tage genau nachbildet. Es besteht im Grunde keine realistische Möglichkeit, dass ein Portfolio aus aktiv gemanagten Fonds Ihnen effektiver und beständiger gute Dienste leistet als der Indexfonds. Einfachheit, Kosteneffizienz und Beständigkeit sollten das Rennen machen.

Falls Sie sich gegen das Indexing entscheiden …

Wir wissen, dass der Indexfonds mehr oder minder so viel abwirft wie der Aktienmarkt. Und von den aktiv gemanagten Fonds wissen wir, dass es unweigerlich früher oder später zu einem Wechsel im Fondsmanagement kommt. Wir wissen, dass viele der Fonds (und leider auch viele ihrer Manager) nicht überleben werden. Wir wissen, dass erfolgreiche Fonds Kapital in solchen Mengen anlocken, dass ihr künftiger Erfolg dadurch voraussichtlich gefährdet wird. Und wir akzeptieren, dass wir nicht in der Lage sind, mit Sicherheit festzustellen, wie viel der Fondsperformance auf Glück basiert und wie viel auf Kompetenz. Bei der Wertentwicklung von Fonds ist die Vergangenheit selten Vorspiel für die Zukunft.

Es gibt schlicht und ergreifend keine systematische Methode, um sich Erfolg zu sichern durch die Auswahl der Fonds, die den Markt schlagen werden – auch (oder vielleicht sogar gerade dann) nicht, wenn wir ihre langfristige frühere Wertentwicklung berücksichtigen. Es ist tatsächlich wie die berühmte Suche nach der Stecknadel im Heuhaufen – mit ähnlichen Erfolgsaussichten.

Wenn Sie mir nicht glauben …

Lesen Sie, wie **Warren Buffett** 2013 in seinem Brief die Aktionäre von Berkshire Hathaway schilderte, welche Anweisungen sein Testament zur Verwaltung des Treuhandfonds für seine Frau enthielt. Statt einen aktiv gemanagten Investmentfonds mit überdurchschnittlicher Erfolgsbilanz auszuwählen, wies er die Treuhänder an, 90 Prozent des Treuhandvermögens in einen »ausgesprochen kostengünstigen Indexfonds auf den S&P 500 (ich schlage Vanguard's vor)« zu investieren. Wir dürfen getrost davon ausgehen, dass Warren Buffett in Betracht gezogen hat, »nach der Stecknadel zu suchen«. Doch letztlich hat er sich dafür entschieden, »den ganzen Heuhaufen zu kaufen«.

Sie brauchen noch mehr Rat? In seiner gewohnten Weisheit brachte der verstorbene **Paul Samuelson** das Problem der Auswahl überlegener Manager mit folgender Parabel auf den Punkt. »Nehmen wir an, es wurde nachgewiesen, dass einer von 20 Alkoholikern lernen könnte, künftig in Gesellschaft maßvoll zu trinken. Dann würde der erfahrene Kliniker antworten: ›Selbst wenn das stimmt, sollten Sie so tun, als wäre es gelogen, denn Sie werden nie den einen unter 20 erkennen, und bei dem Versuch werden Sie jeden Fünften der 20 ruinieren.‹ *Anleger sollten die Suche nach so winzigen Stecknadeln in riesigen Heuhaufen aufgeben.*«

Im *Wall Street Journal* fragte der langjährige Autor der Kolumne »Getting Going«, **Jonathan Clements:** »Können Sie die Gewinner ausfindig machen?« Die Antwort: »Selbst die Fans aktiv gemanagter Fonds räumen oft ein, dass den meisten anderen Anlegern mit Indexfonds besser gedient sei. Doch beflügelt von überbordendem Selbstvertrauen lassen diese Leute nicht von sich aus von aktiv gemanagten Fonds ab. Eine Spur von Irrsinn? Ich glaube schon. Die ertragsstärksten Fonds auszuwählen ist ein bisschen wie ›zu versuchen, vorherzusagen, wie der Würfel fällt, bevor man ihn auf den Würfeltisch fallen lässt‹, sagt ein Anlageberater aus Boca Raton, FL. ›Ich vermag es nicht. Und das Anlegerpublikum ebenso wenig.‹

Um ein breit gestreutes Portfolio aufzubauen, könnten Sie 70 Prozent Ihres Aktienportfolios in einen Indexfonds [auf den gesamten Aktienmarkt] stecken und die übrigen 30 Prozent in einen internationalen Indexfonds.«

Wenn Sie diese Äußerungen eines großen Kapitalverwalters, eines genialen Wissenschaftlers und eines scharfsinnigen Journalisten nicht von den Gefahren einer Fokussierung auf die bisherigen Renditen von Investmentfonds überzeugen, dann glauben Sie doch wenigstens, was Ihnen die Fondsgesellschaften selbst erzählen. Ausnahmslos jede Firma aus der Fondsindustrie bestätigt meine Schlussfolgerung, dass die Wertentwicklung der Vergangenheit nicht dazu geeignet ist, die künftigen Erträge von Investmentfonds zu projizieren. Schließlich steht in jedem Fondsprospekt, in jeder Werbebroschüre und in jeder Investmentfondsanzeige, in der auf die Anlageerträge eines Fonds verwiesen wird (allerdings oftmals so klein gedruckt, dass man es kaum lesen kann) der folgende Warnhinweis: *»Die Wertentwicklung der Vergangenheit ist keine Garantie für zukünftige Ergebnisse.«* Nehmen Sie das bitte ernst!

Elftes Kapitel

»Die Rückkehr zum Mittelwert«

Die Gewinner von gestern sind die Verlierer von morgen

Bei der Fondsauswahl achten zu viele Anleger mehr auf überlegene Performance auf kurze Sicht als auf die nachhaltige Wertentwicklung auf ganz lange Sicht (mit all den ihr eigenen ausgeprägten Schwächen). 2016 flossen über 150 Prozent der Nettokapitalflüsse von Anlegern in Fonds, die von Morningstar mit vier oder fünf Sternen bewertet waren. Dieser statistische Dienst wird von Anlegern am häufigsten herangezogen, um die Rendite eines Fonds einzuschätzen.

In die »Sterne« fließt die Bilanz des Fonds über die vorausgegangenen drei, fünf und zehn Jahre ein. (Bei jüngeren Fonds beziehen sich die Ratings manchmal auch nur auf drei Jahre.) Infolgedessen entfällt die Bewertung eines Fonds mit zehnjähriger Historie zu 35 Prozent auf die Performance der vorausgegangenen zwei Jahre. Bei einem Fonds, der erst drei bis fünf Jahre im Geschäft ist, sind es ganze 65 Prozent. Die zuletzt erzielten kurzfristigen Renditen sind daher stark übergewichtet.

Wie erfolgreich ist die Auswahl von Fonds auf der Grundlage der für so kurzfristige Leistungen vergebenen Sterne? Nicht besonders! Einer 2014 vom *Wall Street Journal* durchgeführten Studie zufolge konnten nur 14 Prozent der Fonds, die 2004 mit fünf Sternen ausgezeichnet worden waren, zehn Jahre später noch mit derselben Bewertung aufwarten. Rund 26 Prozent der ursprünglichen Fünf-Sterne-Fonds hatten einen Stern verloren, die übrigen 50 Prozent waren gleich auf drei oder weniger Sterne abgesackt. Ja, die Fonds-Performance tendiert zum Mittelwert zurück – oder sogar darunter.

Die Rückkehr zum Mittelwert bestätigt sich in umfassenden Daten zur Fondsindustrie

Weitere Daten zur Fondsrendite bestätigen den machtvollen Trend zurück zum Mittelwert. Schauen Sie sich dazu Abbildung 11.1 an, welche die Renditen aller aktiv gemanagten US-Aktienfonds über zwei aufeinanderfolgende Gruppen sich nicht überschneidender Fünfjahreszeiträume vergleicht: 2006 bis 2011 und 2011 bis 2016. Wir sortierten die Erträge für jeden Zeitraum in Quintile ein. Das oberste Quintil enthält die Fonds, die sich am besten entwickelt hatten, das unterste Quintil die mit der schlechtesten Performance. Dann prüften wir, wie sich diese ursprünglichen Fonds im anschließenden Fünfjahreszeitraum entwickelten.

ABBILDUNG 11.1 Rückkehr zum Mittelwert, die ersten fünf Jahre (2006–2011) im Vergleich zu den anschließenden fünf Jahren (2011–2016)

Bewertung 2006–2011			Bewertung 2011–2016					
Anzahl der Fonds			Höchste Rendite	Hoch	Mittel	Niedrig	Niedrigste Rendite	Verschmolzen/geschlossen
Höchste Rendite	353	20 %	13 %	13 %	13 %	25 %	27 %	10 %
Hoch	352	20	18	15	14	21	18	12
Mittel	353	20	17	17	18	14	16	18
Niedrig	352	20	15	18	20	16	8	22
Niedrigste Rendite	352	20	17	18	16	10	12	26
Gesamt	1.762	100 %	16 %	16 %	16 %	17 %	16 %	18 %

Anmerkung: Gesamtzahl der verschmolzenen oder aufgelösten Fonds: 313.

Wenn es so einfach wäre, Fonds auszuwählen, die besser abschneiden als ihre Vergleichsgruppe, indem man schlicht die Gewinner von gestern kauft, dann müsste sich hier ein beständiges Bild ergeben. Will heißen, die meisten Fonds, die im ersten Zeitraum unter den Besten abschlossen, müssten sich auch im nächsten Zeitraum an der Spitze halten, und die vom unteren Rand würden dort verharren. Doch so war es nicht. Wie sich herausstellt, hat die Regression zur Mitte mehr Gewicht als die Beständigkeit.

Werfen Sie einen Blick auf die Fonds, die im ersten Zeitraum (2006–2011) im obersten Quintil rangierten. Dort halten konnten sich im nachfolgenden Fünfjahreszeitraum nur 13 Prozent. Ganze 27 Prozent der Erfolgsfonds aus dem ersten Zeitraum fanden sich im untersten Quintil wieder, weitere 25 Prozent im zweituntersten (vierten) Quintil. Schlimmer noch: 10 Prozent der Gewinner aus der Vorperiode überlebten die nächsten fünf Jahre gar nicht.

Am anderen Ende des Spektrums schafften 17 Prozent der Schlusslichter aus der ersten Periode im Anschlusszeitraum den Sprung ganz nach oben – und schnitten sogar besser ab als die Gewinner der ersten Runde! Lediglich 12 Prozent der Verlierer erzielten im zweiten Zeitraum ähnlich schwache Ergebnisse. 26 Prozent verschwanden von der Bildfläche.

Man muss kein Statistikkünstler sein, um die erstaunliche Zufälligkeit der Erträge in den einzelnen Quintilen zu erkennen. Die stetige Regression zur Mitte konzentrierte sich in jedem Quintil auf rund 16 Prozent – weniger als die 20 Prozent, mit der wir in den ersten Zeitraum gingen. Dieser niedrigere Wert erklärt sich dadurch, dass ganze 18 Prozent der Fonds aus dem ersten Zeitraum vor Ende der zweiten Periode eingestellt wurden – vermutlich wegen schlechter Performance.

Eine zweite Studie bestätigt die erste – und zwar überraschend exakt

Sie fragen sich jetzt womöglich, ob dieses Muster ein Einmalereignis mit geringer Wiederholungswahrscheinlichkeit war.

Die gleiche Frage stellte ich mir auch. Also untersuchten wir den vorangegangenen, sich nicht überschneidenden Fünfjahreszeitraum, 2001 bis 2006, im Vergleich zu 2006 bis 2011. Das Muster bestätigte sich (Abbildung 11.2). Von den ertragsstärksten Fonds der Jahre 2001 bis 2006 konnten sich nur 15 Prozent im obersten Quintil halten, 20 Prozent rutschten ins unterste Quintil ab. Doch das war noch nicht alles: 13 Prozent der Fonds – also 45 an der Zahl – existierten am Ende des Zeitraums nicht mehr.

Von den Fonds, die 2001 bis 2006 im untersten Quintil zu finden waren, schlossen 18 Prozent den Folgezeitraum im obersten Quintil ab – wiederum mit besseren Ergebnissen als die Gewin-

ABBILDUNG 11.2 Rückkehr zum Mittelwert, die ersten fünf Jahre (2001–2006) im Vergleich zu den anschließenden fünf Jahren (2006–2011)

Bewertung 2006–2011			Bewertung 2011–2016					
Anzahl der Fonds			Höchste Rendite	Hoch	Mittel	Niedrig	Niedrigste Rendite	Verschmolzen/geschlossen
Höchste Rendite	356	20 %	15 %	19 %	15 %	19 %	20 %	13 %
Hoch	355	20	13	15	14	15	23	19
Mittel	356	20	14	13	17	17	15	24
Niedrig	355	20	12	16	16	17	10	29
Niedrigste Rendite	355	20	18	13	12	8	6	43
Gesamt	1.777	100 %	14 %	15 %	15 %	15 %	15 %	26 %

Anmerkung: Gesamtzahl der verschmolzenen oder aufgelösten Fonds: 454.

ner der ersten Periode. Von diesen hatten nur 15 Prozent ihre Spitzenposition halten können. Von den Fonds aus dem untersten Quintil wiederholten nur 6 Prozent ihre schwache Leistung. 152 der dort anzusiedelnden Fonds (also 43 Prozent) erreichten das Ende des Zeitraums gar nicht mehr.

Ein Blick auf die Daten dieser beiden Abbildungen zeigt das wiederkehrende Muster der Regression zur Mitte. Wie die Ergebnisse aus Abbildung 11.1 wirken auch die Zahlen für die zweite Periode im Grunde zufällig. Die große Mehrheit der Fonds in allen fünf Quintilen erzielte im Anschluss Erträge, die einigermaßen gleichmäßig über die einzelnen Quintile verteilt waren (mit jeweils zwischen 13 und 18 Prozent).

Aus diesen Daten können wir folgern, dass die Rückkehr zum Mittelwert enormen Einfluss auf die Investmentfondsrenditen hat. Es herrscht erstaunlich wenig Beständigkeit bei den Erträgen, ob bei den stärksten oder bei den schwächsten Fonds. Ich bin nicht so leicht zu beeindrucken, doch diese Daten sind wirklich erstaunlich. Sie widerlegen mit Nachdruck die Annahme der meisten Anleger und Berater, dass sich Managerkompetenz am Ende durchsetzt. Davon scheinen die meisten Anleger auszugehen, doch dem ist nicht so. *Wir sind »Narren des Zufalls«.**

* Titel des gleichnamigen provokativen Buchs von Nassim Nicholas Taleb.

Die leuchtenden Sterne am Investmentfirmament sind selten von Dauer. Allzu oft verglühen sie als Sternschnuppen.

Die Botschaft ist klar: Die Rückkehr zum Mittelwert – die Tendenz von Fonds, deren Bilanz deutlich besser ausfällt als die Branchennorm, wieder auf dem Durchschnitt oder darunter zu landen – ist in der Investmentfondsbranche gegenwärtig und lebendig. Wenn es auf dem Aktienmarkt rund geht, gilt: »Die Ersten werden die Letzten sein.« Doch normalerweise ist eher die Regression zur Mitte an der Tagesordnung. Vergessen Sie also nicht: Die vermeintlichen leuchtenden Sterne am Investmentfirmament sind in Wirklichkeit oft nur Sternschnuppen, die kurz aufleuchten, um dann zu verglühen und ihre Asche sanft zur Erde schweben zu lassen.

Mit jedem Jahr wird klarer, wie es wirklich ist: Die relativen Erträge von Investmentfonds sind ein Zufallsprodukt. In seltenen Fällen scheint tatsächlich Kompetenz im Spiel, doch es würde Jahrzehnte erfordern, um festzustellen, wie viel vom Erfolg eines Fonds dem Glück zuzuschreiben ist und wie viel dem Können des Managers.

Falls Sie anderer Meinung sind und sich für die Anlage in einen Fonds entscheiden, der sich in letzter Zeit überdurchschnittlich entwickelt hat, sollten Sie sich vielleicht die folgenden Fragen stellen: (1) Wie lange wird der Fondsmanager mit demselben Team und derselben Strategie für den Fonds zuständig sein? (2) Wenn sich das Fondsvermögen vervielfacht, wird der Fonds dann noch dieselben Ergebnisse erzielen wie zuvor? (3) In welchem Umfang wurde die Fonds-Performance durch hohe Kostenquoten und/oder einen hohen Portfolioumschlag dezimiert beziehungsweise durch niedrige Kosten und einen geringen Umschlag gesteigert? (4) Wird der Aktienmarkt die Aktien, auf die der Stil des Managers ausgerichtet ist, auch weiterhin begünstigen?

Gewinnbringende Fonds auf der Grundlage der früheren Wertentwicklung auszuwählen, ist ein heikles Unterfangen

Kurz, die Auswahl von Investmentfonds auf der Grundlage der zuletzt verbuchten Wertentwicklung ist eine gefährliche Sache. Da steht quasi schon dran, dass die Rendite weit geringer ausfallen wird als die des Aktienmarkts, die mit einem Indexfonds so leicht zu haben ist.

Vielleicht erkennen wir das besser, wenn wir uns fragen, warum es denn eigentlich so schwer ist, uns mit dem machtvollen Prinzip der Rückkehr zum Mittelwert anzufreunden, das nicht nur die Renditen von Investmentfonds prägt, sondern sich in fast allen Lebensbereichen niederschlägt. In seinem 2013 in der Originalsprache erschienenen Buch *Schnelles Denken, langsames Denken* beantwortete Nobelpreisträger Daniel Kahneman diese Frage folgendermaßen:

> »Unser Intellekt zeichnet sich durch eine starke Neigung zu kausalen Erklärungen aus und kommt nicht gut mit »bloßer Statistik« zurecht. Wenn unsere Aufmerksamkeit auf ein Ereignis gelenkt wird, sucht das assoziative Gedächtnis nach dessen Ursache … aber sie [die kausalen Erklärungen] sind falsch, weil Regressionen zum Mittelwert eine Erklärung, aber keine Ursache haben.«

Wenn Sie mir nicht glauben …

Kurz bevor dieses Buch in Druck ging, schlug der Kommentator **Buttonwood** in *The Economist* ganz ähnliche Töne an wie dieses Kapitel:

»Angenommen, Sie hätten einen der amerikanischen Aktienfonds ausgewählt, die in den zwölf Monaten bis März 2013 zu den ertragsstärksten gehörten. In den folgenden zwölf Monaten, bis März 2014, befanden sich nur noch 25,6 Prozent dieser Fonds im obersten Quartil. Dieses Ergebnis ist reiner Zufall. In den anschließenden Zwölfmonatszeiträumen schrumpfte diese Elite weiter zusammen, auf 4,1 Prozent, 0,5 Prozent und 0,3 Prozent. Diese Zahlen sind sogar noch schlechter als für Zufallswerte anzunehmen. Ähnliche Ergebnisse hätte es gehabt, wenn Sie einen der Fonds ausgewählt hätten, der zu den ertragsstärksten 50 Prozent aller Fonds gehörte. Die Fonds, die es in die obere Hälfte der Charts geschafft hatten, konnten sich dort nicht halten.

Nehmen wir an, Sie hätten einen Fonds herausgepickt, der in den fünf Jahren bis März 2012 im obersten Wertentwicklungsquartil lag. Welcher Prozentsatz dieser Fonds hätte es im anschließenden Fünfjahreszeitraum (bis März 2017) ins oberste Quartil gebracht?

Die Antwort lautet: nur 22,4 Prozent – also erneut weniger als wahrscheinlich. Tatsächlich lagen 27,6 Prozent der herausragenden Fonds der fünf Jahre bis März 2012 in den fünf Jahren bis März 2017 im schlechtesten Quartil. Für die Anleger war die Wahrscheinlichkeit daher größer, eine Niete zu ziehen als einen Gewinner.«

Wenn es heißt, die »Wertentwicklung der Vergangenheit ist nicht aussagekräftig für die Zukunft«, dann ist das mehr als nur ein Compliance-Hinweis. Es ist Mathematik.

Auch **Nassim Nicholas Taleb**, Autor von *Narren des Zufalls*, hat dazu eine Meinung: »Der Monte-Carlo-Generator wirft eine Münze: Bei *Kopf* macht der betreffende Manager im Jahresverlauf einen Gewinn von 10.000 Dollar, bei *Zahl* verliert er 10.000 Dollar. Wir starten das Spiel für das erste Jahr [für 10.000 Manager]. Zum Jahresende erwarten wir, dass 5.000 Manager einen Gewinn von 10.000 Dollar und die anderen 5.000 einen Verlust in gleicher Höhe verbuchen. Jetzt lassen wir das Spiel ein zweites Jahr laufen. Wieder können wir erwarten, dass 2.500 Manager in zwei Jahren in Folge den erforderlichen Gewinn erzielen. Im dritten Jahr sind es 1.250, im vierten 625 und im fünften 313. In einem fairen Spiel haben wir jetzt also 313 Manager, die in fünf aufeinanderfolgenden Jahren Gewinne verbucht haben. [Nach zehn Jahren werden es nur zehn der ursprünglich 10.000 Manager – also nur 0,1 Prozent – sein, die in jedem Jahr beeindrucken konnten.] Nur weil ihnen das Glück hold war … [produziert eine] Gruppe, die ausschließlich aus schlechten Managern besteht, eine geringe Anzahl fantastischer Erfolgsbilanzen … Die Zahl der Manager mit großartigen Erfolgsbilanzen in einem bestimmten

Markt hängt zu einem weitaus größeren Teil von der Anzahl derer ab, die einen Beruf in der Investmentbranche ergreifen (anstatt beispielsweise Zahnmedizin zu studieren), als von ihrer Fähigkeit, Gewinne zu produzieren.«

Das hört sich möglicherweise recht theoretisch an. Deshalb hier die praktische Perspektive – ein Interview der Zeitschrift *Money* mit **Ted Aronson**, Partner des angesehenen Anlageverwaltungsunternehmens AJO aus Philadelphia:

F: Sie sagen, eine Anlage in einen aktiv gemanagten Fonds (im Gegensatz zu einem passiv geführten Indexfonds) sei Glaubenssache. Was meinen Sie damit?

A: Unter normalen Bedingungen muss man [die Wertentwicklung] über 20 bis 800 Jahre [verfolgen], um statistisch nachzuweisen, dass ein Kapitalverwalter nicht nur Glück hat, sondern etwas kann. Um mit 95-prozentiger Wahrscheinlichkeit sagen zu können, dass ein Manager mehr hat als ein glückliches Händchen, braucht man unter Umständen annähernd 1.000 Jahre – und das ist weit länger, als was die meisten Menschen meinen, wenn sie »langfristig« sagen. Selbst um mit nur 75-prozentiger Sicherheit sagen zu können, dass ein Manager kompetent ist, müssten Sie seine Performance im Grunde über 16 bis 115 Jahre überwachen. … Anleger müssen erfahren, wie das Kapitalverwaltungsgeschäft wirklich funktioniert. Da wird mit gezinkten Karten gespielt. Zu unfairen Bedingungen.

F: Wo legen Sie Ihr Geld an?

A: In Vanguard-Indexfonds. Den Vanguard Index 500 halte ich schon seit 23 Jahren. Rechnet man die Steuern ein, spricht sogar noch mehr gegen aktives Management. Ich persönlich glaube, Indexing gewinnt haushoch. Nach Steuern hat aktives Management keine Chance mehr.

Wall Street Journal-Kolumnist und Autor **Jason Zweig** bringt die Jagd nach Performance in einem Satz trefflich auf den Punkt: »Der Kauf von Fondsanteilen ausschließlich auf der Grundlage früherer Leistungen ist so ziemlich das Dümmste, was ein Investor tun kann.«

Zwölftes Kapitel

Auf der Suche nach gutem Rat bei der Fondsauswahl?

Erst wägen, dann wagen

Aus den im zehnten und elften Kapitel präsentierten Indizien lassen sich zwei Lehren ziehen: (1) Die Auswahl gewinnbringender Aktienfonds bietet langfristig dieselben Erfolgschancen wie die Suche nach der Stecknadel im Heuhaufen. (2) Die Auswahl gewinnbringender Fonds auf der Grundlage ihrer bisherigen Leistungen über vergleichsweise kurze Zeiträume führt aller Wahrscheinlichkeit nach zumindest zu Enttäuschung, wenn nicht gar in die Katastrophe. Ist es dann vielleicht besser, diese »Do it yourself«-Ansätze zu vergessen und professionellen Rat einzuholen?

Dabei haben Sie die Wahl zwischen einem Finanzberater (die Bezeichnung, die gewöhnlich Makler an der Wall Street, ja, im Grunde alle Börsenmakler tragen), einem eingetragenen Anlageberater (Registered Investment Adviser, kurz RIA; gewöhnlich keine Makler, die oft – aber nicht immer – rein auf Honorarbasis, nicht auf Provisionsbasis arbeiten) oder auch einem Versicherungsvertreter, der variabel verzinsliche Anlageprodukte vertreibt. (Vorsicht!)

Eingetragene Anlageberater (RIA) können bei der Unterstützung von Anlegern eine wichtige Rolle spielen

In diesem Kapitel werde ich versuchen, die Frage nach dem Wert von Anlageberatern zu beantworten. Sie werden feststellen, dass ich die Fähigkeit der Berater als Gruppe, Ihnen bei der Auswahl von Aktienfonds zu helfen, die überdurchschnittliche Erträge für Ihr Portfolio abwerfen, skeptisch beurteile. (Manche schaffen das, die meisten nicht.) Professionelle Anlageberater erbringen im besten Fall andere wertvolle Dienstleistungen wie Orientierungshilfe bei der Vermögensstrukturierung, Informationen zu steuerlichen Aspekten und Ratschläge dazu, wie viel Sie während der Erwerbstätigkeit ansparen und wie viel Sie wie im Ruhestand ausgeben sollten. Außerdem stehen Ihnen die meisten Berater stets für Gespräche über die Finanzmärkte zur Verfügung.

Berater können Sie dazu animieren, für die Zukunft vorzusorgen. Sie können Ihnen helfen, viele Entscheidungen zu treffen, die nicht direkt mit der Geldanlage zu tun haben, sich aber darauf auswirken (beispielsweise, wenn Sie einen Fonds für die

Ausbildung Ihrer Kinder einrichten oder Kapital für den Kauf einer Immobilie auftreiben möchten). Erfahrene Berater können Ihnen helfen, bestimmte Schlaglöcher auf der Investmentautobahn zu umfahren. (Genauer gesagt, sie können Ihnen helfen, so dumme Fehler zu vermeiden wie der früheren Wertentwicklung nachzujagen, zu versuchen, den richtigen Ein- oder Ausstiegszeitpunkt zu erwischen, oder die Kosten eines Fonds zu ignorieren.) Im Idealfall optimieren diese wichtigen Dienste die Umsetzung Ihres Anlageprogramms und steigern Ihren Ertrag.

Die große Mehrheit aller Anleger verlässt sich auf Makler oder Berater, um den dichten Nebel der Komplexität zu durchdringen, der wohl oder übel unser Finanzsystem einhüllt. Wenn die gängige Schätzung zutrifft, dass rund 70 Prozent der 55 Millionen amerikanischen Familien, die in Investmentfonds investieren, das über Intermediäre tun, dann entscheiden sich rund 15 Millionen Familien für die »Do it yourself«-Methode. Die übrigen 40 Millionen Familien stützen sich bei Anlageentscheidungen auf die Hilfe von Fachleuten. (Das ist im Grunde die erfolglose Strategie, die ich eingangs in meiner Parabel über die Helfer der Familie Gotrocks beschrieben habe.)

Helfer – steigern oder dezimieren sie den Wert?

Wie viel Wert diese Helfer bei der Auswahl von Investmentfonds für Ihr Portfolio beitragen – oder vernichten –, werden wir nie genau sagen können. Ich kann mir aber kaum vorstellen, dass sie als Gruppe besser als, sagen wir, durchschnittlich sind (vor

Abzug ihrer Honorare, wohlgemerkt). Das heißt, ihre Beratung bei der Auswahl von Aktienfonds bringt ihren Kunden Erträge, die sich kaum messbar vom durchschnittlichen Fonds unterscheiden dürften und deshalb um mehrere Prozentpunkte pro Jahr unter dem Aktienmarktergebnis liegen, gemessen vom S&P 500 Index. (Siehe viertes Kapitel.)

Ich bin aber durchaus bereit, die Möglichkeit in Betracht zu ziehen, dass die von den Anlageberatern (den RIAs und Maklern) empfohlene Fondsauswahl besser abschneidet als der Durchschnitt. Wie ich im fünften Kapitel erläutert habe, bringen sie Ihnen schon Vorteile, wenn sie nur die Fonds mit den niedrigsten Gesamtkosten aussuchen – keine Hexerei. Wenn sie so clever sind, zu erkennen, dass Fonds mit hohem Portfolioumschlag steuerlich ungünstig sind, dann ersparen sie Ihnen erhebliche weitere Transaktionskosten und Steuern. Verfolgen sie diese beiden Strategien und empfehlen schwerpunktmäßig kostengünstige Indexfonds – wie es viele Berater tun –, dann umso besser für den Kunden.

Wenn Sie sich verkneifen können, auf jeden Zug aufzuspringen …

Ist ein professioneller Berater dann noch so schlau – oder glücklich –, dass er seine Kunden davon abhalten kann, auf den jeweils letzten, heißesten Zug aufzuspringen (wie den Tech-Aktien-Wahn Ende der 1990er-Jahre, der sich in exzessiver Nachfrage nach Fonds niederschlug, die in »New Economy«-Aktien investierten), dann können seine Kunden locker höhere Erträge erzielen als die enttäuschenden Ergebnisse, die Fondsanleger als Gruppe verbuchen. Wissen Sie noch? Im siebten Kapitel haben wir einen zusätzlichen Rückstand von eineinhalb Prozentpunkten pro Jahr auf den durchschnittlichen Aktienfonds geschätzt. Zur Erinnerung: Der durchschnittliche nominale Anlegerertrag belief sich von 1991 bis 2016 nur auf 6,3 Prozent pro Jahr, obwohl der Aktienmarkt stark anzog und ein einfacher Indexfonds auf den S&P 500 eine Jahresrendite von 9,1 Prozent erzielte.

Bedauerlich (für die Berater): Es gibt schlicht und einfach keinen Beweis dafür, dass die Beratung von RIAs und Maklern bei der Fondsauswahl zu einem besseren Ergebnis geführt hat, als es der durchschnittliche Fondsanleger erzielt hat. Die Indizien vermitteln sogar ein ganz anderes Bild. Die Studie eines von zwei Professoren der Harvard Business School geleiteten Forscherteams kam zu dem Ergebnis, dass »die Unterrendite von über Makler vertriebenen Fonds (Fonds, die vom Arbeitgeber des Vertreibers verwaltet wurden) im Vergleich zu direkt vertriebenen Fonds (die die Anleger direkt kauften) die Anleger [von 1996 bis 2002] rund 9 Milliarden US-Dollar pro Jahr kostete«.

Durchschnittliche Jahresrendite der von Beratern empfohlenen Fonds: 2,9 Prozent; der direkt erworbenen Aktienfonds: 6,6 Prozent

Konkret ergab die Studie, dass sich die Vermögensstruktur durch Makler und Berater nicht verbessert hatte, dass sie den Markttrends hinterherliefen und dass die Anleger, die von ihnen beraten wurden, höhere Ausgabeaufschläge zahlten. Das Fazit der Studie:

Der gewichtete Durchschnittsertrag von Aktienfonds, die von Anlegern gehalten wurden, die sich auf Berater verließen (ohne Ausgabe- oder Rücknahmeaufschläge) belief sich im Schnitt nur auf 2,9 Prozent pro Jahr gegenüber 6,6 Prozent, die Anleger vereinnahmten, die sich selbst um ihre Geldangelegenheiten kümmerten.

Doch auch diese eindrucksvolle Faktenlage veranlasste die Forscher nicht zu der klaren Schlussfolgerung, dass Beratung insgesamt von negativem Wert ist. »Wir schließen nicht aus, dass maßgebliche immaterielle Vorteile vorliegen könnten, und werden diese im Zuge weiterer Studien ermitteln und uns genauer mit der elitären Gruppe von Beratern befassen, die den Wohlstand der Haushalte mehren, die ihnen vertrauen.«

Das Merrill-Lynch-Debakel: eine Fallstudie

Es liegen aber noch überzeugendere Belege dafür vor, dass der Einsatz von Maklern (also nicht von RIAs) ausgeprägte negative Effekte auf die von den Fondsanlegern erzielten Erträge hat. In einer für Fidelity Investments durchgeführten Studie über den Zehnjahreszeitraum von 1994 bis einschließlich 2003 verbuchten von Maklern verwaltete Fonds im Vergleich zu allen anderen Fondsgruppen die niedrigsten Ratings. (Zu den übrigen Gruppen zählten Fonds, die von privat geführten Verwaltern, von Aktiengesellschaften, von Verwaltern, die zu Finanzkonzernen gehörten, und von Bankmanagern gemanagt wurden.)

In der Fidelity-Studie lagen die Fonds von Merrill Lynch 18 Prozentpunkte (!) unter dem Branchendurchschnitt. Bei den Fonds von Goldman Sachs und Morgan Stanley betrug der Rückstand auf den Durchschnitt 9 Prozentpunkte. Und die Fonds von Wells Fargo und Smith Barney lagen bei den zehnjährigen Renditen jeweils um 8 Prozentpunkte zurück.

Diese mangelhafte Leistung ist möglicherweise zumindest zum Teil durch die Aufgabenstellung begründet. Maklerhäuser und ihre Makler/Finanzberater müssen jeden Tag etwas verkaufen, sonst könnten sie nicht überleben. Legt eine Maklerfirma einen neuen Fonds auf, müssen ihn die Makler an den Mann bringen. (Stellen Sie sich vor, an einem beliebigen Tag würde niemand etwas verkaufen, und der Aktienmarkt läge brach – ohne jede Aktivität.)

Zwei Schnapsideen: der Focus Twenty Fund und der Internet Strategies Fund

Dieses imposante Beispiel veranschaulicht das Merrill-Lynch-Debakel und macht schockierend die destruktiven Herausforderungen deutlich, denen Anleger gegenüberstehen können, die sich auf Makler verlassen. Im März 2000, als die vom Internetaktienwahn erzeugte Blase ihren Höhepunkt erreichte, sprang mit Merrill Lynch das größte Maklerhaus der Welt auf den Zug auf und warf zwei neue Fonds auf den Markt. Das war einmal der »Focus Twenty«-Fonds (der auf der damals populären Theorie beruhte, dass ein gutes Abschneiden der 100 favorisierten Titel eines Managers besagte, dass sich seine 20 absoluten Favoriten noch besser entwickeln müssten) und zum anderen der »Internet Strategies«-Fonds.

Als die beiden Fonds auf den Markt kamen, waren sie ein Bombenerfolg. Merrills Makler warben von ihren vertrauensvollen (oder renditehungrigen?) Kunden 2,0 Milliarden US-Dollar ein, 0,9 Milliarden im Focus Twenty und 1,1 Milliarden im Internet Strategies.

Ein Marketingerfolg für Merrill Lynch, eine Fehlinvestition für die Kunden

Die anschließende Renditeentwicklung der Fonds war jedoch ein unglaublicher *Reinfall*. (Das kam nicht so überraschend, denn der beste Zeitpunkt, Anlegern einen neuen Fonds zu *verkaufen* – nämlich wenn er heiß ist –, ist häufig der schlechteste Zeitpunkt, ihn zu *kaufen*.) Der »Internet Strategies«-Fonds brach quasi unverzüglich ein. Sein Inventarwert fiel bis Ende 2000 um 61 Prozent und bis Oktober 2001 um weitere 62 Prozent. Der Gesamtverlust für den Zeitraum belief sich auf erschütternde 86 Prozent.

Die meisten Anleger des Fonds verkauften ihre Anteile mit verheerenden Verlusten. Als das ursprüngliche Fondsvermögen von 1,1 Milliarden US-Dollar auf nur mehr 128 Millionen US-Dollar abgeschmolzen war, beschloss Merrill Lynch, den »Internet Strategies«-Fonds würdig zu beerdigen – durch Verschmelzung mit einem anderen Merrill-Fonds. (Eine Bilanz wie diese fortzuschreiben, wäre für das Unternehmen eine ständige Blamage geworden.)

Die Investmentkatastrophe: Kunden verlieren 80 Prozent ihres Kapitals

Beim Focus Twenty waren die Verluste wohlgemerkt nicht ganz so hoch. Sein Vermögen war zum Jahreswechsel um 28 Prozent geschrumpft und verringerte sich 2001 um weitere 70 Prozent und 2002 noch einmal um 39 Prozent, bis er dann in den drei Folgejahren endlich schwarze Zahlen verbuchte. Per saldo betrug der insgesamt bis Ende 2006 erzielte Ertrag minus 79 Prozent. Die Anleger zogen immer wieder Kapital ab, und das Fondsvermögen, das im Jahr 2000 die Marke von 1,5 Milliarden US-Dollar angepeilt hatte, pendelt derzeit bei 82 Millionen US-Dollar – ein Rückgang um 95 Prozent. Anders als der »Internet Strategies«-Fonds macht der Focus Twenty weiter, heißt aber inzwischen BlackRock Focus Growth. Die Lehre bleibt die gleiche: Der 2-Milliarden-US-Dollar-Marketingerfolg der beiden Fonds Merrill Lynch Internet Strategies und Focus Twenty war für Merrills Kunden, die rund 80 Prozent ihrer sauer verdienten Ersparnisse einbüßten, eine Katastrophe.

Was Finanzberater wert sind

Obwohl sie (als Gruppe) so enttäuschende Ergebnisse erzielen und trotz des geschilderten kolossalen Fehlschlags des Maklerhauses Merrill Lynch können RIAs Anlegern in vieler Hinsicht Mehrwert bieten. Ich vertrete die Auffassung, dass Finanzberater vielen – sogar den meisten – Anlegern wertvolle Dienste leisten können, indem sie sie ruhig schlafen lassen. Indem sie ihnen helfen, ein vernünftiges Portfolio aufzubauen, das ihren Renditevorstellungen und ihrer Risikotoleranz entspricht. Indem sie sie bei der Komplexität, den Feinheiten und den steuerlichen Auswirkungen einer Anlage in Investmentfonds unterstützen. Und indem sie dafür sorgen, dass sie auch in heiklen Phasen am Ball bleiben. Dennoch bestätigen die von mir bislang vorgelegten Fakten meine Ausgangshypothese, dass Berater als Gruppe, so wichtig ihre Dienste auch sein mögen, keine zuverlässige Wertsteigerung durch die Auswahl von Fonds bieten, die den Markt schlagen.

Der Aufstieg der Robo-Adviser

In den letzten Jahren ist eine neue Beratungsmethode für Anleger entstanden. Ein paar junge Unternehmen nutzen die Datentechnologie und bieten Anlegern direkt computerisierte »Robo-Beratung« an, die oft wenig oder gar keine persönlichen Kontakte erfordert. Diese Unternehmen nutzen nach eigenen Angaben Verlustvorträge, empfehlen aber ansonsten generell Buy-and-hold-Portfolios, deren Anlagen auf Renten- und Aktienindexfonds aufgeteilt werden. In aller Regel fokussieren sie sich auf börsengehandelte Indexfonds und verfügen jederzeit über Liquidität ohne die Begrenzungen der Handelshäufigkeit, denen Fondsverwalter häufig unterliegen.

Die Robo-Adviser wachsen schnell. 2017 wiesen die beiden Pioniere der Roboterberatung rund 10 Milliarden US-Dollar an verwaltetem Kundenvermögen aus. Bislang entfällt nur ein kleiner Bruchteil des insgesamt von RIAs betreuten Anlegerkapitals auf die Robo-Adviser. Mit extrem niedrigen Jahresgebühren (von rund 0,25 Prozent) könnten sie sich aber künftig einen beträchtlichen Anteil am Beratungsmarkt sichern.

Einfach geht vor komplex

Die im vorliegenden Kapitel geschilderten Fakten mögen angestaubt oder anekdotenhaft sein. Dennoch öffnen sie die Augen für die Problematik komplexer Anlagestrategien. Unter dem Strich belegen sie wieder einmal, dass die Einfachheit marktbreiter kostengünstiger Indexfonds, die man einmal kauft und für immer hält, vermutlich die optimale Strategie für die große Mehrheit der Anleger darstellt.

Denken Sie darüber nach, sich einen RIA, einen Makler oder Versicherungsvertreter als Anlageberater zu suchen, berücksichtigen Sie diese Feststellungen bitte. Sind Sie trotzdem dazu entschlossen, achten Sie unbedingt darauf, dass Sie nicht mehr zahlen als angemessen, denn die Beraterhonorare mindern die etwaige Rendite Ihres Fondsportfolios beträchtlich. Da Anlageberater meist Honorare in der Größenordnung von 1 Prozent pro Jahr verlangen, die sich mit zunehmendem Volumen verringern, sollten Sie abwägen, ob die vom Berater erbrachten Rahmendienstleistungen die Minderung der Rendite wert sind, die seine Gebühren längerfristig mit sich bringen. Und schließlich – was Sie kaum überraschen dürfte – sollten Sie besonders solche Berater in die engere Auswahl ziehen, die in ihren Modellportfolios Aktien- und Rentenindexfonds empfehlen.

Der Treuhänderstandard

Abschließen möchte ich dieses Kapitel mit einer guten Nachricht für alle Kunden, die sich bei der Auswahl und Verwaltung ihrer Investmentfondsportfolios auf professionelle Beratung verlassen. In den USA gibt es derzeit einen Trend zur Einführung eines US-Standards für treuhänderische Pflichten für Berater. Das bedeutet schlicht gesagt, dass Berater in erster Linie Ihre Interessen verfolgen müssen. Der 2016 vom US-Arbeitsministerium verabschiedete Standard würde nur für Unternehmen und Personen gelten, die Anlegern bestimmte Altersvorsorgeprogramme anbieten wie Individual Retirement Accounts (IRAs), 401(k)-Sparpläne und 403(b)-Sparpläne. Für RIAs gilt bereits ein gesetzlicher Treuhänderstandard für alle ihre Kunden, doch die Anwendung eines solchen Standards auf Makler und Versicherungsvertreter stellt eine maßgebliche Ausweitung des Grundsatzes dar, dass das Wohl des Kunden im Vordergrund stehen muss.

Am Ende muss der neue Standard nicht nur für Altersvorsorgeprogramme gelten, sondern für *alle* Anlagen *aller* Kunden. Doch bereits jetzt gibt es parteipolitisch motivierte Bestrebungen, den geltenden Standard aufzuweichen oder abzuschaffen, was 2017 in Kraft treten soll. Realität ist aber, dass sich – selbst wenn der aktuelle Vorschlag letztlich scheitert –, das Prinzip der treuhänderischen Pflicht durchsetzt. Der Investmentbogen ist weit gespannt, geht aber in die Richtung treuhänderischer Verpflichtung.

Wenn Sie mir nicht glauben …

Hören Sie auf den weithin angesehenen Anlageberater **William Bernstein**, der in seinem Buch *The Four Pillars of Investment Wisdom* Folgendes geschrieben hat: »Sie sollten sicher sein können, dass Ihr Berater Ihre Anlagen allein nach ihrem Nutzen für den Anleger auswählt, nicht danach, wie viel er daran verdient.

Diesbezügliche Warnsignale sind Fonds mit hohen Ausgabeaufschlägen, Versicherungsprodukte, Limited Partnerships oder Spezialfonds. Die beste und einzige Methode, um dafür zu sorgen, dass Sie und Ihr Berater im selben Team spielen, ist seine Bezahlung auf reiner Honorarbasis, sodass er von keiner anderen Stelle vergütet wird als von Ihnen. …

Doch auch eine Vergütung auf Honorarbasis ist nicht ohne Tücken. Das Beraterhonorar sollte angemessen sein. Es lohnt sich nicht, jemandem mehr als 1 Prozent dafür zu zahlen, dass er Ihr Geld verwaltet. Handelt es sich um Beträge von mehr als 1 Million US-Dollar, sollten Sie höchstens 0,75 Prozent zahlen, und ab 5 Millionen US-Dollar maximal 0,5 Prozent. …

Ihr Berater sollte nach Möglichkeit passive Indexfonds einsetzen. Erzählt er Ihnen, er sei in der Lage, Manager ausfindig zu machen, die die Indizes schlagen, macht er Ihnen und sich etwas vor. Ich bezeichne eine Verpflichtung zur passiven Investition in Indizes als ›Anlageklassenreligion‹. Engagieren Sie keinen Berater, der ihr nicht anhängt.«

Dreizehntes Kapitel

Profitieren Sie vom erhabenen Prinzip der Einfachheit und Sparsamkeit

Halten Sie traditionelle kostengünstige Indexfonds, die den Aktienmarkt nachbilden

Was haben wir aus den Vorkapiteln gelernt?

- Es kommt auf die Kosten an (fünftes, sechstes und siebtes Kapitel).
- Es ist nicht sinnvoll, Aktienfonds aufgrund ihrer langfristigen früheren Wertentwicklung auszuwählen (zehntes Kapitel).

- Fondserträge tendieren zum Mittelwert zurück (elftes Kapitel).
- Ratschläge, so gut diese auch gemeint sein mögen, sind nicht immer zuverlässig (zwölftes Kapitel).

Wenn niedrige Kosten positiv sind (und dieser These würde wohl kaum ein Analyst, Wissenschaftler oder Fachmann widersprechen), dann sollte die logische Konsequenz eigentlich sein, sich auf die allergünstigsten Fonds zu verlegen – die traditionellen Indexfonds, die den gesamten Aktienmarkt halten, oder? Die jährlichen Kostenquoten der größten solchen Fonds liegen mitunter nur bei 0,04 Prozent und ihre Umschlagkosten tendieren gegen null. Alles eingerechnet, können sich die Kosten auf nur vier Basispunkte pro Jahr belaufen. Sie liegen damit noch um 96 Prozent unter den 91 Basispunkten für das im fünften Kapitel beschriebene kostengünstigste Fondsquartil.

Und diese Strategie funktioniert. Sie müssen sich nur die faktische Überlegenheit des S&P-500-Indexfonds gegenüber dem durchschnittlichen Aktienfonds über die vergangenen 25 Jahre und das vorausgegangene Jahrzehnt vor Augen führen, wie in den Vorkapiteln geschildert. Die Argumente für den Erfolg des Indexing sind mit Blick auf die Vergangenheit ausgesprochen überzeugend – quasi unwiderlegbar. Und angesichts der Aussichten auf geringere Aktienerträge in den kommenden zehn Jahren wollen wir unseren anekdotischen Spaziergang durch die unerbittlichen Regeln einfacher Arithmetik mit einem letzten statistischen Beispiel abschließen, das mögliche künftige Entwicklungen vorwegnimmt.

Die Monte-Carlo-Simulation

Es ist möglich, auf der Grundlage statistischer Daten die Wahrscheinlichkeit hochzurechnen, dass ein passiv gemanagter Indexfonds über verschiedene Zeiträume besser abschneidet als ein aktiv gemanagter Aktienfonds. Diese komplexe Rechenaufgabe nennt sich »Monte-Carlo-Simulation«.* Dafür werden ein paar einfache Annahmen zur Volatilität von Aktienfondserträgen und zu der Größenordnung getroffen, in der sie vom Aktienmarktertrag abweichen, und noch eine Annahme zu den Gesamtkosten der Anlage in Aktien. Das vorliegende Beispiel geht konkret davon aus, dass sich die Indexfondskosten auf 0,25 Prozent pro Jahr belaufen und alle mit dem aktiven Management verbundenen Kosten auf 2 Prozent pro Jahr. (Es gibt Indexfonds mit viel niedrigeren Kosten, und viele Aktienfonds verursachen sogar noch höhere Kosten. Im Zweifel werden aktiv gemanagte Fonds bei dieser Herangehensweise also unverhältnismäßig positiv dargestellt.)

Das Ergebnis: Über ein Jahr dürften im Schnitt rund 29 Prozent der aktiven Manager erwartungsgemäß den Index schlagen, und über fünf Jahre noch rund 15 Prozent. Nach 50 Jahren würden demnach nur noch 2 Prozent der aktiven Manager besser abschneiden als der Index (Abbildung 13.1).

---

* Bei einer gängigen Monte-Carlo-Simulationsmethode werden sämtliche von einer Aktie über einen langen Zeitraum (sogar ein ganzes Jahrhundert) vereinnahmten Monatserträge herangezogen, nach dem Zufallsprinzip durcheinandergewürfelt und dann die jährlichen Renditen errechnet, die von jedem der vielen tausend hypothetischen Portfolios erzielt wurden.

ABBILDUNG 13.1 Wahrscheinlichkeit einer Überrendite eines aktiv gemanagten Portfolios über einen passiven Indexfonds

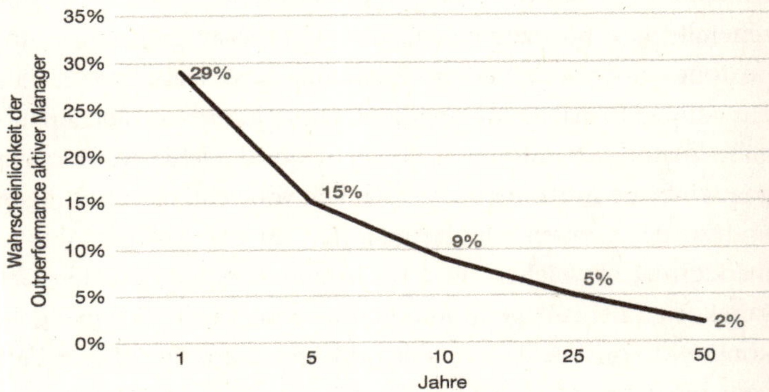

Im Reich der Sparsamkeit ist die Einfachheit König

Wie die Zukunft ganz konkret aussehen wird, können wir natürlich nicht sagen. Aber wir kennen die Entwicklungen der letzten 25 Jahre, und wir wissen aus dem zehnten Kapitel, dass seit 1970 nur zwei der 355 zu Anfang des Zeitraums betriebstätigen Fonds den Aktienmarktindex um 2 oder mehr Prozent pro Jahr schlagen konnten. Hinzu kommt: Einer dieser Gewinner büßte seinen zunächst erzielten Vorsprung schon vor 20 Jahren wieder ein. Es sieht also ganz so aus, als lägen wir mit unserer statistisch ermittelten Wahrscheinlichkeit nicht so sehr daneben. Unsere Rechnung spricht demnach mehr als deutlich dafür, dass Indexfonds in Ihrem Portfolio eine wichtige Stellung einnehmen sollten. In meinem stellen sie ohnehin den Löwenanteil dar.

In einer Zeit mit verhaltenen Aktien- und Rentenmarktrenditen, wie sie uns vermutlich ins Haus steht, sind die Fondskosten bedeutsamer denn je – umso mehr, wenn wir uns von der Illusion verabschieden, dass Investmentfonds als Gruppe alle Erträge mitnehmen können, die die Finanzmärkte bieten, um uns der noch größeren Illusion hinzugeben, dass sich die meisten Investmentfondsanleger mit ihren Fondsportfolios zumindest diese dezimierten Erträge sichern können. Für den Indexfonds spricht, wie ich gern sage, dass »im Reich der Sparsamkeit die Einfachheit König ist«.

Noch einmal: All die lästigen Kosten – die Aufwandsquoten der Fonds, die Ausgabeaufschläge, die Umschlagkosten, die Steuerabzüge und dann noch die steigenden Lebenshaltungskosten (Inflation) als heimtückischste aller Kostenfallen – garantieren praktisch, dass sich die reale Kaufkraft Ihrer Anlagen mit der Zeit aufzehrt. Hinzu kommt, dass die Fondsanleger nur in den seltensten Fällen tatsächlich in den Genuss der Erträge kommen, die die Fonds ausweisen.

Meine Schlussfolgerungen beruhen auf mathematischen Fakten – auf den unerbittlichen Regeln einfacher Arithmetik

Natürlich ist es möglich, dass ich mit meinen Schlussfolgerungen zu den Markterträgen, die in den kommenden Jahren zu erwarten sind, falschliege. Sie könnten niedriger oder höher ausfallen. Doch was den Anteil an den Erträgen angeht, welche die Fonds erzielen können, und den Anteil dieser Erträge, der de facto den

Anlegern zugutekommt, so weisen meine Schlussfolgerungen dazu eine Gemeinsamkeit auf: Sie basieren nicht auf meiner persönlichen Meinung, sondern weitgehend auf mathematischen Fakten – *auf den unerbittlichen Regeln einfacher Arithmetik*. Und ihnen zufolge gleicht die Auswahl gewinnbringender Fonds der sprichwörtlichen Suche nach der Stecknadel im Heuhaufen. Wenn Sie diese Regeln missachten, so tun Sie das auf eigene Gefahr.

Wenn die Straße zum Anlageerfolg von gefährlichen Kurven und gähnenden Schlaglöchern durchzogen ist, vergessen Sie darüber nicht, dass Ihnen einfache Arithmetik helfen kann, diese Kurven sicher zu nehmen und die Schlaglöcher zu umfahren. Diversifizieren Sie also nach Kräften, minimieren Sie Ihre Anlagekosten und fokussieren Sie Ihre Emotionen dort, wo Sie keinen solchen Schaden anrichten können, wie ihn die meisten anderen Anleger erleben. Verlassen Sie sich auf Ihren gesunden Menschenverstand. Investieren Sie überwiegend in einen S&P-500-Indexfonds oder einen Indexfonds, der den gesamten Aktienmarkt abbildet (was aufs Gleiche hinausläuft). Überlegen Sie sich gut, wie viel Risiko Sie eingehen wollen und welchen Teil Ihres Anlagekapitals Sie in Aktien investieren möchten. Und bleiben Sie dann einfach am Ball.

Nicht alle Indexfonds sind gleich. Die Kosten für die Anleger können ganz unterschiedlich ausfallen.

Ich sollte unbedingt noch anmerken, dass nicht alle Indexfonds gleich sind. Ihre indexbasierten Portfolios sind zwar im Wesentlichen identisch, nicht aber die Kosten. Manche haben extrem niedrige Kostenquoten, andere so hohe, dass das nicht mehr nachvollziehbar ist. Manche Fonds werden ohne Ausgabe- und Rücknahmeabschläge angeboten, doch knapp ein Drittel ist, wie sich herausstellt, mit erheblichen Ausgabeaufschlägen verbunden – oft mit der Option, diese über einen Zeitraum von (gewöhnlich) fünf Jahren zu zahlen. Für andere fällt eine marktübliche Maklerprovision an.

Der Abstand bei den Kostenquoten für die günstigsten und die kostspieligsten Fonds, die bei zehn großen Fondsgesellschaften für ihre S&P-500-Indexfonds anfallen, beläuft sich auf über 1,3 Prozent des Vermögens pro Jahr (Abbildung 13.2) – eine gewaltige Diskrepanz. Erschwerend kommt hinzu, dass die kostenintensiven Indexfonds dem Anleger auch noch Ausgabeaufschläge aufbürden.

Selbst unter den günstigen S&P-500-Indexfonds liegen die Kosten in einer großen Spanne. Während der Indexfonds von Vanguard – die Königsklasse – mit einer minimalen Kostenquote von 0,04 Prozent zu Buche schlägt, fallen für den Fonds von T. Rowe Price 0,25 Prozent an. Damit ist er zwar immer noch billiger als die kostspieligsten Indexfonds, doch kaum als »günstig« zu bezeichnen. Wenn wir von einem Jahresertrag von 6 Prozent über 25 Jahre ausgehen, würde eine Erstanlage von 10.000 US-Dollar im T.-Rowe-Price-Indexfonds über diesen Zeitraum auf 40.458 US-Dollar anwachsen. Bei einem wirklich kostengünstigen Indexfonds mit einer Kostenquote von 0,04 Prozent wären es 42.516 US-Dollar – also 2.058 US-Dollar mehr als bei dem teureren Indexprodukt. Ja, auch scheinbar kleine Preisunterschiede wirken sich aus.

ABBILDUNG 13.2 Kosten ausgewählter S&P 500-Indexfonds

Fünf kostengünstige S&P 500-Indexfonds	Jährliche Kostenquote	Ausgabe-aufschlag
Vanguard 500 Index Admiral	0,04 %	0,0 %
Fidelity 500 Index Premium	0,045	0,0
Schwab S&P 500 Index	0,09	0,0
Northern Stock Index	0,10	0,0
T. Rowe Price Equity Index 500	0,25	0,0
Fünf kostenintensive Fonds		
Invesco S&P 500 Index	0,59 %	1,10 %
State Farm S&P 500 Index	0,66	1,00
Wells Fargo Index	0,45	1,15
State Street Equity 500 Index	0,51	1,05
JPMorgan Equity Index	0,45	4,80

Heute sind rund 40 traditionelle Indexinvestmentfonds im Angebot, die den S&P 500 Index nachbilden. Davon sind 14 mit Ausgabeaufschlägen zwischen 1,5 und 5,75 Prozent belegt. Ein kluger Anleger wird sich nur solche Indexfonds aussuchen, die ohne Ausgabeaufschlag erhältlich sind und die niedrigsten laufenden Kosten ausweisen. Diese Kosten stehen erwartungsgemäß in direktem Zusammenhang mit dem für die Anteilsinhaber dieser Fonds erzielten Nettoertrag.

Zwei Fonds. Ein Index. Unterschiedliche Kosten.

Den ersten Indexfonds legte Vanguard 1975 auf. Erst neun Jahre später kam der zweite Indexfonds auf den Markt – der im Januar 1984 errichtete Wells Fargo Equity Index Fund. Seine bisherige Ertragsentwicklung ist mit der des ursprünglichen Vanguard 500 Index Fund vergleichbar.

Beide Fonds entschieden sich für den S&P 500 Index als Benchmark. Die Abschlussprovision auf den Vanguard Index 500 Fund wurde schon in den ersten Monaten nach seiner Auflegung gestrichen. Heute liegt seine Kostenquote für Anleger, die mindestens 10.000 US-Dollar in den Fonds investiert haben, bei 0,04 Prozent (4 Basispunkten).

Der Fonds von Wells Fargo dagegen erhob einen Ausgabeaufschlag von 5,5 Prozent, und seine durchschnittliche Kostenquote lag bei 0,80 Prozent pro Jahr (derzeit sind es 0,45 Prozent). Der Fonds geriet damit von Anfang an ins Hintertreffen und mit jedem Jahr, das vergeht, vergrößert sich sein Rückstand.

Ihr Indexfonds sollte nicht die Cash Cow Ihres Fondsverwalters sein – sondern Ihre

In den 33 Jahren seit 1984 summierten sich diese scheinbar geringfügigen Unterschiede für den Vanguard-Fonds zu einer Wertsteigerung von 27 Prozent. Aus einer ursprünglichen Anlage von 10.000 US-Dollar im Vanguard 500 Index Fund waren Anfang 2017 294.900 US-Dollar geworden. Beim Wells Fargo Equity Index Fund waren es nur 232.100 US-Dollar. *Indexfonds ist nicht gleich Indexfonds.* Kluge Anleger entscheiden sich für die kostengünstigsten Indexfonds seriöser Anbieter.

Vor ein paar Jahren antwortete ein Vertreter von Wells Fargo auf die Frage, wie sein Unternehmen diese hohen Kosten rechtfertige: »Sie verstehen das nicht. Das ist unsere Cash Cow.« (Will heißen, die Verwaltungsgesellschaft verdient daran kontinuierlich gut.) Indem Sie sich sorgfältig die kostengünstigsten Indexfonds für Ihr Portfolio aussuchen, sorgen Sie dafür, dass der Fonds nicht die Cash Cow des Verwalters ist, sondern Ihre.

Ob die Märkte nun effizient sind oder nicht – Indexing funktioniert immer

Der gängigen Meinung zufolge ist Indexing vielleicht in besonders effizienten Marktbereichen sinnvoll, etwa beim S&P 500 für US-Large-Caps, während in anderen Marktsegmenten aktives Management unter Umständen Vorteile bringen kann – zum Beispiel bei Small-Caps oder auf Nicht-US-Märkten. Diese Behauptung ist aber inzwischen widerlegt.

Wie aus Abbildung 3.3 im dritten Kapitel ersichtlich, funktioniert Indexing gut, wo immer es auch zum Einsatz kommt. *Das muss so sein.* Denn ob Märkte effizient sind oder nicht, als Gruppe erzielen alle Anleger in einem bestimmten Segment den Ertrag dieses Segments. Schon möglich, dass die erfolgreichsten Manager auf ineffizienten Märkten ungewöhnlich hohe Erträge erzielen. Das bedeutet aber, dass irgendein anderer Manager ungewöhnlich hohe Verluste erleidet. Nicht vergessen: Als Gruppe bilden alle Anleger in einem bestimmten Aktienmarktsegment zwangsläufig den Durchschnitt.

Auch internationale Fonds verfehlen ihre Referenz-Indizes

Auch von internationalen Fonds wird gern behauptet, es sei für Manager leichter, auf (vermeintlich) weniger effizienten Märkten Gewinne zu erzielen. Stimmt aber nicht. S&P berichtet, dass sein internationaler Index (für die globalen Märkte ohne US-Aktien) in den vergangenen 15 Jahren 89 Prozent der aktiv gemanagten internationalen Aktienfonds überrundet hat.

Ebenso schnitt der S&P-Schwellenländerindex besser ab als 90 Prozent der Schwellenländerfonds. Angesichts der Erfolge des Indexing auf effizienteren und weniger effizienten Märkten in den USA und weltweit frage ich mich, was noch für Daten erforderlich sind, damit sich alle grundsätzlich für Indexfonds entscheiden.

Vorsicht – lassen Sie sich nicht auf Glücksspiel ein

Ein Wort der Warnung: Eine Anlage in bestimmten Marktsektoren erfolgt zwar am effizientesten über Indexfonds, doch wenn sie dabei erst auf einen, dann auf einen anderen gewinnbringenden Sektor setzen, dann läuft das auf eine Wette hinaus. *Beim Wetten können Sie aber nur verlieren.*

Warum? In erster Linie deshalb, weil sich Emotionen mit ziemlicher Sicherheit sehr negativ auf den Ertrag auswirken, den ein Anleger erzielt. Welche Erträge ein Sektor auch abwirft, die Erträge der Anleger in eben diesen Sektoren dürften vermutlich, wenn nicht gar sicherlich, deutlich darunter bleiben. Es gibt jede Menge Indizien dafür, dass die jeweils gefragtesten Sektorfonds stets solche sind, die zuletzt die spektakulärste Performance verbucht haben. Infolgedessen torpediert eine Handelsstrategie, die auf postfaktischer Popularität beruht, quasi garantiert den Anlageerfolg.

Passen Sie gut auf, wenn Sie versuchen, den Marktsektor zu ermitteln, auf den Sie setzen wollen. Die Anlage in einen traditionellen Aktienmarktindexfonds zu möglichst niedrigen Kosten mag weniger aufregend sein als Glücksspiel, ist aber dennoch letztlich die überlegene Strategie. Über sie ist mit mathematischer Gewissheit zu sagen, dass sie den Goldstandard der Kapitalanlage darstellt. So eifrig sie es auch versuchen, die Alchemisten des aktiven Managements können ihr Blei, Kupfer oder Eisen nicht zu Gold verwandeln. Meiden Sie Komplexität, entscheiden Sie sich für Einfachheit und Sparsamkeit. Dann sollten Ihre Kapitalanlagen florieren.

Wenn Sie mir nicht glauben ...

Vielleicht halten Sie mich ja für zu pessimistisch, weil ich davon ausgehe, dass nur 2 Prozent aller Aktieninvestmentportfolios über einen Zeitraum von 50 Jahren besser abschneiden als der Aktienmarkt. Dann werfen Sie mal einen Blick auf die von **Michael J. Mauboussin** ermittelten Wahrscheinlichkeiten. Er ist Marktstrategieleiter bei Credit Suisse, Lehrbeauftragter der Columbia Business School und Autor des Bestsellers *Mehr, als man denkt.* Meine 2-Prozent-Schätzung läuft darauf hinaus, dass ein Portfolio aus 50 den Aktienmarkt über 50 Jahre schlägt. Nach Mauboussins Rechnung liegt die Wahrscheinlichkeit, dass ein Fonds 15 Jahre in Folge überdurchschnittliche Renditen erzielt, bei 1 zu 223.000, und für 21 Jahre bei 1 zu 31 Millionen. So oder so, die Chancen, einen Indexfonds auf den Gesamtmarkt zu übertreffen, sind verschwindend gering.

Warren Buffetts weithin geschätzter Partner bei Berkshire Hathaway, **Charlie Munger**, macht sich wortgewaltig dafür stark, bei Kapitalanlagen unsinnige Komplexität zu meiden und sich stattdessen für Einfachheit zu entscheiden: »Bei großen gemeinnützigen Stiftungen hat es in den letzten Jahren einen Ruck zu mehr Komplexität gegeben. Manche konsultieren inzwischen nicht nur ein paar wenige, sondern richtig viele Anlageberater, die von einer zusätzlichen Beraterebene ausgewählt werden, die entscheiden soll, welche Anlageberater die besten sind, Unterstützung bei der Aufteilung der Mittel auf die verschiedenen Kategorien leisten und sicherstellen soll, dass die vorgeblichen Anlagestile auch wirklich penibel eingehalten werden … [hinzu kommt] eine dritte Ebene von Wertpapieranalysten, die von den Investmentbanken beauftragt werden.

Eines steht angesichts dieser ganzen Komplexität fest: Die Gesamtkosten der Anlageverwaltung zuzüglich der Reibungsverluste, die sich aus dem eher häufigen Ein- und Ausstieg in viele große Anlagepositionen ergeben, können leicht 3 Prozent des Nettovermögens einer Stiftung pro Jahr ausmachen. In ihrer Gesamtheit müssen dann die Anleger jedes Jahr einen Performance-Nachteil hinnehmen, der den Gesamtkosten für die Croupiers entspricht, die sie nach eigenem gemeinschaftlichem Entschluss tragen wollen. …

Das unweigerliche Ergebnis: Genau die Hälfte der Anleger wird nach den Abzügen für die Croupiers ein geringeres Resultat erzielen als das Medianergebnis, welches an sich schon zwischen unspektakulär und lausig liegen kann. Besser beraten ist, wer auf die Berater verzichtet und den Portfolioumschlag verringert, indem er sich auf Indexanlagen in Aktien verlegt.« (Familie Gotrocks lässt wieder einmal grüßen.)

Vierzehntes Kapitel

Rentenfonds

Auch dafür gelten die unerbittlichen Regeln einfacher Arithmetik

Bisher habe ich meinen auf Vernunft gegründeten Ansatz nur auf den Aktienmarkt angewendet – auf Aktienfonds und Aktienindexfonds. Doch die unerbittlichen Regeln einfacher Arithmetik, mit denen ich Sie beglückt habe, gelten auch – und womöglich sogar umso mehr – für Rentenfonds.

Der Grund dafür ist ja vielleicht offensichtlich. Während der Aktienmarkt und jeder einzelne dort gehandelte Titel von einer scheinbar grenzenlosen Fülle von Faktoren beeinflusst werden, bestimmt nur ein einziger Faktor über den Ertrag, den Anleger auf dem Rentenmarkt erzielen: das herrschende Zinsniveau nämlich.

Die Rentenfondsmanager können wenig bis gar nichts tun, um die Zinsentwicklung zu beeinflussen. Gefallen ihnen die Sätze nicht, die der Markt festlegt, wird es kaum etwas bringen, das Finanzministerium oder die Notenbank anzurufen oder anderweitig zu versuchen, das Angebot-Nachfrage-Verhältnis zu verändern.

Warum sollte ein intelligenter Anleger in Anleihen investieren?

Langfristig haben Aktien in der Vergangenheit generell höhere Renditen gebracht als Anleihen. Das sollte auch in den kommenden zehn Jahren so bleiben, wenngleich vernünftigerweise zu erwarten ist, dass die Erträge von Aktien und Anleihen mit einiger Sicherheit deutlich geringer ausfallen werden, als es der historischen Norm entspricht.

Wie im neunten Kapitel erwähnt, schätze ich den Durchschnittsertrag von Anleihen für die kommenden zehn Jahre auf 3,1 Prozent. Zusammenfassend haben Anleihen seit 1900 im Schnitt 5,3 Prozent pro Jahr abgeworfen, seit 1974 waren es 8,0 Prozent und im anstehenden Jahrzehnt dürften es plus/minus 3,1 Prozent werden.

Warum sollte ein intelligenter Anleger dann heute überhaupt Anleihen halten? Erstens, weil sich ein langer Lauf aus einer Reihe kurzer Läufe zusammensetzt – und kurzfristig haben Anleihen schon oft höhere Renditen erzielt als Aktien. In den 117 Jahren seit 1900 haben Anleihen in 42 Jahren besser abgeschnitten als Aktien. In 29 von 112 Fünfjahreszeiträumen konnten Anleihen Aktien überrunden, und sogar in 13 von 103 Fünfzehnjahreszeiträumen.

Zweitens, und das könnte ungleich bedeutsamer sein, kann Ihnen die Verringerung der Schwankungsbreite Ihres Portfolios in längeren rückläufigen Marktphasen Schutz in Abwärtsrichtung bieten – einen Anker im Wind sozusagen. Der konservative Charakter eines Mischportfolios aus Aktien und Anleihen kann die Wahrscheinlichkeit kontraproduktiven Anlegerverhaltens verringern (also die kalten Füße bei einem Einbruch der Aktienmärkte, die Sie veranlassen könnten, Ihre Aktienposition abzustoßen).

Drittens haben die Anleiherenditen seit Anfang der 1960er-Jahre fast den tiefsten Stand erreicht. Dennoch liegt die Umlaufrendite von Anleihen (3,1 Prozent) immer noch über der Dividendenrendite von Aktien (2 Prozent).

Der Abstand zwischen Anleihe- und Aktienrenditen ist ähnlich

Tatsächlich fällt das positive Renditegefälle von 1,1 Prozentpunkten für Anleihen vor Aktien erstaunlich ähnlich aus wie der 1,4-prozentige Renditevorsprung, den Anleihen in der letzten Ära halten konnten (seit 1974 betrug die durchschnittliche Rendite für Anleihen 6,9 Prozent, für Aktien 5,5 Prozent). Also waren Anleihen selbst in dieser Phase niedriger Zinsen (und Dividendenrenditen) im Verhältnis durchaus wettbewerbsfähig.

Unter diesem Aspekt stellt sich daher nicht die Frage, warum man Anleihen halten sollte. Es fragt sich eher: »Welchen Anteil meines Portfolios sollte ich auf Anleihen entfallen lassen?« Mit dieser Frage befassen wir uns im achtzehnten Kapitel noch.

Rentenfondsmanager bilden den Rentenmarkt nach

Als Gruppe erwirtschaften Rentenfondsmanager nahezu unweigerlich einen Bruttoertrag, der sich nach dem Ausgangsniveau richtet, das durch das aktuelle Zinsumfeld vorgegeben ist. Sicher, ein paar Manager erzielen womöglich bessere Ergebnisse – vielleicht sogar über einen längeren Zeitraum –, weil sie besonders schlau sind, besonders viel Glück haben oder besonders hohe Risiken eingehen.

Leider holen einen schlechte Entscheidungen immer wieder ein – und können die längerfristigen Renditen beeinträchtigen. (Auch die Rückkehr zum Mittelwert schlägt oft zu Buche.) Hinzu kommt: Auch wenn es ein Rentenmanager schafft, den Bruttoertrag eines Fonds um ein paar Prozentbruchteile zu steigern, reicht das selten aus, um die Aufwendungen, Gebühren und Ausgabeaufschläge auszugleichen, die für seine Dienste anfallen.

Anleihen tragen unterschiedliche Risiken

Diese Kosten erschweren die Aufgabe der Ertragssteigerung enorm. Sehr selbstbewusste Rentenfondsmanager könnten daher in Versuchung geraten, die Risiken ein bisschen zu erhöhen, indem sie die Laufzeiten der Anleihen im Portfolio etwas verlängern. (Langläufer mit, sagen wir, 30 Jahren Laufzeit, sind schwankungsanfälliger als kurzfristige Papiere mit vielleicht zweijähriger Laufzeit, liefern aber gewöhnlich höhere Renditen.)

Unter Umständen lassen sich die Manager auch dazu verleiten, den Ertrag in die Höhe zu treiben, indem sie die Bonität des Portfolios verringern und weniger US-Schatzanleihen (mit einem Rating von AA+) oder Investment-Grade-Unternehmensanleihen (mit einem Rating von mindestens BBB) halten, dafür aber mehr Anleihen ohne Anlagequalität (mit einem Rating von BB oder schlechter) oder sogar sogenannte Ramschanleihen oder Junk Bonds, die mit CC oder gar nicht geratet sind. Erhöhen Sie den Anteil an Junk Bonds an Ihrem Portfolio, um den laufenden Ertrag zu verbessern, setzen Sie sich mit Ihren Renteninvestments dadurch hohen Risiken aus. (Wie sollte es anders sein?) Anleger, die die Rendite ihrer Bondportfolios durch Anlage in Ramschanleihen aufbessern möchten, sollten sich dabei auf kleine Positionen beschränken. Vorsicht ist angezeigt!

Drei grundlegende Arten von Rentenfonds

Ein Vorteil von Rentenfonds ist, dass Sie den Anlegern oft drei (oder mehr) Optionen beim Rendite-Risiko-Verhältnis bieten. Kurzfristige Portfolios sind für Anleger gedacht, die bereit sind, auf Renditechancen zu verzichten, um Volatilitätsrisiken zu verringern. Langfristige Portfolios sind für Anleger geeignet, die ihre Rendite maximieren möchten und bereit sind, höhere Volatilität in Kauf zu nehmen. Mittelfristige Portfolios sind dagegen auf ein ausgewogenes Verhältnis zwischen Ertragschancen und Marktvolatilität angelegt. Diese Optionen machen Rentenfonds für Anleger mit verschiedenen Strategien attraktiv.

Wie bei Aktienfonds gilt: Auch aktiv gemanagte Rentenfonds liegen hinter ihren Referenz-Indizes. Warum? Aufgrund der Arithmetik der Kosten

Letzten Endes sollten Rentenfonds mit vergleichbarer Laufzeit und Kreditqualität den Bruttoertrag der ihnen durch ihre Strategien vorgegebenen Rentenmarktsegmente erzielen. Nach Abzug ihrer Kostenquoten, Betriebskosten und (gegebenenfalls) Ausgabeauf- und Rücknahmeabschläge bleibt ihr Nettoertrag hinter dem Markt zurück. Wenn es um Anleihen geht, sind Brandeis' mahnende Worte besonders bedeutsam: »*Vergiss nicht, Fremder. Die Arithmetik ist die erste der Wissenschaften, und die Mutter der Sicherheit.*«

Es gibt zu viele Arten von Rentenfonds, um Ihre Geduld damit auf die Probe zu stellen, die Wertentwicklung jedes einzelnen zu untersuchen. Ich fokussiere mich daher auf Fonds in den drei Hauptlaufzeitbereichen (kurz-, mittel- und langfristige Anleihen) und den beiden wichtigsten Qualitätssegmenten (US-Staatspapiere und Investment-Grade-Unternehmensanleihen).

Im dritten Kapitel habe ich geschrieben, dass die Erträge von 90 Prozent der aktiv gemanagten Aktienfonds hinter ihren Benchmark-Indizes lagen, wie vom S&P in einem SPIVA(Standard and Poor's Indices versus Active)-Bericht ausgewiesen.

Der SPIVA-Bericht vergleicht auch die Erträge der Rentenfonds in unterschiedlichen Kategorien mit ihren entsprechenden Benchmark-Indizes. Während der 15 Jahre von 2001 bis 2016 erzielten die Bond-Indizes ebenfalls eine eindrucksvolle Performance und schnitten besser ab als 85 Prozent aller aktiv gemanagten Rentenfonds aus den sechs Kategorien – kurz-, mittel- und langfristig, jeweils unterteilt in US-Staatsanleihen und Unternehmensanleihen mit Anlagequalität (Abbildung 14.1). Die entsprechenden Indizes stellten auch die Manager von auf Kommunalobligationen und hochverzinslichen Anleihen spezialisierten Fonds (jeweils 84 beziehungsweise 96 Prozent) in den Schatten.

ABBILDUNG 14.1 Prozentualer Anteil aktiv gemanagter Rentenfonds, die schlechter abschnitten als S&P-Indizes, 2001–2016

Fondskategorie	US-Staatsanleihen	Investment Grade
Kurzfristige Anleihen	86 %	73 %
Mittelfristige Anleihen	82	73
Langfristige Anleihen	97	97
Durchschnitt	88 %	81 %

Kosten haben maßgeblichen Einfluss auf die Erträge von Rentenfonds

Der durchschnittliche Rückstand der Renditen mittel- und kurzfristiger US-Staatsanleihen- und Unternehmensanleihenfonds auf Indexfonds wird für die vergangenen 15 Jahre vom SPIVA auf rund 0,55 Prozent pro Jahr geschätzt. Die Kosten eines Rentenindexfonds lagen im Schnitt bei rund 0,10 Prozent pro Jahr, während die Kostenquote aktiv gemanagter Rentenfonds durchschnittlich 0,75 Prozent betrug. Der Unterschied bei den Kostenquoten belief sich im Schnitt auf rund 0,65 Prozent und fiel damit etwas größer aus als das Gefälle bei der Wertentwicklung. Wieder einmal wird deutlich, dass ein Großteil des Vorsprungs von Indexfonds auf niedrigere Kosten zurückzuführen ist.

Der Indexfonds für den gesamten Rentenmarkt

Der erste Indexfonds für den gesamten Rentenmarkt – 1986 aufgelegt und bis heute der größte – bildet den Bloomberg Barclays U.S. Aggregate Bond Index ab. Daran haben sich fast alle der großen Indexfonds orientiert, die den gesamten Rentenmarkt abdecken. Solche Indexfonds zeichnen sich durch äußerst hohe Bonität aus (63 Prozent von der US-Regierung garantierte Anleihen, weitere 5 Prozent in Unternehmensanleihen mit AAA-Rating, 32 Prozent mit einem Rating zwischen AA und BAA und gar keine Emissionen ohne Investment Grade). In den zurückliegenden zehn Jahren erwirtschaftete ein Indexfonds auf den gesamten Rentenmarkt 4,41 Prozent Ertrag pro Jahr und lag damit nur 0,05 Prozentpunkte hinter der von seinem Zielindex verbuchten Jahresrendite von 4,46 Prozent – eine erstaunliche Parallele.

Da hochwertige Portfolios fast immer niedrigere Renditen abwerfen als Portfolios von geringerer Bonität, war die Rendite für den Indexfonds auf den gesamten Rentenmarkt Mitte 2017 mit 2,5 Prozent relativ gering, während der von uns zuvor in diesem Kapitel herangezogene Stellvertreter für den Rentenmarkt 3,1 Prozent auswies. Die Ursache: Das von uns für diese Analyse konstruierte Bondportfolio ist in US-Staatsanleihen (50 Prozent) geringer und in Unternehmensanleihen mit Investment Grade (50 Prozent) höher gewichtet als der Index und konnte dadurch eine höhere Rendite erzielen.

Um ein solches jeweils hälftig in Staats- und Unternehmensanleihen investiertes Bondportfolio aufzubauen, sollten Anleger, die auf höhere Renditen angewiesen sind, als sie der Indexfonds auf den gesamten Rentenmarkt abwirft (aber trotzdem Wert auf die Kreditqualität des Portfolios legen), ein Portfolio in Erwägung ziehen, das sich zu 75 Prozent aus dem Indexfonds auf den gesamten Rentenmarkt und zu 25 Prozent aus einem Indexfonds auf Investment-Grade-Unternehmensanleihen zusammensetzt.

Rentenindexfonds liegen die gleichen Wertschöpfungskräfte zugrunde wie Aktienindexfonds

Im Grunde beziehen Rentenindexfonds ihren Wert aus denselben Faktoren wie Aktienindexfonds: breite Streuung, möglichst niedrige Kosten, disziplinierte Portfolioaktivität, steuerliche Effizienz und Fokussierung auf Anteilsinhaber, die auf langfristige Strategien setzen. Diese vernunftbetonten Merkmale sind es, durch die Indexfonds garantieren können, dass Sie den Anteil an den Erträgen der Aktien- und Rentenmärkte erhalten, der Ihnen zusteht – was übrigens für alle Finanzmärkte gilt.

De facto treffen viele der Vorkapitel dieses Buches, in denen es um Aktienfonds ging, genauso gut auch auf Rentenfonds zu – allen voran »Die kostengünstigsten Fonds im Fokus«, »Langfristige Gewinner auswählen«, »Profitieren Sie vom erhabenen Prinzip der Einfachheit und Sparsamkeit«. Die Regeln sind allgemeingültig.

Wenn Sie mir nicht glauben …

Im festverzinslichen Segment gewinnen Indexfonds an Einfluss. **Peter Fisher**, Ex-Chef der Rentengruppe beim globalen Investmentgiganten BlackRock, stellt fest: »Wir gehen in die zweite Phase der Index-Revolution über. Die Welt ist ein erschreckender, unsicherer Ort, und die Anleger möchten ihre [Renten-]Portfolios so einfach gestalten, dass sie nachts ruhig schlafen können.«

Über die erstaunlichen (und erstaunlich offensichtlichen) Vorzüge von Indexfonds, die in Anleihen investieren, ist noch nicht so viel geschrieben worden. Dennoch erhielten die in diesem Kapitel formulierten Überzeugungen kräftige Unterstützung durch **Walter R. Good, CFA,** und **Roy W. Hermansen, CFA**, in dem Buch *Index Your Way to Investment Success*. »Ein Vergleich der Aufwendungen, Transaktionskosten und gegebenenfalls der Ausgabeauf- und Rücknahmeabschläge ergibt einen Kostenvorteil für Rentenindexfonds. … Gegenüber aktiv gemanagten, mit Vertriebsgebühren beaufschlagten Indexfonds beläuft sich dieser auf 1,2 Prozentpunkte pro Jahr.

Die Daten vermitteln ein ernüchterndes Bild von der Herausforderung, vor der aktive Rentenfondsmanager stehen … und einen Eindruck von dem zusätzlichen Ertrag, den das aktive Management – im Durchschnitt über längere Zeiträume – erwirtschaften muss, um auch nur kostendeckend zu arbeiten!«

Schützenhilfe kommt auch von der anderen Seite des Atlantiks. Aus England schreibt **Tim Hale**, Autor von *Smarter Investing: Simpler Decisions for Better Results*: »Sie sollten die Effizienz der Anlage in Renten-Indizes nicht außer Acht lassen, wenngleich sie bisher eher nicht an die große Glocke gehängt wurde. Die Indizien sind eindeutig und sprechen klar für eine Anlage in Indexfonds. … In den zehn Jahren von 1988 bis 1998 brachten US-Bondindexfonds 8,9 Prozent pro Jahr gegenüber 8,2 Prozent bei aktiv gemanagten Rentenfonds … [wobei] Indexfonds besser abschnitten als 85 Prozent aller aktiven Fonds. Dieses Renditegefälle ist hauptsächlich auf die Gebühren zurückzuführen.«

Fünfzehntes Kapitel

Der börsengehandelte Indexfonds

Ein Verräter an der Sache – Trader to the Cause?

In den letzten zehn Jahren wurde der traditionelle Indexfonds (Traditional Index Fund, TIF) von einer Art Wolf im Schafspelz herausgefordert, dem börsengehandelten Indexfonds (Exchange-Traded Fund, ETF). Bei einem solchen ETF handelt es sich schlicht gesagt um einen Indexfonds, der auf einen leichteren Handel mit seinen Anteilen abgestellt ist und in der Verkleidung eines traditionellen Indexfonds daherkommt.

Wenn es bei der vor 42 Jahren konzipierten Urform des TIF um langfristige Kapitalanlage ging, können Indexfonds als Handelsvehikel eigentlich nur als kurzfristige Spekulation bezeichnet werden. Wenn das ursprüngliche Paradigma auf möglichst breite Streuung setzte, dann bietet ein Engagement in bestimmten, wenn auch stark diversifizierte Marktsektoren natürlich keine so breite Streuung und ist mit entsprechend höheren Risiken verbunden. Und wenn minimale Kosten Teil des ursprünglichen Paradigmas waren, dann fällt dieser Punkt flach, wenn man auf Marktsektoren bezogene Indexfonds hält, die mit höheren Kosten einhergehen, Maklerprovisionen verursachen, wenn sie gehandelt werden, und mit Steuern beaufschlagt sind, wenn man das Glück hat, dass die Geschäfte gut laufen.

Lassen Sie mich Klartext reden. Es spricht nichts dagegen, in solche Index-ETFs zu investieren, die den breiten Aktienmarkt abbilden, *wenn Sie damit nicht handeln*. Kurzfristige Spekulation bringt Verluste. Die langfristige Investition ist eine bewährte Strategie, für die breite Marktindexfonds richtig aufgestellt sind.

Wer mit ETFs handelt, hat keine Ahnung, in welchem Verhältnis seine Anlageerträge zu den auf dem Aktienmarkt erzielten Renditen stehen

Die Quintessenz des ursprünglichen TIF-Paradigmas ist, dafür zu sorgen, ja, praktisch zu garantieren, dass der Anleger den Anteil am Aktienmarktertrag erhält, der ihm zusteht. Wer mit ETFs handelt, hat aber keine solche Garantie. Nach all den Herausforderungen der Auswahl, der mit der Wahl des richtigen Zeitpunkts verbundenen Risiken, der zusätzlichen Kosten und Steuern haben ETF-Händler de facto keine Ahnung, in welchem Verhältnis ihre Anlageerträge zur Aktienmarktrendite stehen.

Diese Unterschiede zwischen dem *traditionellen* Indexfonds – dem TIF – und dem *neuen* Indexfonds, für den der ETF steht, sind gewaltig (Abbildung 15.1). ETFs ticken anders als die traditionellen Indexfonds. Um mit einem alten Lied zu sprechen, frage ich mich manchmal: »What have they done to my song, Ma?«

ABBILDUNG 15.1 Traditionelle Indexfonds und börsengehandelte Indexfonds im Vergleich

	TIFs	ETFs		
		Breite Indexfonds		
		Anlegen	Handeln	Spezialisierte Indexfonds
Möglichst breite Streuung	Ja	Ja	Ja	Nein
Längster Zeithorizont	Ja	Ja	Nein	Selten
Minimale Kosten	Ja	Ja	Ja*	Ja*
Maximale steuerliche Effizienz	Ja	Ja	Nein	Nein
Maximaler Anteil am Marktertrag	Ja	Ja	Unbekannt	Unbekannt

* Aber nur ohne Berücksichtigung der Handelskosten.

Wie die »Spinne« entstand

Der erste US-amerikanische ETF wurde 1993 von Nathan Most aufgelegt, hieß »Standard & Poor's Depositary Receipts« (SPDRs) und lief deshalb bald nur noch unter dem Spitznamen »Spider« – die Spinne. Die Idee war genial: Man investierte zu Echtzeitbewertungen kostengünstig und steueroptimiert in den S&P-500-Index. Bei langfristiger Investition versprach das heftige Konkurrenz für den traditionellen S&P-500-Indexfonds.* (Die Maklerprovisionen ließen ihn jedoch für Anleger, die regelmäßig kleinere Beträge investierten, weniger geeignet erscheinen).

Der Spider 500 ist nach wie vor der größte ETF. Anfang 2017 belief sich sein Vermögen auf über 240 Milliarden US-Dollar. 2016 wurden rund 26 Milliarden Anteile am Spider S&P 500 gehandelt, was ein Gesamtdollarvolumen von beachtlichen 5,5 Billionen US-Dollar ergab – und eine jährliche Umschlagsquote von 2.900 Prozent. Nach dem Dollarvolumen war der Spider an jedem einzelnen Tag die am breitesten gehandelte Aktie der Welt.

Spiders und andere ähnliche ETFs werden vornehmlich von kurzfristigen Anlegern verwendet. Die größten Abnehmer, die rund die Hälfte aller ETF-Anlagen halten, sind Banken, aktive Kapitalverwalter, Hedgefonds und professionelle Händler, die ihre ETF-Anteile eifrig handeln. Der Umschlag dieser großen Trader lag 2016 im Schnitt bei knapp 1.000 Prozent (!).

---

* Der mittlerweile verstorbene Nathan Most, ein feiner Mensch, hat Vanguard ursprünglich eine Partnerschaft angeboten. Er wollte unseren S&P 500 Index Fund als Handelsvehikel nutzen. Da ich aber den Handel als für die Makler lukrativ und für die Anleger nachteilig betrachte, lehnte ich ab. Wir trennten uns jedoch als Freunde.

Explosives ETF-Wachstum

Die ETF-Landschaft hat sich von diesem ersten S&P-500-ETF so stark entwickelt, dass inzwischen immerhin die Hälfte des Gesamtvermögens aller Indexfonds darauf entfällt. Anfang 2017 lag der Anteil bei 2,5 von insgesamt 5 Billionen US-Dollar. Der Marktanteil von 50 Prozent hatte 2007 noch 41 Prozent und 1997 erst 9 Prozent betragen.

ETFs sind inzwischen eine feste Größe auf den Finanzmärkten. Das Dollarvolumen ihrer Handelsaktivitäten beläuft sich mitunter auf ganze 40 Prozent oder sogar noch mehr des gesamten täglichen Handelsvolumens am ganzen US-Aktienmarkt. ETFs erfüllen nachweislich die Bedürfnisse von Anlegern und Spekulanten, haben sich aber auch für die Makler als Geschenk des Himmels erwiesen. Das atemberaubende Wachstum der ETFs sagt sicherlich etwas über die Energie der Finanzunternehmer an der Wall Street aus, über den Fokus der Kapitalverwalter auf Kapitalakquise, über die Marketingmacht der Maklerhäuser und darüber, wie groß die Bereitschaft, ja, der Eifer ist, mit dem die Anleger komplexe Strategien und aggressiven Handel favorisieren, weil sie immer noch glauben, dass sie den Markt schlagen können – obwohl so viel dagegen spricht. Wir werden ja sehen.

Die ETF-Flut

Aus dem Wachstum der ETFs ist eine richtige Springflut geworden – nicht nur nach Zahlen, sondern auch hinsichtlich ihrer

Bandbreite. Inzwischen stehen über 2.000 ETFs zur Verfügung (vor zehn Jahren waren es noch nur 340), und die Auswahl an Anlagemöglichkeiten ist wirklich beachtlich.*

ETF-Angebote unterscheiden sich vom Profil her wesentlich von TIF-Angeboten (Abbildung 15.2). Beispielsweise sind nur 32 Prozent der ETF-Anlagen in breit (über den US-Markt und international) diversifizierte Aktienmarktindexfonds wie den Spider investiert – dagegen ganze 62 Prozent der TIF-Anlagen. Es existieren 950 ETFs, die konzentrierte, spekulative, inverse und gehebelte Strategien anbieten. Auf sie entfallen 23 Prozent der ETF-Anlagen. Unter den TIFs trifft das nur auf 137 Produkte zu (mit einem Anteil an den TIF-Anlagen von 5 Prozent).

Außerdem gibt es 669 ETFs mit Fokus auf Smart-Beta- und Faktorstrategien, 244, die auf Aktienmarktsektoren basieren, und 156, die ihre Anlagen auf bestimmte andere Länder als die USA konzentrieren. Außerdem sind da noch 196 breit aufgestellte Renten-ETFs und 422 ETFs, die stark gehebelt sind (was es Spekulanten ermöglicht, auf die Richtung der Aktienmarktentwicklung zu setzen und tägliche Schwankungen des Aktienmarkts zu verdoppeln, zu verdreifachen oder sogar zu vervierfachen!), die Rohstoffpreise und Währungen nachbilden und andere hochriskante Strategien verfolgen.

---

* In den zwölf Monaten bis zum Abgabetermin dieses Buches sind rund 250 weitere ETFs auf den Markt gekommen, und rund 200 wurden eingestellt. Die vielen ETF-Auflegungen und -Schließungen deuten auf eine neue Investmentmode hin. Solche Modeerscheinungen waren selten gut für die Anleger.

ABBILDUNG 15.2 Zusammensetzung von TIF-Anlagen und ETF-Anlagen, Dezember 2016

Traditionelle Indexfonds (TIFs)				
	Anlagen (Milliarden)		Anzahl der Fonds	
Diversifizierte US-Aktien	1.295 USD	47 %	67	16 %
Diversifizierte Nicht-US-Aktien	421	15	43	10
Diversifizierte Anleihen	489	18	50	12
Faktor/Smart Beta	423	15	129	30
Konzentriert/spekulativ	132	5	137	32
Summe	2.760 USD	100 %	426	100 %
Exchange-Traded Funds (ETFs)				
	Anlagen (Milliarden)		Anzahl der Fonds	
Diversifizierte US-Aktien	477 USD	20 %	40	2 %
Diversifizierte Nicht-US-Aktien	287	12	94	5
Diversifizierte Anleihen	355	15	196	10
Faktor/Smart Beta	756	31	669	34
Konzentriert/spekulativ	562	23	950	49
Summe	2.438 USD	100 %	1.949	100 %

Hinzu kommt, dass die Kapitalzuflüsse in ETFs äußerst volatil sind, vor allem im Vergleich zu den relativ stabilen Kapitalströmen in TIFs. In den 24 Monaten vom Aktienmarkthoch im April 2007 bis April 2009 (kurz nach dem Tief infolge des Markteinbruchs um 50 Prozent) verzeichneten TIFs *keinen einzigen Monat mit Abflüssen*. Die Kapitalflüsse in ETFs fielen dagegen in 10 der 24 Monate negativ aus. Die Bandbreite reichte von Zuflüssen von 31 Milliarden US-Dollar im Dezember 2007 (um das Markthoch herum) bis zu Abflüssen von 18 Milliarden US-Dollar im Februar 2009, als die Aktienkurse ihren absoluten Tiefststand erreichten. Das ist kontraproduktives Anlegerverhalten in Reinkultur.

Die meisten ETFs sind also ganz klar stark von den Konzepten des Buy-and-hold, der Diversifizierung und der minimalen Kosten abgewichen, die für den traditionellen Indexfonds charakteristisch sind.

Die bekannte Purdey-Flinte eignet sich hervorragend für die Großwildjagd in Afrika, ist aber auch eine ideale Waffe für potenzielle Selbstmörder

Marktbreite ETFs stellen den einzigen Umstand dar, unter dem ein ETF die fünf vorstehend für den ursprünglichen Indexfonds aufgelisteten Paradigmen replizieren oder vielleicht sogar optimieren kann – *aber nur, wenn er gekauft und langfristig gehalten wird*. Die jährlichen Kostenquoten von ETFs gleichen in aller Regel denen von TIF-Produkten, wenngleich ihre Transaktionsprovisionen den Ertrag mindern, den Anleger vereinnahmen können.

Für den Spider wurde in der ersten Zeit mit dem Slogan geworben: »*Jetzt können Sie jederzeit den S&P 500 handeln – in Echtzeit.*« Können Sie. Doch wieso sollten Sie? Mich erinnert der ETF – ein clever konzeptioniertes Finanzinstrument – unwillkürlich an die berühmte Purdey-Flinte, die angeblich die beste ihrer Art sein soll. Mag sein, dass man in Afrika damit hervorragend Großwild jagen kann. Doch sie ist auch eine ideale Waffe für potenzielle Selbstmörder. Ich befürchte, dass sich allzu viele ETFs für ihre Anteilsinhaber wenn nicht als selbstmörderisch, dann zumindest als vermögensvernichtend erweisen werden.

Die Versuchung, früheren Renditen hinterherzulaufen

Welchen Ertrag die einzelnen Sektor-ETFs auch erwirtschaften – wer in solche eng gefasste ETFs investiert, erzielt vermutlich, wenn nicht sogar sicher, deutlich geringere Gewinne. Es lässt sich vielfach belegen, dass jeweils die Sektorfonds am gefragtesten sind, die zuletzt bei der Wertentwicklung brillierten. Doch solche Erfolge sind nicht von Dauer. (Schließlich ist da die Rückkehr zum Mittelwert.)

De facto ist derartige postfaktische Popularität ein Garant für Misserfolg. Das haben wir aus dem siebten Kapitel gelernt – nämlich, dass Investmentfondsanleger fast immer beträchtlich weniger Gewinn erzielen als die von ihnen gehaltenen Fonds, und sogar noch weniger, wenn sie sich für Fonds entscheiden, die nicht so breit gestreut sind und volatiler reagieren. Das Muster dürfte sich bei ETFs in verstärkter Form wiederholen.

Bei 19 von 20 der ertragsstärksten ETFs fielen die Erträge der Anleger geringer aus als die Erträge des ETF

Um diesen Aspekt zu veranschaulichen, wollen wir die Bilanz der 20 ertragsstärksten ETFs von 2003 bis 2006 betrachten. Lediglich ein einziger von ihnen brachte seinen Anteilsinhabern mehr Ertrag, als er für sich auswies. Im Schnitt bekamen die Anleger 5 Prozentpunkte pro Jahr weniger. Im extremsten Fall waren es sogar ganze 14 Prozentpunkte (der iShares Austria wies 42 Prozent Ertrag aus, die Anleger bekamen nur 28 Prozent).

»Mit Vorsicht zu genießen«, sollte als Warnhinweis ganz oben auf jedem ETF-Etikett stehen, doch das ist zumindest bisher nicht der Fall. Alternativ würde sich anbieten: »Achtung – Renditejäger bei der Arbeit.«

Gleich zweimal daneben: Wer auf heiße Marktsektoren setzt (Emotionen) und hohe Kosten in Kauf nimmt (Aufwand), gefährdet auf jeden Fall sein Vermögen

Gleich zweimal daneben greifen Anleger, die sich dafür entscheiden (oder von ihren Maklern dazu überredet werden), aktiv mit ETFs zu handeln. Sie stehen nahezu unweigerlich vor dem kontraproduktiven Problem, den richtigen Ein- und Ausstiegszeitpunkt zu erwischen, da Anleger in aller Regel dann auf Sektoren setzen, wenn sie heiß werden – und dagegen, wenn sie abkühlen. Zweitens kumulieren sich die hohen Provisionen und Gebühren mit der Zeit, und der Aufwand fordert einen wachsenden Tribut vom ETF-Ertrag.

Im Zusammenspiel gefährden diese beiden Feinde des Aktienanlegers – Emotionen und Kosten – unweigerlich Ihr Vermögen, von dem enormen Aufwand an Lebenszeit ganz zu schweigen, die Sie produktiver und vergnüglicher verbringen könnten.

So haben sich etwa seit 2006 ETFs zum Vorreiter aller Strategien entwickelt, mit denen der Markt angeblich zu schlagen ist und auf die ich im Folgekapitel noch näher eingehe. Die Anbieter und Vermarkter der sogenannten Smart-Beta-Strategien glauben offenbar, ihre »fundamentalen Indexing«- und »Faktor«-Methoden seien gewinnbringende langfristige Strategien. Doch durch die Entscheidung für das ETF-Format ist ihre Prämisse, dass noch höhere kurzfristige Gewinne drin sind, wenn man die Makler in den Vertriebsmix einbezieht – und die Anleger dazu animiert, ihre ETFs rege zu kaufen und zu verkaufen.

Für Anbieter und Makler ist mit den ETFs ein Traum in Erfüllung gegangen – und für Anleger?

Für Anbieter, Makler und Fondsmanager ist mit ETFs ganz klar ein Traum Wirklichkeit geworden. Vielleicht ist aber die Frage erlaubt, ob diese börsengehandelten Indexfonds auch für die Anleger zu schön sind, um wahr zu sein? Profitieren sie wirklich davon, dass sie nunmehr in der Lage sind, »rund um die Uhr in Echtzeit« mit ETFs zu handeln? Ist weniger Diversifizierung mehr?

Ist die Trendfolge ein Spiel, das Anleger gewinnen können? Oder nicht? Sind ETFs wirklich kostengünstige Instrumente, wenn wir die Maklerprovisionen und Steuern auf die kurzfristigen Gewinne zu ihren Kostenquoten hinzuaddieren? Ist Buy-and-sell (oft mit hoher Frequenz) wirklich eine bessere Strategie als Buy-and-hold?

Und schließlich: Wenn der traditionelle Indexfonds dafür konzipiert war, von der Weisheit der langfristigen Kapitalanlage zu profitieren, sind Anleger in solchen ETFs dann nicht zu oft mit unsinniger kurzfristiger Spekulation befasst?

Sicher sagt Ihnen Ihr Hausverstand, wie diese Fragen zu beantworten sind.

Was geht vor – geschäftliche Interessen oder die Interessen des Kunden?

Wo in dem breiten Spektrum zwischen der Förderung der Interessen aller im Investmentgeschäft Tätigen und den Interessen ihrer Kunden sind ETFs anzusiedeln? Wenn Sie auf einmal eine größere Position in einem der beiden klassischen Vertreter des Indexing – dem Vanguard 500 ETF oder dem Spider 500 ETF – mit einer geringen Provision erwerben und die Anteile langfristig halten, dann profitieren Sie von der breiten Streuung und den geringen Kostenquoten, die beide Produkte bieten. Vielleicht bringen Ihnen diese marktbreiten ETFs sogar noch den einen oder anderen Steuervorteil.

Handeln Sie aber mit diesen beiden ETFs, dann verstoßen Sie gegen die unerbittlichen Regeln einfacher Arithmetik, die Voraussetzung sind für den Anlageerfolg. Sagt Ihnen die Vorstellung von Sektor-ETFs zu, dann investieren Sie in die richtigen und handeln Sie nicht.

Die Antwort auf meine Frage

Lassen Sie mich jetzt die eingangs in diesem Kapitel gestellte Frage beantworten: »What have they done to my song, Ma?« Als Erfinder des seinerzeit – vor all den Jahren – ersten traditionellen Indexfonds der Welt kann ich darauf angesichts des ETF-Phänomens nur sagen: »Sie haben mein Konzept in eine Plastiktüte gewickelt und auf den Kopf gestellt.«

Kurz, der ETF verrät die Sache des TIF. Ich rate allen klugen Anlegern, bei der bewährten Indexstrategie zu bleiben. Ich kann Ihnen zwar nicht zusichern, dass die Anlage in traditionelle Indexfonds die beste Strategie aller Zeiten ist, aber eines können Sie mir glauben: Es gibt unzählige schlechtere Strategien.

Wenn Sie mir nicht glauben …

In einem Essay mit dem Titel »Indexing Goes Hollywood« schreibt Morningstar-Chef **Don Philips**: »Indexing hat auch eine dunkle Seite, die die Anleger nicht übersehen sollten. Der potenzielle Schaden für Anleger wächst mit zunehmender Spezialisierung der Indexangebote – und genau das passiert in der Welt der ETFs. … Richtig eingesetzt, können Präzisionswerkzeuge Großartiges bewirken. In den falschen Händen können Sie jedoch erheblichen Schaden anrichten. Durch die Entwicklung komplexerer Angebote hat sich die Index-Community neue Einnahmequellen erschlossen aus … hoch spezialisierten Werkzeugen. Das geschieht jedoch auf Kosten potenziell erheblicher Schäden für weniger versierte Anleger. Eine Charakterprobe für die Index-Community ist die Entscheidung, dieses Risiko zu ignorieren oder es entschlossen zu verringern. Auf dem Spiel steht dabei der gute Name der Indexing-Strategie.«

Jim Wiandt, Gründer von ETF.com (das zuvor ironischerweise IndexUniverse.com hieß) äußerte sich folgendermaßen: »Ich habe schon immer eine gewisse Ironie darin gesehen, dass Indexing – wie fast alles andere in der Finanzwelt auch – in Wellen erfolgt. Hedgefonds-Indizes, Microcap-Indizes, Dividenden-Indizes, Rohstoff-Indizes, China-Indizes und ›optimierte‹ Indizes sind allesamt Modeerscheinungen. Dreimal dürfen Sie raten, was alle diese Indizes gemein haben: (1) Sie laufen der Rendite hinterher. (2) Sie laufen der Rendite hinterher oder (3) sie laufen der Rendite hinterher?

Wenn Sie an Indexing glauben, dann wissen Sie, dass nichts umsonst ist. Am Ende geht es beim Trend zum optimierten Indexing um die Optimierung der Gewinne der Manager. … Wir dürfen den Ball dabei nicht aus den Augen verlieren und müssen uns vor Augen führen, was Indexing ausmacht: nämlich geringere Gebühren, breite Streuung und ein ultralangfristiger Horizont. Glauben Sie nicht an den Hype. Wer versucht, den Markt zu schlagen – ganz gleich wie –, der wird am Ende vermutlich geschlagen werden … und zwar durch die damit verbundenen Kosten.«

Hören Sie nun noch die unverblümten Warnungen zweier leitender Mitarbeiter eines großen ETF-Sponsors. **Chief Executive:** »Für die meisten Leute sind Sektorfonds nicht zielführend. … Weichen Sie [nicht] zu stark vom Marktkurs ab.« **Chief Investment Officer:** »Es wäre keine gute Idee, gezielt auf sehr eng gefasste ETFs zu setzen. Damit sind fast so hohe Risiken verbunden wie mit der Konzentration auf bestimmte Einzeltitel. … Sie gehen damit enorme Risiken ein. Manchmal gibt es auch zu viel des Guten. … *Wer braucht das eigentlich?*«

Sechzehntes Kapitel

Indexfonds, die versprechen, den Markt zu schlagen

Das neue Paradigma?

Seit Auflegung des ersten Indexinvestmentfonds im Jahr 1975 haben sich für langfristig orientierte Anleger gedachte traditionelle Indexfonds (TIFs) sowohl als erstaunlicher Kunstgriff als auch als unglaublicher kommerzieller Erfolg erwiesen.

In den Vorkapiteln haben wir ziemlich eindeutig nachgewiesen, dass Indexfonds für Anleger erfolgreich langfristige Erträge erzielen, die deren mit aktiv gemanagten Fonds erwirtschaftete Renditen bei Weitem übersteigen.

Angesichts dieses Kunststücks überrascht der kommerzielle Erfolg des Indexing eher nicht. (Auch wenn er eine ganze Weile auf sich warten ließ!) Die Grundsätze des ursprünglichen S&P-500-Index-Modells haben sich bewährt. Heute bildet der Löwenanteil des in TIFs investierten Kapitals den breiten US-Aktienmarkt (den S&P 500 oder den Gesamtaktienmarktindex), den breiten internationalen Aktienmarkt und den breiten US-Rentenmarkt ab.

Die Anlagen in solche traditionellen Aktienindexfonds sind von 16 Millionen US-Dollar im Jahr 1976 auf 2 Billionen US-Dollar Anfang 2017 gewaltig gestiegen und belaufen sich auf insgesamt 20 Prozent aller Anlagen in Aktienfonds. Auch die Anlagen in traditionelle Rentenindexfonds sind in die Höhe geschossen – von 1986 bis 2017 von 132 Millionen US-Dollar auf 407 Milliarden US-Dollar beziehungsweise 13 Prozent aller steuerpflichtigen Rentenfondsanlagen. Seit 2009 haben TIF-Anlagen um 18 Prozent pro Jahr zugenommen, also etwas schneller als die Kapitalströme in die verwandten ETFs.

Erfolg sorgt für Konkurrenz

In vielen Bereichen herrscht beim Indexing inzwischen Konkurrenzdruck. Die größten TIF-Manager liefern sich erbitterte Preiskriege und senken ihre Kostenquoten, um das Kapital der Anleger einzuwerben, die so klug sind, zu merken, dass es auf die Kosten ankommt.

Für Indexfondsanleger ist das toll. Allerdings drückt es auf die Gewinne der Indexfondsmanager und wirkt abschreckend auf Unternehmer, die sonst vielleicht in der Hoffnung, durch den Aufbau von Fondsimperien reich zu werden, neue Fondsgesellschaften gründen würden.*

Passive ETF-Strategien, die mehr Ertrag bringen sollen als der Aktienmarkt

Wie aber machen sich Indexfondspromoter dann die Vorteile der nachweislichen Attribute zunutze, die dem Erfolg der TIFs zugrunde liegen? Na ja, sie legen neue Indizes auf und reihen sich in die ETF-Parade ein! Dann behaupten sie (oder lassen das zumindest nachdrücklich durchblicken), dass ihre neuen Indexstrategien die breiten Markt-Indizes beständig übertreffen, die bislang mehr oder minder definiert haben, wie wir über Indexing denken.

Für diese potenziell höhere Rendite berechnen ETF-Manager eine höhere Gebühr – ganz gleich, ob sie diese Rendite auch tatsächlich erzielen (was gewöhnlich nicht der Fall ist). Mit dem Versprechen von Überrenditen sind eine Fülle von ETFs auf den Markt gekommen, um Anleger wie Spekulanten anzulocken.

* Die Vanguard-Fonds arbeiten gerade kostendeckend, sodass es eher Skaleneffekte als der Wettbewerb sind, welche die von den Anteilseignern getragenen Kosten verringern.

Aktive Manager im Vergleich zu aktiven Strategien

Werfen wir einen Blick auf die methodischen Unterschiede zwischen traditionellen aktiven Kapitalverwaltern und ETF-Managern. Aktive Manager wissen, dass man ein Marktportfolio nur schlagen kann, wenn man von dessen Aufbau abweicht. Und genau das versuchen aktive Manager – jeder für sich.

Allen zusammen kann das nicht gelingen, denn durch ihre Handelsgeschäfte verschiebt sich das Eigentum nur von einem Halter auf einen anderen. All das Hin- und Herschieben von Aktienzertifikaten kann sich zwar für den einen oder anderen Käufer oder Verkäufer auszahlen, doch insgesamt verdienen daran nur die Finanzvermittler.

Doch aktive Manager haben ein handfestes finanziell motiviertes Interesse daran, zu propagieren, eventuelle in der Vergangenheit verbuchte Erfolge auch künftig fortschreiben zu können. Und wenn sie bisher nicht so erfolgreich waren, tja, dann kann es künftig ja nur besser werden.

ETF-Sponsoren dagegen geben kein Vorauswissen vor. Sie setzen mehrheitlich auf eine der beiden folgenden Strategien: (1) Sie bieten marktbreite Indexfonds an, die Anleger in Echtzeit mit Gewinn handeln können (eine Behauptung, die fragwürdig erscheint.) (2) Sie legen Indizes für ein breites Spektrum eng gefasster Marktsektoren auf, die Anleger hin- und herschieben können, um zusätzliche Gewinne zu erzielen. (Belegt ist aber eher das Gegenteil.)

In Wirklichkeit wird dadurch die Zuständigkeit für die Anlageverwaltung und die Portfoliostrategie von aktiven Fondsmanagern auf aktive Fondsanleger verlagert. Diese maßgebliche Veränderung hat enorme Auswirkungen für das breite Anlegerpublikum. Und ich gebe offen zu, dass ich große Zweifel hege, ob den Anlegern damit wirklich gut gedient sein dürfte.

Die neuen passiven Indexnachbilder sind in Wirklichkeit aktive Strategen

Die neue Generation passiver Indexnachbilder hat sich weitgehend deshalb für die ETF-Struktur entschieden, um ihre Produkte an den Mann zu bringen. Der Markt ist leicht zugänglich. In den letzten Jahren sind sogenannte »Smart Beta«-ETFs (was auch immer das heißen mag) zum Renner geworden.

Smart-Beta-Manager stellen ihre Indizes selbst zusammen. Dabei handelt es sich nicht um Indizes im herkömmlichen Sinn, sondern um aktive Strategien, die als Indizes ausgegeben werden. Sie fokussieren sich auf die Gewichtung ihrer Portfolios anhand sogenannter Faktoren – Aktien, deren Erträge von ähnlichen Treibern bestimmt werden. Statt ihre Portfoliopositionen nach Marktkapitalisierung zu gewichten, konzentrieren sie sich mitunter auf nur einen Faktor (Value, Momentum, Volumen und so weiter) oder setzen eine Kombination von Faktoren ein wie Unternehmensumsätze, -Cashflows, -gewinne und -dividenden. So ist ein Smart-Beta-ETF-Portfolio beispielsweise nach der Höhe der von den einzelnen Unternehmen ausgeschütteten Dividenden gewichtet, nicht nach der Marktkapitalisierung seiner Komponenten.

Keine so schlechte Idee, aber auch keine weltbewegende

Als Konzept ist Smart Beta gar nicht so dumm – aber eben auch nicht spektakulär. Smart-Beta-ETF-Manager stützen sich auf Computeranalysen einer Fülle erhobener Daten zur früheren Entwicklung von Aktien, die es den Fondsmanagern ermöglichen, Faktoren zu ermitteln, die sich leicht in ETFs verpacken lassen. Ihr Ziel ist dabei, dem Manager hohe Gewinne einzufahren, indem Kapital von Anlegern eingeworben wird, die sich einen Renditevorteil versprechen.

Was diese Strategien angeht, dürfen Sie mir gerne ein gewisses Misstrauen unterstellen. Mir ist das zu schön, um wahr zu sein. Den Markt beständig zu überrunden, ist schwierig – unter anderem schon wegen der starken Tendenz von Investmentfondserträgen, zum Mittelwert zurückzukehren. Die Faktoren, die heute Gewinne bringen, sind mit großer Wahrscheinlichkeit die Verlustbringer von morgen. Und Anleger, welche die Rückkehr zum Mittelwert verkennen, machen mit ziemlicher Sicherheit einen großen Fehler.

»Auf der Suche nach der verlorenen Zeit«

Rufen Sie sich mit Blick auf die zunehmende Popularität von ETFs den Fondswahn der »Go-Go-Ära« von 1965 bis 1968 oder den »Nifty Fifty«-Hype von 1970 bis 1973 ins Gedächtnis, als die Fondsindustrie ihr Produktangebot ebenfalls am Zeitgeschmack orientierte. Solche Produkte sind meist äußerst einträglich für

Fondssponsoren, aber fast immer absolut verheerend für Fondsanleger. Ich darf Sie an folgendes bewährtes Prinzip erinnern: *Erfolgreiche kurzfristige Marketingstrategien sind selten – wenn überhaupt – optimale langfristige Anlagestrategien.*

Erwartungsgemäß haben die fundamentalen Faktoren, die ETF-Anbieter gewöhnlich als Grundlage für ihre Portfoliostrategien angeben, die traditionellen Indizes in der Vergangenheit tatsächlich übertroffen. (Das bezeichnen wir als *Datenlage*. Sie können sicher sein, dass sich niemand trauen würde, eine neue Strategie zu bewerben, die in der Vergangenheit schlechter abgeschnitten hat als ein traditioneller Indexfonds.) Doch in der Investmentwelt ist die Vergangenheit eben selten ein Vorbote für die Zukunft.

Jüngste Entwicklungen bestätigen die skeptische Beurteilung der Wirkung von Smart Beta

Dessen ungeachtet sind die Anlagen solcher Smart-Beta-ETFs (von Morningstar in »Strategic Beta« umgetauft) förmlich explodiert – von 100 Milliarden US-Dollar im Jahr 2006 auf zuletzt über 750 Milliarden US-Dollar. In den ersten vier Monaten 2017 entfielen auf dieses Segment ganze 26 Prozent der Kapitalflüsse in der Investmentfondsbranche.

Gleichzeitig haben die beiden maßgeblichen Strategic-Beta-Anlagestile – Value und Growth – eine Kehrtwende vollzogen. 2016 stieg der Value-Index um 16,9 Prozent, während der Growth-Index mit 6,2 Prozent weit geringer zulegte. 2017 erhöhte sich der Growth-Index (bis einschließlich April) sprunghaft um 12,2 Prozent. Der Value-Index erzielte mit viel Mühe ein Plus von 3,3 Prozent. Zugegeben, das sind beides eher kurze Zeiträume, um Faktorstrategien zu bewerten. Doch – und vielleicht wenig überraschend: Es scheint, dass die Rückkehr zum Mittelwert wieder zuschlägt.

»The new Copernicans«?

Die Vertreter dieser neuen Gattung von Smart-Beta-ETF-Indexnachbildern halten mit ihrer weisen Voraussicht nicht hinter dem Berg. Sie behaupten – vielleicht ein bisschen großspurig – in unterschiedlicher Aufbereitung, sie repräsentierten eine »neue Welle« des Indexing, eine »Revolution«, die Anlegern ein »neues Paradigma« böte – eine Kombination aus höheren Erträgen und geringeren Risiken.

Tatsächlich haben sich die Anhänger faktorbasierter Indizes selbst als die »neuen Kopernikaner« bezeichnet, nach dem Astronomen des 16. Jahrhunderts, der darauf kam, dass nicht die Erde der Mittelpunkt unseres Sonnensystems ist, sondern die Sonne. Sie stellten die traditionellen marktkapitalisierungsgewichteten Indexnachbilder mit den alten Astronomen gleich, die das Ptolemäische Weltbild von der Erde als Mittelpunkt des Universums fortschreiben wollten. Und sie versicherten der Welt, uns stünde ein »gewaltiger Paradigmenwechsel« beim Indexing bevor. In den vergangenen zehn Jahren hat Smart Beta nur einen geringfügigen Paradigmenwandel dargestellt. Doch selbst sein frühester Befürworter, der sogenannte »Godfather of Smart Beta«, bezeichnete einen Smart-Beta-Crash unlängst als »relativ wahrscheinlich«. (Ich habe da sowieso meine Zweifel.)

Ein Blick auf die bisherige Bilanz

In den letzten zehn Jahren hatten sowohl der ursprüngliche »fundamentale« Indexfonds als auch der erste »dividendengewichtete« Indexfonds Gelegenheit, den Wert ihrer Theorien zu beweisen. Und was haben sie bewiesen? Im Grunde *gar nichts*. Die Vergleiche sind Abbildung 16.1 zu entnehmen.

ABBILDUNG 16.1 »Smart Beta«-Erträge: Zehnjahreszeitraum zum 31. Dezember 2016

	Fundamentaler Indexfonds	**Dividenden-Indexfonds**	**S&P-500-Indexfonds**
Jahresrendite	7,6 %	6,6 %	6,9 %
Risiko (Standardabweichung)	17,7	15,1	15,3
Sharpe Ratio*	0,39	0,38	0,40
Korrelation mit dem S&P-500-Index	0,97	0,97	1,00

* Messgröße für den risikobereinigten Ertrag

Sie werden feststellen, dass der fundamentale Indexfonds höhere Erträge erzielte und dabei höhere Risiken einging als der S&P-500-Fonds. Der Dividendenindex dagegen verbuchte niedrigere Renditen bei geringeren Risiken. Doch einer Berechnung der risikobereinigten Sharpe Ratio zufolge liegt der S&P-500-Indexfonds bei beiden Vergleichen vorn.

Dass die Risiko-Rendite-Profile aller drei Fonds ähnlich ausfallen, dürfte nicht überraschen. Schließlich halten sie jeweils ein diversifiziertes Portfolio aus ähnlichen Aktien – die lediglich unterschiedlich gewichtet sind. Faktisch ließen sich die beiden Smart-Beta-ETFs angesichts der erstaunlich hohen Korrelation von 0,97 mit den Erträgen des S&P 500 beide als kostspielige »verkappte Indexfonds« beschreiben.

Das S&P-500-Index-Portfolio bietet die Gewissheit, dass Anleger so gut wie den gesamten Ertrag des Aktienmarktindex erhalten. Das tun die beiden Smart-Beta-ETFs vielleicht auch. Wir können aber nicht sicher sein. Sie sollten sich Folgendes fragen: »Ist mir bei ähnlichen Portfolios ein sicheres (relatives) Ergebnis lieber als ein ungewisses? Ist Vorsicht besser als Nachsicht?« Das können nur Sie entscheiden.

Behauptet ein aktiver Aktienfondsmanager, er wüsste, wie sich auf unserem hoch- (aber nicht vollkommen) effizienten US-amerikanischen Aktienmarkt zusätzlicher Wert erschließen lässt, dann schauen sich die Anleger seine bisherige Bilanz an, prüfen die Strategien und investieren – oder auch nicht. Viele dieser neuen Smart-Beta-ETF-Manager sind eigentlich aktive Manager. Sie geben aber nicht nur vor, zu wissen, was kommt, sondern ziehen aus diesem Wissen das nötige Selbstvertrauen, um zu behaupten, dass bestimmte Marktsektoren (wie Dividendenwerte) den breiten Index auf absehbare Zeit schlagen werden. Diese These widerspricht der Vernunft – und den Lehren der Geschichte.

»Der größte Feind eines guten Plans ist der Traum von einem perfekten« – halten Sie sich daher an den guten

Traditionelle marktkapitalisierungsgewichtete Indexfonds (wie der Standard & Poor's 500) garantieren, dass Sie den Anteil an den Aktienmarkterträgen erhalten, der Ihnen zusteht, und sichern Ihnen praktisch auch zu, dass Sie langfristig zumindest besser abschneiden als 90 Prozent aller übrigen Anleger auf dem Markt. Vielleicht funktioniert dieses neue Paradigma des Faktor-Indexing – anders als alle anderen neuen Paradigmen, die mir bisher untergekommen sind – ja tatsächlich. Vielleicht aber auch nicht.

Ich rate Ihnen eindringlich, nicht dem Sirenengesang von Paradigmen zu erliegen, die Ihnen weit größere Reichtümer versprechen, als sie der traditionelle Indexfonds abwirft. Denken Sie an die prophetische Warnung des Militärtheoretikers und preußischen Generals Carl von Clausewitz aus dem frühen 19. Jahrhundert: ›Der größte Feind eines guten Plans ist der Traum von einem perfekten.‹ Hängen Sie nicht solchen Träumen nach. Benutzen Sie Ihren Verstand und halten Sie sich an den guten Plan – den traditionellen Indexfonds.

Wenn Sie mir nicht glauben …

Mir liegt dieses Thema sehr am Herzen – und nicht nur mir allein. Harvard-Professor und Ex-Vorsitzender des Wirtschaftsrats des US-Präsidenten **Gregory Mankiw** unter George W. Bush hat zum Wettstreit zwischen traditionellen Indexfonds und Smart Beta Folgendes zu sagen: »Ich setze in dieser Frage auf Bogle.« (Und er hatte Recht.)

Aber auch **William Sharpe,** Professor für Finanzwesen an der Stanford University und Träger des Wirtschaftsnobelpreises, hat dazu eine Meinung: »Smart Beta ist dumm. … Erstaunlich, dass Menschen glauben, dass ein System, in dem Aktien anders gewichtet werden als nach Kapitalisierung, einen kapitalisierungsgewichteten Index schlagen kann. … Neue Paradigmen kommen und gehen. Gegen den Markt zu wetten (und darauf hohe Summen zu setzen) dürfte ein ausgesprochen riskantes Unterfangen sein.«

Und auch Wharton School-Professor **Jeremy Siegel**, Autor von *Aktien für die Ewigkeit* und Berater von Wisdom Tree Investments, dem Promoter eines dividendenorientierten Faktormodells, spricht sich für die traditionelle Indexnachbildung aus. »Es ist nachweisbar, dass sich eine maximale Streuung erreichen lässt, indem man jede Aktie *im Verhältnis zu ihrem Wert auf dem Gesamtmarkt* [Hervorhebung des Autors] hält. … Der Rückblick verklärt manches … verzerrt die Vergangenheit und animiert uns, auf unseren Instinkt zu setzen und zu versuchen, klüger zu sein als andere Anleger, die ihrerseits dasselbe Spielchen spielen. Für die meisten führt es zu katastrophalen Ergebnissen, wenn wir versuchen, den Markt zu schlagen … unser Vorgehen bringt uns viel geringere Erträge, als möglich gewesen wären, wenn wir einfach engagiert geblieben wären … und den Markt Jahr um Jahr mit Indexfonds [wie] dem Vanguard-500-Portfolio nachgebildet hätten … und dem Total Stock Market Index Fund von Vanguard.« (Dieses Zitat stammt aus der ersten Auflage von Dr. Siegels Buch aus dem Jahr 1994. Mir ist natürlich bewusst, dass er jedes Recht hat, seine Meinung zu ändern.)

Siebzehntes Kapitel

Was wohl Benjamin Graham vom Indexing gehalten hätte?

Warren Buffett bestätigt, dass Ben Graham für den Indexfonds plädiert hätte

Die erste Auflage von *Intelligent Investieren* erschien 1949. Geschrieben hat dieses Buch Benjamin Graham, der angesehenste Kapitalverwalter seiner Zeit. *Intelligent Investieren* gilt als bestes Buch seiner Art – umfassend, analytisch, scharfsichtig und geradeheraus: ein echtes Standardwerk.

Benjamin Graham ist zwar vor allem für seinen Fokus auf der Value-Investing-Strategie bekannt, für die eine Aktienkategorie steht, die er als »Schnäppchen« bezeichnete, gab jedoch zu bedenken: »Der aggressive Investor muss ein enormes Wissen über den Wert der Aktien haben – so viel, dass er seine Anlageentscheidungen so zu treffen in der Lage ist, als müsste er damit seinen Lebensunterhalt verdienen … [mit einem mentalen Rüstzeug, das ihn vom Anlegerpublikum unterscheidet]. Aus dieser Überlegung folgt, dass *sich die Mehrheit der Besitzer von Wertpapieren der defensiven Kategorie zuordnen sollte.*«

Anleger sollten sich mit den einigermaßen ordentlichen Gewinnen zufriedengeben, die sie mit einem defensiven Portfolio erzielen können

Warum? Ganz einfach: »[Die meisten Besitzer von Wertpapieren] haben nicht die Zeit, nicht die Entschlossenheit und auch nicht die mentale Einstellung, die Kapitalanlage als einen Beruf oder ein Geschäft zu betrachten. Sie sollten sich deshalb auch mit den Gewinnen zufriedengeben, die sie derzeit mit einem defensiven Portfolio erzielen können …, und sie sollten der Versuchung widerstehen, diesen Gewinn dadurch zu erhöhen, dass sie den für sie passenden Weg verlassen.«

Der erste Indexinvestmentfonds wurde erst 1974 aufgelegt, ein Vierteljahrhundert nach dem Erscheinen der Erstauflage von *Intelligent Investieren* im Jahr 1949. Dennoch beschreibt Graham vorausschauend das Wesen dieses beispiellosen Fonds. (Zufällig ebenfalls im Jahr 1949 brachte mich ein Artikel aus der Zeitschrift *Fortune* mit der Investmentfondsindustrie in Berührung und regte mich dazu an, 1951 meine Abschlussarbeit in Princeton über Investmentfonds zu schreiben. Darin spielte ich bereits auf das Konzept vom Indexfonds an: »[Investmentfonds] können keine Überrenditen über den jeweiligen Marktdurchschnitt für sich beanspruchen.«

Dem defensiven Anleger, der Unterstützung brauchte, empfahl Graham ursprünglich professionelle Anlageberater, denn diese »verlassen sich hauptsächlich auf ihre Erfahrung … [und] behaupten auch nicht, sie seien brillant, sondern verweisen stolz darauf, dass sie vorsichtig, konservativ und kompetent sind. Ihr vielleicht wichtigster Wert für die Kunden besteht darin, dass sie diese vor teuren Fehlern schützen.«

Graham warnte die Anleger vor zu hohen Erwartungen an Maklerhäuser: »Die Bruderschaft der Broker an der Wall Street … strebt … immer noch nach den Standards und dem hohen Ansehen eines wirklichen Berufs.« (Was sie auch 50 Jahre später noch nicht erreicht hat.)

Die Wall Street – ein »falstaffischer Witz«

Ebenso profund stellte er das Offensichtliche fest: Dass die Aktienbroker der Wall Street »im Geschäft sind, um Provisionen zu kassieren, und dass der Weg zum geschäftlichen Erfolg darin besteht, dem Kunden das zu geben, was er haben will. … Deshalb sind sie bemüht, ihren Kunden zu helfen, in einem Bereich Geld zu verdienen, in dem diese allerdings dazu verurteilt sind, letztlich Geld zu verlieren.« Später, 1976, beschrieb Graham seine Ansicht von der Wall Street als »höchst negativ … sie ist ein falstaffischer Witz, der oft sogar zu einem Irrenhaus verkommt … eine große Wäscherei, in der sich die einzelnen Institute gegenseitig körbeweise die Wäsche wegnehmen.« (Das erinnert an die Gedanken zweier hochkarätiger Verwalter von Universitätsstiftungen – Jack Meyer, früher bei Harvard, und David Swensen von Yale, von denen bereits die Rede war.)

In dieser ersten Auflage von *Intelligent Investieren* empfahl Graham Anlegern führende Investmentfonds als Alternative zum Aufbau von Portfolios in Eigenregie. Die seinerzeit etablierten Investmentfonds bezeichnete Graham als kompetent geführt – von Managern, die weniger Fehler machen als der typische Kleinanleger – und schrieb ihnen zu, zu annehmbaren Kosten eine nützliche Funktion zu erfüllen, indem sie eine angemessen diversifizierte Liste von Stammaktien kauften und hielten.

Die Wahrheit über Investmentfondsmanager

Was Fondsmanager leisten konnten, beurteilte Graham knallhart realistisch. Diesen Punkt veranschaulichte er in seinem Buch mit Daten, die von 1937 bis 1947 belegten, dass der durchschnittliche Investmentfonds einen Gesamtertrag von 54 Prozent erzielte, während der Standard & Poor's 500 Index insgesamt 57 Prozent Rendite abwarf. Die bedrückende Wirkung von Ausgabeaufschlägen blieb dabei unberücksichtigt. (Manche Dinge verändern sich nicht.)

Graham folgerte daraus, dass die Zahlen nicht besonders beeindruckend seien – weder in die eine noch in die andere Richtung. Insgesamt haben sich die Manager gerade mal in der Lage gezeigt, die Kosten und die Belastung durch nicht investierte Barmittel aufzufangen. 1949 waren die Fondsaufwendungen und die mit dem Portfolioumschlag verbundenen Kosten allerdings noch deutlich geringer als heute. Diese Veränderung erklärt vielleicht, warum die Zahlen, als diese Kosten in den letzten Jahrzehnten deutlich über die Fondserträge hinausgingen, eher einen negativen als einen positiven Eindruck vermittelten.

»Werden sie nicht vernünftig gemanagt, können sie für kurze Zeit spektakuläre, aber weitgehend illusorische Gewinne erzielen, auf die aber unweigerlich verhängnisvolle Verluste folgen«

1965 war Grahams Vertrauen darauf, dass Fonds den Marktertrag abwerfen, bereits erschüttert. »Werden sie nicht vernünftig gemanagt«, so schrieb er in der Auflage von *Intelligent Investieren* aus dem Jahr 1973, »können sie für kurze Zeit spektakuläre, aber weitgehend illusorische Gewinne erzielen, auf die aber unweigerlich verhängnisvolle Verluste folgen.« Er schrieb über die sogenannten Performance-Fonds aus der Go-Go-Ära Mitte der 1960er-Jahre, in der »eine ganz neue ›Art‹ im Finanzbereich« entstand, mit einem besonderen »Talent, auf Gewinner zu setzen. … Schlaue Menschen, voller Energie – normalerweise ziemlich jung –, [waren es, die die Fonds managten. Sie] haben schon immer versprochen, mit dem Geld anderer Wunder wirken zu können …, doch letztlich brachten sie immer nur Verluste ein.«

Damit hätte Graham genauso gut vorausschauend die Hunderte riskanter »New Economy«-Fonds meinen können, die während der gewaltigen, von Tech-Werten getriebenen Hausse Ende der 1990er-Jahre entstanden, und ihren letztlichen Wertkollaps, der noch höher ausfiel als der verheerende Markteinbruch um 50 Prozent, der sich anschließen sollte. (Siehe Abbildung 7.2 im siebten Kapitel.)

»Um an einer Anlage richtig Geld zu verdienen, ... muss man Wertpapiere nicht kaufen und verkaufen, sondern besitzen und halten ... wegen ihrer Dividenden ... und um von ihrem langfristigen Wertzuwachs zu profitieren«

Grahams zeitlose Lektionen zum intelligenten Investieren gelten heute noch genauso wie damals, als er sie in seiner Erstauflage verfasste. Benjamin Grahams immerwährende Botschaft:

> »Um an einer Anlage richtig Geld zu verdienen, muss man – wie es schon bisher überwiegend der Fall war – Wertpapiere nicht kaufen und verkaufen, sondern besitzen und halten, Zinsen und Dividenden vereinnahmen und von ihrem langfristigen Wertzuwachs profitieren.«

Grahams Philosophie kommt im vorliegenden Buch immer wieder zum Tragen. Die besten Beispiele dafür sind die Parabel von der Familie Gotrocks aus dem ersten Kapitel und die Unterscheidung zwischen dem realen Markt für den Substanzwert von

Unternehmen und dem Erwartungsmarkt der flüchtigen Aktienkurse, der im zweiten Kapitel beschrieben wurde.

Die Graham-Strategie von 1949 – der Vorläufer des Indexfonds von 1976

Eine diversifizierte Liste von Aktien besitzen und halten? Spricht sich Graham damit nicht für einen Fonds aus, der im Grunde den gesamten Aktienmarkt kauft und für alle Zeiten hält und dabei geduldig Zinsen, Dividenden und Wertzuwächse vereinnahmt? Erinnert seine Ermahnung, sich »strikt auf normale, konservative Formen der Kapitalanlage fest[zu]legen«, nicht unheimlich an das Konzept des Aktienmarktindexfonds? Wenn Benjamin Graham defensiven Anlegern rät, »mehr Wert auf Diversifizierung zu legen als auf die Einzeltitelauswahl«, ist er dann nicht schon ganz dicht dran an der Beschreibung des heutigen Aktienindexfonds?

Das Scheitern der Investmentmanager

In hohem Alter, in einem 1976 veröffentlichten Interview, räumte Graham unumwunden ein, dass die Investmentmanager unweigerlich bei dem Versuch gescheitert seien, den Markt zu schlagen. Zufällig wurde dieses Gespräch im August 1976 geführt – also fast zeitgleich mit dem Börsengang des ersten Indexfonds der Welt, des First Index Investment Trust, der heute Vanguard 500 Index Fund heißt.

Graham wurde gefragt: »Kann der durchschnittliche Manager über Jahre bessere Ergebnisse erzielen als der Standard & Poor's Index?« Seine unverblümte Antwort: »Nein.« Erläuternd schob er nach: »Das würde ja im Grunde heißen, dass sich die Aktienmarktexperten in ihrer Gesamtheit selbst schlagen könnten – ein Widerspruch in sich.«*

»Ich sehe keinen Grund, weshalb sie [die Anleger] sich mit niedrigeren Erträgen zufriedengeben sollten, als sie ein Indexfonds erwirtschaftet«

Dann kam die Frage, ob sich die Anleger mit dem Marktertrag zufriedengeben sollten. Grahams Antwort: »*Ja*.« So viele Jahre später geht es in diesem *kleinen Handbuch* im Kern darum, Anleger in die Lage zu versetzen, ihren gerechten Anteil am Aktienmarktertrag zu erzielen. Und das ist *nur* mit einem kostengünstigen traditionellen Indexfonds zu garantieren.

Im selben Interview wurde Benjamin Graham zu dem Einwand gegen den Indexfonds befragt, dass jeder Anleger andere Bedürfnisse hat. Wieder antwortete er glasklar:

»Im Grunde ist das nur ein billiges Klischee – eine Ausrede, um die mittelmäßigen bisher erzielten Ergebnisse zu rechtfertigen. Alle Investoren wünschen sich gute Anlageergebnisse, wo-

* Es gibt weder Belege dafür, dass hauptberufliche Fachleute höhere Renditen erzielen als einzelne Amateure, noch dafür, dass irgendeine Klasse institutioneller Investoren (also Pensionskassenverwalter oder Investmentfondsmanager) höhere Erträge erwirtschaftet als eine andere.

rauf sie auch Anspruch haben, soweit sie tatsächlich erzielbar sind. *Ich sehe keinen Grund, weshalb sie sich mit niedrigeren Erträgen zufriedengeben sollten, als sie ein Indexfonds erwirtschaftet – oder für derart unterdurchschnittliche Ergebnisse die üblichen Gebühren zahlen sollten.*«

Die nüchternen Grundlagen der Portfoliopolitik

Der Name Benjamin Graham ist eng verknüpft oder sogar nahezu gleichzusetzen mit dem »Value Investing« und der Ermittlung unterbewerteter Wertpapiere. Sein Buchklassiker widmet aber den nüchternen Grundlagen der Portfoliopolitik – den klaren, einfachen Grundsätzen der Diversifizierung und den rationalen langfristigen Erwartungen, die auch die übergreifenden Themen des vorliegenden *kleinen Handbuchs* sind – viel mehr Aufmerksamkeit als der Lösung des sphinxwürdigen Rätsels, wie man durch gründliche Wertpapieranalyse überdurchschnittliche Aktien auswählt.

Früher lohnte sich die Ermittlung überdurchschnittlicher Werte – heute ist das anders

Graham wusste genau, dass die überdurchschnittlichen Erträge, die er persönlich durch Beachtung seiner Bewertungsgrundsätze erzielt hatte, künftig schwieriger zu realisieren sein würden. 1976 machte er in einem Interview folgendes bemerkenswertes Zugeständnis:

> »Ich war die längste Zeit ein Verfechter ausgeklügelter Methoden zur Wertpapieranalyse, um Chancen auf überdurchschnittliches Wertpotenzial zu ermitteln. Das lohnte sich vor, sagen wir, 40 Jahren noch. Inzwischen hat sich vieles geändert. Früher konnte jeder qualifizierte Wertpapieranalyst durch gründliche Untersuchung professionell unterbewertete Emissionen auswählen. *Doch angesichts der gewaltigen Vielzahl an Analysen, die heute durchgeführt werden, bezweifle ich, ob solche aufwändigen Bestrebungen zu einer Auswahl führen, die so weit über dem Durchschnitt liegt, dass sie ihre Kosten rechtfertigen.*«

Man darf sicher sagen, dass nach Grahams anspruchsvollen Standards die überwiegende Mehrheit der heutigen Investmentfonds nicht hält, was sie verspricht – vor allem wegen der hohen Kosten und des spekulativen Verhaltens. Infolgedessen konnte sich der traditionelle Indexfonds in der Gunst der Anleger inzwischen eine Vorrangstellung sichern.

Warum? Weil er tut, was er tut – nämlich möglichst breite Diversifizierung gewährleisten –, und weil er lässt, was er lässt: Weder stellt er hohe Managementgebühren in Rechnung, noch sorgt er für hohen Portfolioumschlag. Diese Umschreibungen von Grahams Maximen sind ein wesentlicher Teil seines Vermächtnisses für die große Mehrheit der Aktionäre, die sich seiner Ansicht nach an die für defensive Anleger konzipierten Grundsätze halten sollten.

»Zufriedenstellende Anlageergebnisse zu erzielen, ist einfacher, als die meisten Leute meinen«

Benjamin Grahams bleibendes Erbe sind sein gesunder Menschenverstand, seine Intelligenz, sein klarer Blick, seine Verständlichkeit und sein Gespür für Finanzgeschichte – in Kombination mit seiner Bereitschaft, an soliden Grundsätzen für die langfristige Kapitalanlage festzuhalten. Er selbst bringt seine Empfehlungen folgendermaßen auf den Punkt:

»Zum Glück für den normalen Investor ist es für seinen Erfolg überhaupt nicht erforderlich, dass [er bewährte Eigenschaften wie … Mut, Kenntnisreichtum, Urteilsvermögen und Erfahrung mitbringt … die sich auf sein Programm auswirken können] – *vorausgesetzt*, er begrenzt seine Ambitionen auf sein Können und seine Aktivitäten auf den engen und sicheren Pfad der normalen und defensiven Kapitalanlage. Befriedigende Anlageergebnisse zu erzielen ist leichter, als die meisten Menschen wissen. Überragende Erfolge zu erzielen ist schwieriger, als es aussieht.«

Wenn es doch so einfach ist – geradezu unglaublich einfach sogar –, sich mittels eines Indexfonds den Ertrag des Aktienmarkts zu sichern, dann muss man keine zusätzlichen Risiken eingehen – oder sich mit überhöhten Kosten belasten –, um überdurchschnittliche Ergebnisse zu erzielen. Mit Blick auf Benjamin Grahams langfristige Perspektive, seine Vernunft, seinen knallharten Realismus und seine Klugheit besteht meines Erachtens kein Zweifel daran, dass er dem Indexfonds Beifall gezollt hätte. Folgende Äußerungen Warren Buffetts belegen genau das.

Wenn Sie mir nicht glauben …

Obwohl Benjamin Grahams klar formulierte Kommentare ohne Weiteres als Befürwortung eines kostengünstigen Gesamtmarkt-Indexfonds gewertet werden können, müssen Sie mir das nicht glauben. Hören Sie stattdessen, was Grahams Protegé und Kollege **Warren Buffett** dazu zu sagen hat, dessen Rat und praktische Unterstützung Graham in seiner letzten Ausgabe von *Intelligent Investieren* ausdrücklich würdigte. Buffett sprach sich 1993 eindeutig für den Indexfonds aus. 2006 ging er sogar noch weiter und bekräftigte seine Empfehlung nicht nur, sondern versicherte mir persönlich, dass Graham selbst bereits Jahrzehnte zuvor für den Indexfonds plädiert hätte.

Folgendes hat mir Buffett bei einem Dinner in Omaha 2006 persönlich gesagt: »Für die große Mehrheit der Anleger ist ein kostengünstiger Indexfonds die vernünftigste Aktienanlage. Mein Mentor Ben Graham war schon vor vielen Jahren dieser Ansicht, und alles, was ich bisher beobachtet habe, bestärkt mich darin.«

Dem habe ich nur frei nach Forrest Gump hinzuzufügen: »Das ist alles, was ich dazu zu sagen habe.«

Achtzehntes Kapitel

Vermögensstrukturierung, die Erste: Aktien und Anleihen

Einstieg in die Kapitalanlage, Vermögensaufbau, Ruhestand

In diesem und dem nächsten Kapitel befassen wir uns mit zwei komplexen Themen: Den allgemeinen Grundsätzen der Vermögensstrukturierung und der Allokation von Kapital, das für die Altersvorsorge gedacht ist. Auf diese Fragen gibt es keine einfachen Antworten.

Wieso nicht? Nun, erstens, weil wir Anleger so viele verschiedene Anlageziele, Risikotoleranzen und Verhaltensmerkmale haben.

Zweitens, weil Aktien- und Rentenmarkt in den vergangenen 35 Jahren außergewöhnlich hohe Erträge abgeworfen haben, was sich im kommenden Jahrzehnt eher nicht wiederholen dürfte. (Siehe neuntes Kapitel: »Wenn die Party vorbei ist«.)

Drittens sind die Autoren von Büchern über Kapitalanlage im eigentlichen Wortsinn Gefangene der Epochen, die sie erlebt haben. So hatte Benjamin Graham, als er 1949 *Intelligent Investieren* schrieb, *nie* ein Jahr erlebt, in dem die Verzinsung von Anleihen die Dividendenrendite von Aktien übertroffen hätte. Ich dagegen, der ich 2017 dieses Kapitel schreibe, habe über 60 Jahre in Folge erlebt, wie die Dividendenrendite von Aktien *nicht ein einziges Mal* die Verzinsung von Anleihen überstiegen hätte. Da erscheint eine Trendwende nur fair.

Statt im Rückblick den Datenwust zu früheren Renditen und Risiken von Aktien und Anleihen zu durchforsten, will ich nachvollziehbare Prinzipien erörtern, die Sie in Ihrer aktuellen Situation anwenden können. Ob Sie während Ihrer Erwerbstätigkeit ein Anlageportfolio aufbauen oder im Ruhestand Kapital entnehmen – ich hoffe, ich kann Ihnen helfen, Ihr Vermögen für Ihre Zukunft richtig zu strukturieren.

Der Unterschied bei der Portfoliorendite geht zu 94 Prozent auf die Asset-Allokation zurück

Benjamin Graham war sich sicher: Die erste Anlageentscheidung sollte die Aufteilung Ihrer Anlagen betreffen: Wie viel Kapital sollten Sie in Aktien halten? Und wie viel in Anleihen? Graham hielt diese strategische Entscheidung für die womöglich wichtigste im Leben eines Anlegers.

Eine richtungweisende wissenschaftliche Studie aus dem Jahr 1986 bestätigte seine Ansicht. Sie ergab, dass erstaunliche 94 Prozent der Unterschiede beim erzielten Gesamtertrag institutionell verwalteter Pensionskassen auf die Asset-Allokation zurückgingen – also auf die Aufteilung des Kapitals auf die verschiedenen Anlageklassen. Der Wert von 94 Prozent lässt vermuten, dass langfristige Fondsanleger davon profitieren könnten, wenn sie der Aufteilung ihrer Anlagen auf Aktien- und Rentenfonds etwas mehr Beachtung schenkten – und der Entscheidung für oder gegen bestimmte Fonds etwas weniger.

Benjamin Grahams Standardaufteilung: 50/50

Wo sollen wir ansetzen? Beginnen wir bei Benjamin Grahams Rat zur Vermögensstrukturierung aus seinem Klassiker *Intelligent Investieren* von 1949:

> »Als Grundregel haben wir vorgeschlagen, dass der Investor nie weniger als 25 Prozent und nie mehr als 75 Prozent seines Vermögens in Aktien anlegen sollte, umgekehrt aber auch nicht weniger als 25 Prozent und nicht mehr als 75 Prozent in Anleihen. Darin liegt eigentlich die Folgerung, dass die Aufteilung der wichtigsten Anlageinstrumente im Verhältnis 50:50 erfolgen sollte. … Außerdem wird ein wirklich konservativer Anleger sich mit dem zufriedengeben, was die Hälfte seines Portfolios in einem stei-

> genden Markt einbringt, während ein ernsthafter Abschwung ihn tröstet,* wenn er darüber nachdenkt, dass es ihm wesentlich besser ergeht als vielen seiner unternehmungslustigeren Freunde.«

Vermögensstrukturierung und Renditeunterschiede

Heutzutage mag Anlegern und ihren Beratern die 50/50-Aufteilung auf Aktien und Anleihen (und die Bandbreite von 75/25 bis 25/75) zu konservativ erscheinen. Doch 1949, als Graham sein Buch schrieb, brachten Aktien 6,9 Prozent Rendite und Anleihen 1,9 Prozent. Heute liegt die Rendite von Aktien bei 2,0 Prozent und von Anleihen bei 3,1 Prozent – ein gewaltiger Unterschied für die Entscheidung, wie viel Kapital man in Aktien beziehungsweise Anleihen investieren soll.** Messbar ist dieser Unterschied auf zweierlei Arten: (1) Die Bruttorendite eines hälftig in Aktien und Anleihen investierten Portfolios ist um ganze 40 Prozent zurückgegangen, nämlich von 4,4 auf 2,6 Prozent. (2) Die Renditetabellen haben sich umgekehrt: Aktien lieferten 1949 einen jährlichen Rendite*aufschlag* von (wirklich erstaunlichen) 5,0 Prozent und 2017 einen Rendite*abschlag* von 1,1 Prozent.

Als ich Grahams Philosophie 1993 in meinem Buch *Bogle on Mutual Funds: New Perspectives for the Intelligent Investor* erör-

---

* Offensichtlich bezieht sich Graham hier auf die Maxime »Um zu ertragen, was anderen zustößt, sind wir allemal stark genug«.

** Die Bondrendite steht für ein Portfolio, das sich zur Hälfte aus Unternehmensanleihen (3,9 Prozent) und zur Hälfte aus zehnjährigen US-Schatzanweisungen (2,3 Prozent) zusammensetzt.

terte, ging ich von der Verwendung nur dieser beiden Anlageklassen aus. Meine Empfehlung für Anleger in der erwerbstätigen Vermögensbildungsphase ihres Lebens war auf einen Mix aus Aktien und Anleihen im Verhältnis von 80/20 bei jungen Anlegern und 70/30 bei älteren ausgerichtet, die sich zur Ruhe setzen wollten und am Anfang der Ausschüttungsphase standen. Für jüngere Anleger empfahl ich 60/40 und für ältere Anleger 50/50.

Kleine Turbulenzen

Trotz des heute weitaus niedrigeren Niveaus der Zinsen und Dividendenrenditen, der gewaltigen Hausse seit Grahams Zeiten und der zwischenzeitlichen Turbulenzen (wie die Börsencrashs von 1973/74 und 1987, das Platzen der Dotcom-Blase 2000 und die globale Finanzkrise von 2008/2009) gelten die von Graham vor all den Jahren formulierten allgemeinen Grundsätze erstaunlicherweise weitgehend unverändert. Die von ihm für die Vermögensaufteilung vorgeschlagenen Prozentsätze bilden nach wie vor eine solide Ausgangsbasis für ein vernünftiges Anlageprogramm.

Wie viel Risiko ein Anleger verkraften kann beziehungsweise will

Zwei grundlegende Faktoren bestimmen, wie Sie Ihr Portfolio zwischen Aktien und Anleihen aufteilen sollen: (1) Wie viel Risiko Sie in Kauf nehmen *können* und (2) wie viel Sie in Kauf nehmen *wollen*. Wie viel Risiko Sie verkraften können, richtet sich nach einer Konstellation von Faktoren wie Ihrer Finanzlage, Ihren künftigen Verbindlichkeiten (beispielsweise Ihr Ruhestandseinkommen, die Kosten für das Studium Ihrer Kinder und/oder Enkelkinder, der Eigenkapitalanteil für den Kauf einer Immobilie) und der Anzahl der Jahre, die Ihnen zur Finanzierung dieser Verbindlichkeiten zur Verfügung stehen. Generell können Sie höhere Risiken eingehen, wenn solche Verbindlichkeiten noch Zukunftsmusik sind. Desgleichen gilt: Je mehr Vermögen Sie im Verhältnis zur Höhe Ihrer Verbindlichkeiten aufbauen, desto mehr Risiko können Sie verkraften.

Ihre Risikobereitschaft ist dagegen eine sehr persönliche Angelegenheit. Manche Anleger können mit dem Auf und Ab des Marktes gut umgehen, ohne sich Sorgen zu machen. Wenn Ihnen die Wertschwankungen Ihres Portfolios aber nachts den Schlaf rauben, dann sind Ihre Risiken vermutlich zu hoch für Sie. Im Zusammenspiel ergibt sich aus der Höhe der Risiken, die Sie verkraften können, und Ihrer Risikobereitschaft Ihre *Risikotoleranz*.

Ein fundamentales Allokationsmodell für Anleger, die Vermögen aufbauen – und für solche, die bereits im Ruhestand sind

Befassen wir uns zunächst mit einem grundlegenden Allokationsmodell für den Vermögensaufbau eines Anlegers in der entsprechenden Lebensphase. Die Vernunft diktiert die Hauptpunkte, die dabei zu berücksichtigen sind. (1) Anleger, die Vermögen aufbauen wollen, indem sie regelmäßig Geld anlegen, können sich etwas mehr Risiko erlauben – also aggressiver vorgehen – als Anleger mit einem mehr oder minder festen Kapitalpool, die von laufenden Erträgen und auch von Kapitalauszahlungen abhängig sind, um ihre Lebenshaltungskosten zu bestreiten. (2) Jüngere Anleger, die den Zinseszinseffekt länger für sich arbeiten lassen können, können es sich ebenfalls leisten, aggressiver anzulegen, während ältere Investoren wohl eher einen konservativeren Kurs einschlagen sollten.

Grahams Leitlinien für die Vermögensstrukturierung sind vernünftig. Meine sind ganz ähnlich, aber etwas flexibler. In Stammaktien sollten Sie so viel investieren, wie es Ihre Risikotoleranz zulässt. Als Höchstwert für die allgemeine Zielallokation in Aktien empfehle ich beispielsweise 80 Prozent, wenn es sich bei den Anlegern um jüngere Menschen handelt, die sehr langfristig Vermögen bilden wollen.

Meine niedrigste Aktienallokation von 25 Prozent gilt für ältere Anleger, die schon lange im Ruhestand sind. Sie sollten den kurzfristigen *Folgen* Ihres Vorgehens mehr Gewicht beimessen als den *Wahrscheinlichkeiten* künftiger Erträge. Ihnen muss klar sein, dass die Ertragsvolatilität für sie kein ideales Risikomaß darstellt. Weitaus bedeutsamer ist das Risiko, dass sie unerwartet Mittel flüssig machen müssen, um ihre Lebenshaltung zu bestreiten – oftmals in gedrückten Märkten – und die erzielten Erlöse unter Umständen unter den ursprünglichen Anschaffungskosten der Anlagen liegen. Bei der Kapitalanlage gibt es keine Garantie.

Vier Entscheidungen

Als intelligenter Investor müssen Sie für Ihr Konzept zur Vermögensstrukturierung vier Entscheidungen treffen:

- Erstens und vor allem müssen Sie eine strategische Entscheidung für die Aufteilung Ihres Vermögens auf Aktien und Anleihen treffen. Je nach ihren persönlichen Umständen und Bedürfnissen werden unterschiedlich situierte Anleger natürlich unterschiedliche Entscheidungen treffen.

- Zweitens können Sie sich nicht vor der Entscheidung drücken, entweder ein festes Verhältnis beizubehalten oder die Anteile je nach Ertragslage der Märkte zu verändern. Ein festes Verhältnis (das regelmäßig so umgewichtet wird, dass es wieder der ursprünglichen Asset-Allokation entspricht) ist eine kluge Entscheidung, die Risiken begrenzt, und für viele Anleger vermutlich die bessere Wahl. Ein Portfolio, das niemals neu gewichtet wird, dürfte langfristig höhere Renditen bringen.

- An dritter Stelle steht die Entscheidung für oder gegen ein taktisches Allokationselement zur Veränderung des Verhältnisses zwischen Aktien und Anleihen, wenn sich die Marktbedingungen verändern. Die taktische Allokation ist mit bestimmten Risiken verbunden. Eine Veränderung der Aktien-/Anleiheanteile wirkt vielleicht wertsteigernd, vielleicht aber auch nicht (und Letzteres ist meines Erachtens wahrscheinlicher). In unserer von Unsicherheit geprägten Welt sollten taktische Änderungen sparsam vorgenommen werden, da sie ein gewisses Vorauswissen voraussetzen, über das die wenigsten verfügen – wenn überhaupt. Generell sollten Anleger die Finger von taktischer Allokation lassen.

- Vielleicht am wichtigsten ist viertens die Entscheidung, ob man sich auf aktiv gemanagte Investmentfonds oder traditionelle Indexfonds fokussiert. Die Indizien sprechen klar und eindeutig für die Indexfondsstrategie.

Diese vier Entscheidungen stellen den intelligenten Investor ausnahmslos vor eine schwere, anspruchsvolle Wahl. Gehen Sie sie mit Bedacht, Gründlichkeit und Umsicht an, damit Sie vernünftige Ergebnisse erzielen.

Der Zusammenhang zwischen Risikoaufschlägen und Mehrkosten

Wie Sie Ihr Anlagenportfolio auf Aktien und Anleihen aufteilen, dürfte sich wesentlich auf Ihre Vermögensbildung auswirken, so viel steht fest. Dabei sind sich viel zu wenige Anleger des entscheidenden Zusammenhangs zwischen Fondskosten und Asset-Allokation bewusst.

Ein kostengünstiges Portfolio mit einer *geringeren* Allokation in Aktien (und deshalb auch *geringeren* Risiken) kann denselben oder sogar einen *höheren* Nettoertrag abwerfen wie ein Portfolio mit einer weit höheren Aktienallokation (und entsprechend *höheren* Risiken), sofern die Kosten einer Anlage in die risikoärmere Alternative deutlich unter den Kosten für eine riskantere Option liegen.

Folgendes einfaches Beispiel macht das vielleicht deutlich (Abbildung 18.1). Hier gehen wir davon aus, dass ein Anleger ein Portfolio hält, das im Verhältnis 75 zu 25 auf Aktien und Anleihen aufgeteilt ist. Die voraussichtliche jährliche Bruttorendite beläuft sich auf 6 Prozent für Aktien und 3 Prozent für Anleihen.

ABBILDUNG 18.1 Durch Kostensenkung können Sie bei geringeren Risiken höhere Erträge erzielen

Kostenintensive aktiv gemanagte Fonds				**Kostengünstige Indexfonds**			
	Aktien	Anleihen	Portfolio-effekt		Aktien	Anleihen	Portfolio-effekt
Allo-kation	75 %	25 %	–	Allo-kation	25 %	75 %	–
Brutto-rendite	6	3	5,25 %	Brutto-rendite	6	3	3,75 %
Kosten	2	1	1,75	Kosten	0,05	0,10	0,09
Netto-rendite	4,0 %	2,0 %	3,50 %	Netto-rendite	6,0 %	2,9 %	3,66 %

Für einen Anleger, der sich für aktiv gemanagte Fonds entschieden hat, fallen jeweils Gesamtkosten von 2 beziehungsweise 1 Prozent pro Jahr an. Der zu erwartende Nettoertrag des betreffenden Portfolios liegt bei 3,5 Prozent.

Nehmen wir nun – bei konstanten Erträgen auf Aktien und Anleihen – an, dass ein konservativerer Anleger ein Portfolio im Verhältnis 25 zu 75 hält – also genau die umgekehrte Aufteilung. Der Anleger ersetzt aber die kostenintensiven aktiv gemanagten Investmentfonds durch kostengünstige Indexfonds, die bei Aktien nur mit 0,05 Prozent zu Buche schlagen, bei Anleihen mit 0,10 Prozent. Der erwartete Nettoertrag dieses Index-Mischportfolios würde de facto auf 3,66 Prozent pro Jahr ansteigen.

Niedrige Kosten ermöglichen risikoärmeren Portfolios höhere Erträge als Portfolios mit höheren Risiken

Nimmt man bei diesem Beispiel schlicht die Belastung durch überhöhte Kosten aus der Gleichung heraus, dann schneidet ein Portfolio mit 25 Prozent Aktien und 75 Prozent Anleihen besser ab als eines mit umgekehrter Aufteilung. *Der Indexfonds verändert die landläufige Anschauung zur Vermögensstrukturierung.*

Es kommt auf die Kosten an! Risikoaufschläge und Kostennachteile, die einander ständig bekriegen, müssen Eingang finden in die Gewichtung von Aktien und Anleihen in Ihrem Portfolio. Es ist höchste Zeit.

Lassen Sie mich ganz deutlich werden: Ich sage nicht, dass sie Ihre Aktienallokation zusammenstreichen sollen, wenn Sie

Ihre kostspieligen aktiv gemanagten Fonds gegen günstige Indexfonds austauschen. Ich sage nur, wenn Sie aktiv gemanagte Aktien- und Rentenfonds in Ihrer Vermögensstruktur halten, die mit weit höheren Gebühren beaufschlagt sind als kostengünstige Indexfonds, dann sollten Sie sich gut überlegen, womit Sie wohl den höchsten Nettoertrag erzielen. Rechnen Sie doch einfach nach!

Der Faktor Mensch – ein Rat für den besorgten Anleger

Es ist nicht so schwer, eine klare Strategie zur Vermögensaufteilung festzulegen. Wir könnten sicher Schlimmeres tun, als mit Ben Grahams zentralem Ziel von 50 Prozent Aktien und 50 Prozent Anleihen anzufangen – mit einer auf 75 zu 25 bzw. 25 zu 75 begrenzten Schwankungsbreite, jeweils bestehend aus Standard-Aktien- und Rentenindexfonds.

Doch so genau muss eine Allokation gar nicht sein. Dabei geht es auch um Urteilsvermögen, Hoffnungen, Ängste und Risikotoleranz. Eine absolut wasserdichte Strategie für Anleger gibt es nicht. Selbst ich mache mir um die Allokation meines Portfolios Gedanken.

In folgendem Brief erläutere ich einem jungen Anleger meine Bedenken, der sich um künftige Katastrophen in unserer fragilen Welt und unserer schnelllebigen Gesellschaft sorgt und versucht, eine vernünftige Vermögensstruktur für sein persönliches Portfolio zu ermitteln:

Ich gehe davon aus, dass die US-Wirtschaft langfristig weiterwächst, und dass der Substanzwert des Aktienmarkts dieses Wachstum widerspiegelt. Warum? Weil sich der Substanzwert aus Dividendenrenditen und Ertragssteigerungen zusammensetzt, die in der Vergangenheit eine Korrelation von etwa 0,96 mit dem Wirtschaftswachstum des Landes, gemessen am BIP, verzeichnet haben (was einer vollständigen Korrelation von 1,00 schon sehr nahe kommt).

Natürlich kommt es vor, dass die Kurse auf dem Aktienmarkt über diesen Substanzwert steigen (oder darunter fallen). Zu solchen Zeiten liegt dann eine gewisse Überbewertung vor. (Oder auch nicht – wir können uns da nie ganz sicher sein.) Doch auf lange Sicht sind die Marktkurse am Ende immer mit dem Substanzwert zusammengefallen. Ich bin (wie Warren Buffett) davon überzeugt, dass das, ganz rational betrachtet, eben so ist.

Maßgebliche Risiken – bekannte wie unbekannte – gibt es natürlich. Sie und ich wissen so viel oder wenig wie jeder andere darüber, wann diese eintreten. Die Beurteilung der Wahrscheinlichkeiten und der möglichen Folgen bleibt ganz uns überlassen. Aber wenn wir gar nicht investieren, stehen wir am Ende mit leeren Händen da.

Mein persönliches Gesamtportfolio setzt sich zu jeweils rund 50 Prozent aus indexierten Aktien und Anleihen zusammen, überwiegend kurz- und mittelfristig indexiert. In meinem Alter (ich bin jetzt 88) fühle ich mich mit dieser Aufteilung wohl. Ich gebe jedoch offen zu, dass ich die halbe Zeit befürchte, zu viel in Aktien investiert zu haben, und die andere halbe Zeit, es könnte zu wenig sein. Am Ende sind wir alle nur Menschen, die im Nebel der Unwissenheit agieren und uns auf unsere Umstände und unseren gesunden Menschenverstand verlassen bei der Festlegung der richtigen Vermögensaufteilung.

Um mit Churchills Worten über die Demokratie zu sprechen, so ist »meine Anlagestrategie die schlechteste, die je entwickelt wurde … abgesehen von jeder anderen bisher ausprobierten.« Ich hoffe, das hilft Ihnen weiter. Viel Glück.

J.C.B.

Viel Glück auch den Lesern dieses Kapitels. Machen Sie's, so gut Sie können, denn es gibt keinen Königsweg, um das Problem der Vermögensstrukturierung zu lösen.

Neunzehntes Kapitel

Vermögensstrukturierung, die Zweite

Altersvorsorge und Fonds, die Ihre Asset-Allokation vorab festlegen

In meinem 1993 verfassten Buch *Bogle on Mutual Funds* erläutere ich eine Vielzahl von Asset-Allokationsstrategien, die Anlegern zur Verfügung stehen, und spreche im Anschluss an, dass »weniger mehr« sein könnte – dass nämlich einfach die konventionelle (Lösung), also ein (Index-)Mischfonds aus 60 Prozent US-Aktien und 40 Prozent US-Anleihen, der außergewöhnlich breite Streuung bietet und mit minimalen Kosten betrieben wird, genauso gut funktioniert wie die Betreuung Ihres gesamten Portfolios durch ein Anlageberatungsunternehmen. 1992 beschloss ich, bei Vanguard genauso einen Mischfonds im Verhältnis 60 zu 40 aus Aktien und Anleihen aufzulegen. Rückblickend über die nachfolgenden 25 Jahre betrachtet, war dieser Fonds ein enormer Erfolg (Abbildung 19.1).

Sehen wir uns die erstaunliche Bilanz dieses Index-Mischfonds an: Über seine 25-jährige Laufzeit erzielte der Fonds eine Jahresrendite von 8,0 Prozent, verglichen mit 6,3 Prozent für seine Vergleichsgruppe – ein Vorsprung von 1,7 Prozentpunkten pro Jahr. Dieser Unterschied belief sich insgesamt auf einen kumulierten Ertrag von 202 Prozentpunkten.

Der Vorteil des Index-Mischfonds liegt vor allem in seinen niedrigen Kosten begründet – mit einer Kostenquote von 0,14 Prozent gegenüber 1,34 Prozent für die Mischfonds-Vergleichsgruppe.

ABBILDUNG 19.1 Das kostengünstige Index-Mischportfolio im Vergleich zu kostenintensiveren Konkurrenzangeboten, 1992 bis 2016

	Rendite		
	Jährlich*	Kumuliert	Kostenquote
Index-Mischfonds	8,0 %	+536 %	0,14 %
Durchschnittlicher Mischfonds	6,3	334	1,34
Indexvorteil	1,7 %	+202 %	1,20 %

* Korrelation der Jahresrendite: 0,98.

Dieser Kostenvorteil und die bemerkenswerte Korrelation seines Jahresertrags von 0,98 mit anderen Fonds aus der Vergleichsgruppe (1,00 entspricht einer vollkommenen Korrelation) lässt uns mit Fug und Recht vermuten, dass der Index-Mischfonds seine Vergleichsgruppe auch in den kommenden Jahren schlagen dürfte.

Ja, ein Anleger wäre mit einem kostengünstigen Indexfonds auf den S&P 500 besser dran gewesen – mit einer Jahresrendite von 9,3 Prozent für diesen Zeitraum gegenüber dem Ertrag eines Index-Mischfonds von 8,1 Prozent. Bei seiner geringeren Volatilität (Index-Mischfonds: 8,9 Prozent, S&P-500-Indexfonds: 14,3 Prozent) wäre der Vorteil beim risikoadjustierten Ertrag sogar noch größer gewesen. Doch wenn es Probleme gab, bot der Index-Mischfonds außergewöhnlichen Schutz. 2000/2002, als der S&P 500 um 38 Prozent einbrach, verlor der Index-Mischfonds nur 14 Prozent. 2008, als der S&P 500 um 37 Prozent abrutschte, waren es beim Mischfonds nur 22 Prozent.

Anleger mit einem sehr langen Anlagehorizont und viel Schneid – Anleger, die sich von den immer wieder auftretenden Börsencrashs nicht ins Bockshorn jagen lassen – sind mit einer 100-prozentigen Allokation im S&P-500-Index fast immer besser bedient (wobei der Abstand in den vergangenen 25 Jahren ungewöhnlich knapp ausfiel und meiner Erwartung nach künftig größer werden dürfte).

Doch wenn Ihr Zeithorizont begrenzt ist oder Sie sich von der Volatilität des Aktienmarkts einschüchtern lassen und in Versuchung geraten, Ihren Aktienanteil in stürmischen Zeiten abzustoßen? Dann sollten Sie die Strategie, auf einen Index-Mischfonds mit fester Aufteilung von 60 zu 40 in Aktien und Anleihen zu setzen und unbeirrt daran festzuhalten, ernsthaft in Erwägung ziehen.

Und wieder: die Weisheit von Benjamin Graham

Ich sehe auch für einen Anleger im Ruhestand keinen Grund, stärker von der Empfehlung Benjamin Grahams abzuweichen, die er vor so vielen Jahren allen Anlegern erteilte, wie im Vorkapitel nachzulesen – nämlich einer grundlegenden Aufteilung in 50 Prozent Aktien und 50 Prozent Anleihen, mit einer Bandbreite von 75 zu 25 bzw. 25 zu 75. Der höhere Aktienanteil ist für risikotolerantere Anleger geeignet, die für sich und ihre Erben nach größerem Reichtum streben, das geringere Verhältnis für risikoscheue Anleger, denen ihr ruhiger Nachtschlaf wichtiger ist als die Aussicht auf höhere Erträge.

Ich bin oft als Verfechter einer ähnlichen einfachen und scheinbar starren Vermögensaufteilung bezeichnet worden: Ihre Position in Anleihen sollte Ihrem Lebensalter entsprechen. Der Rest wird in Aktien investiert. Diese Strategie zur Asset-Allokation erfüllt die Bedürfnisse vieler, wenn nicht der meisten Anleger recht gut, sollte aber nie mehr sein als eine grobe Faustregel, bei der Ihre Überlegungen ansetzen können. Sie beruht (oder jedenfalls war das früher einmal so) auf der Vorstellung, dass wir in jüngerem Alter nur begrenztes Anlagekapital zur Verfügung haben, keine laufenden Anlageerträge benötigen, höhere Risiken verkraften können und glauben, dass Aktien langfristig höhere

Renditen abwerfen als Anleihen. und wir deshalb stärker in Aktien als in Anleihen engagiert sein sollten.

Wenn wir älter werden und uns irgendwann zur Ruhe setzen, haben die meisten ein erkleckliches Anlageportfolio aufgebaut. Dann sind wir in aller Regel risikoscheuer, eher bereit, auf maximalen Kapitalzuwachs zu verzichten und stärker von den höheren laufenden Erträgen abhängig, die Anleihen in den vergangenen 60 Jahren abgeworfen haben. Unter diesen Umständen sollten wir mehr Anleihen als Aktien halten.

Die nötige Flexibilität

Es war keinesfalls meine Absicht, eine solche altersbasierte Faustregel strikt anzuwenden. So gibt es sicherlich viele junge Anleger, die, wenn sie ihre erste Vollzeitstelle angetreten haben, in diesen frühen Jahren regelmäßig nicht 75, sondern 100 Prozent ihrer Ersparnisse in Aktien stecken könnten.

Dagegen ist eine Aktienquote von null Prozent selbst für einen frischgebackenen Hundertjährigen eher ein zweifelhaftes Ziel. (Und Hundertjährige dürfte es in Zukunft immer mehr geben.) Laufend Aktien zu verkaufen, um den Aktienanteil zu senken, ist für einen solchen Anleger nicht unbedingt sinnvoll – vor allem in Anbetracht der potenziell hohen Steuern auf Veräußerungsgewinne, die realisiert werden, wenn Aktien mit erheblichem Wertzuwachs abgestoßen werden.

Ein flexibler altersorientierter Plan klingt für uns vernünftiger. Doch die vielen Studien, die durchgeführt wurden, um die große Vielzahl ähnlicher (wenngleich genauerer und komplexerer) Allokationsstrategien zu bestätigen, haben alle ein und denselben Fehler: Sie stützen sich auf die vergangenen Renditen von Anleihen und Aktien, die sich in den kommenden zehn Jahren kaum wiederholen dürften. (Siehe neuntes Kapitel.)

»Die Schecks sind in der Post«

Das bringt mich zu einem noch wichtigeren Punkt. Mit zunehmendem Alter verlassen wir uns immer weniger auf unser Humankapital, das uns im Großen und Ganzen dorthin gebracht hat, wo wir heute sind, und mehr auf unser Anlagekapital. Schließlich ist im Ruhestand am allerwichtigsten, dass Erträge in der nötigen Höhe fließen, um unseren Bedarf zu decken – in Form der Dividendenschecks für unsere Fondsanlagen und der monatlichen Überweisungen von der Rentenversicherung.

Natürlich ist der Marktwert unseres Kapitals von Bedeutung. Doch ständig auf den Wert unserer Anlagen zu schauen, ist nicht nur un-, sondern sogar kontraproduktiv. In Wirklichkeit brauchen wir im Ruhestand stetige Einnahmen, die nach Möglichkeit mit der Inflation steigen.

Die Rente entspricht exakt diesen Kriterien. Ein Mischfondsportfolio kann bei mäßigen Risiken eine effektive Ergänzung zur Rente darstellen (oder umgekehrt). Etwa die Hälfte der Erträge eines Mischportfolios stammen aus Anleihezinsen, die andere Hälfte aus Dividenden, überwiegend von Large-Caps. Mit nur drei nennenswerten Ausnahmen sind die Dividenden auf den S&P-500-Index in jedem der 90 Jahre seit seiner Auflegung 1926 gestiegen. (Siehe Abbildung 6.2 im sechsten Kapitel.)

Rentenzahlungen plus Indexfondsdividenden sind eine solide Grundlage für stetige, wachsende Einnahmen

Eine Kombination aus Rentenzahlungen und Dividenden aus Indexfonds* (bei Bedarf ergänzt durch Kapitalauszahlungen) ist vermutlich ein effektiver Weg, sich regelmäßiger monatlicher Einnahmen aus der Altersvorsorge zu erfreuen. (Zwar schütten nur wenige Aktienfonds monatlich Dividenden aus, doch die meisten bieten Programme an, die regelmäßige monatliche Zahlungen vorsehen.)

Die Ertragsrenditen von Aktien und Anleihen befinden sich auf einem historischen Tiefpunkt (mit 2 Prozent für Aktien und 3 Prozent für Anleihen). Aufgrund der verheerenden Effekte der mit Investmentfonds verbundenen Kosten sind die Renditen aktiv gemanagter Fondsprodukte weit niedriger, wie dem sechsten Kapitel zu entnehmen ist. Derart geringe Renditen dürften kaum ausreichen, um den Bedarf an laufenden Einnahmen zu befriedigen, den viele Anleger haben. Daher sind sie besser beraten, wenn sie in Betracht ziehen, ihr Alterseinkommen mithilfe eines Gesamtertragsansatzes zu sichern – anhand einer Kombination

* Wie in Abbildung 6.3 im sechsten Kapitel dargestellt, schlucken aktiv gemanagte Fonds den Großteil der oder gar die gesamten Bruttodividenden, die sie vereinnahmen. Nicht so der Indexfonds.

aus Fondsdividenden und regelmäßigen Kapitalentnahmen, um so im Ruhestand einen steten Strom monatlicher Zahlungen herbeizuführen.

Nicht-US-Aktien – ein neues Allokationsparadigma?

In den letzten zehn Jahren wurde das klassische *aus zwei Fonds bestehende* Modellportfolio (US-Anleihen und -Aktien) in der Akzeptanz weitgehend verdrängt von einem Modellportfolio aus *drei Fonds*: 33 Prozent in einem Bond-Indexfonds, 33 Prozent in einem US-Aktienindexfonds und 33 Prozent in einem Indexfonds für Nicht-US-Aktien.

Aus einer solchen Portfolio-Allokation auf drei Fonds spricht im Grunde die breite Akzeptanz eines globalen Portfolios bei vielen Beratern und Anlegern. Ein solches Portfolio basiert im Wesentlichen auf den Marktkapitalisierungen der Aktien aus fast allen Ländern der Welt.

1993 habe ich dem Anlegerpublikum in meinem Buch *Bogle on Mutual Funds* erklärt, sie müssten keine Aktien aus anderen Ländern als den USA in ihren Portfolios halten und sollten auf keinen Fall mehr als 20 Prozent ihres Aktienanteils in Nicht-US-Aktien investieren.

Meine Auffassung, dass ein ausschließlich aus US-Aktien bestehendes Portfolio die Bedürfnisse der meisten Anleger erfüllt, wurde (und wird immer noch) von, sagen wir, so gut wie allen infrage gestellt. Sie argumentieren wie folgt: »Ist es denn nicht ebenso willkürlich, Nicht-US-Aktien aus einem diversifizierten

Portfolio auszuschließen, wie, sagen wir, den Technologiesektor aus dem S&P 500?«

Ich hielt dagegen. Wir Amerikaner verdienen unser Geld in Dollar, geben es in Dollar aus, sparen in Dollar und investieren in Dollar – wieso sollten wir Währungsrisiken eingehen? Haben sich US-Institute in aller Regel nicht als stärker erwiesen als die anderer Länder? Stammt nicht die Hälfte der Umsätze und Gewinne von US-Unternehmen schon aus anderen Ländern? Dürfte das US-Bruttoinlandsprodukt (BIP) nicht zumindest ebenso schnell wachsen wie das BIP in der übrigen Welt – vielleicht sogar schneller?

Die Ratschläge aus meinem Buch von 1993 haben sich bezahlt gemacht

Aus welchem Grund auch immer – meine Ratschläge haben sich bezahlt gemacht. Seit 1993 hat der US-amerikanische S&P-500-Index im Schnitt eine Jahresrendite von 9,4 Prozent erzielt (kumuliert +707 Prozent). Das Nicht-US-Portfolio – dabei beziehe ich mich auf den MSCI Europe, Australasia and Far East Index (EAFE) – erwirtschaftete 5,1 Prozent im Jahr (+216 Prozent).

Abgesehen davon könnte schon sein, dass sich der im vergangenen Vierteljahrhundert verzeichnete relative Vorsprung der US-Aktienmärkte inzwischen wegarbitragiert hat und dass die lange Phase relativer Rückstände von Nicht-US-Aktien in anderen Ländern zu attraktiven Bewertungen geführt hat. Wer weiß das schon? Sie müssen daher die Wahrscheinlichkeiten abwägen und Ihr eigenes Urteil fällen.

Ein festes Verhältnis zwischen Aktien und Anleihen? Oder eines, das sich gemäß den Anlagezielen oder mit der Zeit verändert?

Das Ziel eines Mischindexfonds mit festem Verhältnis zwischen Aktien und Anleihen bestand darin, den Anlegern die lästige Aufgabe der Aufteilung ihres Vermögens abzunehmen, während sich die Märkte veränderten. Ich gelangte aber bald zum (offensichtlichen!) Schluss, dass das willkürliche Mischportfolio im Verhältnis 60 zu 40 – vielleicht die vernünftigste Quote für Anleger, die ein ausgewogenes Risiko-Ertrags-Profil anstreben – womöglich nicht für alle Anleger geeignet ist. Warum also nicht Fonds mit anderen Allokationen anbieten?

Daher offerierte Vanguard vier sogenannte »LifeStrategy«-Fonds (Abbildung 19.2) – Growth (80 Prozent Aktien), Moderate Growth (60 Prozent Aktien), Conservative Growth (40 Prozent Aktien) und Income (20 Prozent Aktien). Inzwischen entfallen diese Aktienallokationen allesamt zu 60 Prozent auf US-Aktien und zu 40 Prozent auf Aktien aus anderen Ländern. Bei den Bond-Allokationen sind es 70 Prozent US-Anleihen und 30 Prozent Anleihen aus anderen Ländern.

Der Aufstieg des Target-Date-Fund (TDF)

Die LifeStrategy-Fonds sind keinesfalls die einzige Abwandlung des Mischfondskonzepts. In den vergangenen zehn Jahren ist die Nachfrage der Anleger nach sogenannten Target-Date-Funds

ABBILDUNG 19.2 Die Vermögensaufteilung verschiedener Mischfonds

	Balanced Index	LifeStrategy Growth	LifeStrategy Moderate Growth	LifeStrategy Conservative Growth	LifeStrategy Income	Target Retirement 2060	Target Retirement 2065	Target Retirement 2050
US-Aktien	60 %	48 %	36 %	24 %	12 %	54 %	54 %	54 %
Nicht-US-Aktien	0	32	24	16	8	36	36	36
Aktien gesamt	60 %	80 %	60 %	40 %	20 %	90 %	90 %	90 %
US-Anleihen	40 %	14 %	28 %	42 %	56 %	7 %	7 %	7 %
Nicht-US-Anleihen	0	6	12	18	24	3	3	3
Anleihen gesamt	40 %	20 %	40 %	60 %	80 %	10 %	10 %	10 %
	Target Retirement 2045	Target Retirement 2040	Target Retirement 2035	Target Retirement 2030	Target Retirement 2025	Target Retirement 2020	Target Retirement 2015	Target Retirement Income
US-Aktien	54 %	52 %	48 %	43 %	39 %	34 %	27 %	18 %
Nicht-US-Aktien	36	35	32	29	26	23	18	12
Aktien gesamt	90 %	87 %	80 %	72 %	65 %	56 %	44 %	30 %
US-Anleihen	7 %	9 %	15 %	20 %	25 %	32 %	42 %	54 %
Nicht-US-Anleihen	3	4	6	8	11	12	14	16
Anleihen gesamt	10 %	13 %	21 %	28 %	35 %	44 %	56 %	70 %

(TDFs) förmlich explodiert – Fonds, die diversifizierte Portfolios aus Aktien und Anleihen halten und immer konservativer agieren, je näher ihr Zieldatum rückt: gewöhnlich das Jahr, in dem der Anleger voraussichtlich in Rente geht.

Target-Fonds für die Altersvorsorge sind mit Abstand die beliebtesten und verwalten mittlerweile ein Vermögen von knapp 1 Billion US-Dollar. Ihr Konzept – im Grunde die Umschichtung von Aktien in Anleihen, je näher der Zeitpunkt rückt, an dem daraus Zahlungsverpflichtungen gedeckt werden müssen – kann aber auch auf andere Anlageziele Anwendung finden, etwa für die Ausbildung der Kinder. Einer der Gründe für die Popularität von Target-Date-Funds ist ihre Schlichtheit. Sie müssen lediglich abschätzen, in welchem Jahr Sie in Ruhestand gehen oder Ihr Kind ein Studium aufnehmen wird, und dann in den Fonds investieren, der diesem Zieldatum am nächsten liegt nach dem Motto »einmal eingerichtet, nie wieder darüber nachgedacht«.

TDFs können eine ausgezeichnete Wahl sein – nicht nur für Anleger, die gerade in die Kapitalanlage einsteigen, sondern auch für solche, die sich für eine einfache Strategie zur Finanzierung ihrer Altersversorgung entscheiden. Doch wenn Ihr Vermögen wächst und Ihre private Bilanz und Ihre Anlageziele komplexer werden, kann es sich lohnen, über einzelne Bausteine wie kostengünstige Aktien- und Rentenindexfonds nachzudenken, um daraus ein Portfolio aufzubauen.

Wenn Sie sich für TDFs entscheiden, empfehle ich Ihnen dringend, erst einmal »einen Blick unter die Haube« zu werfen. (Nie verkehrt!) Vergleichen Sie die Kosten von TDFs und achten Sie auf die zugrunde liegenden Strukturen. Viele TDFs halten aktiv gemanagte Fonds als Komponenten, während andere kostengünstige Indexfonds verwenden.

Verschaffen Sie sich unbedingt Einblick in Ihr TDF-Portfolio und einen Überblick über die Kosten, die Ihnen dafür entstehen. Aktiv gemanagte TDFs haben überwiegend jährliche Kostenquoten von durchschnittlich 0,70 Prozent. Indexfonds-TDFs kommen dagegen mit 0,13 Prozent aus. Es wird Sie kaum überraschen, dass ich preiswerte, indexbasierte Target-Date-Funds für Ihre beste Option halte.

Rente nicht vergessen

Welche Strategie zur Vermögensaufteilung Sie für sich auch für die beste halten, die Rolle der Rente müssen Sie dabei unbedingt berücksichtigen, denn sie stellt für viele Ruheständler den wichtigsten Einkommensanteil. Rund 93 Prozent aller US-Amerikaner beziehen im Ruhestand Rente. Bei der Ermittlung ihrer Asset-Allokation müssen Anleger diese Zahlungen als anleihenähnlichen Vermögenswert ins Kalkül ziehen.

Die Rente macht einen wesentlichen Bestandteil Ihres Portfolios aus. Ich will das an einem Beispiel verdeutlichen. Die durchschnittliche verbleibende Lebenserwartung eines 62-jährigen US-Amerikaners beträgt rund 20 Jahre. Ich gehe daher davon aus, dass ein 62-jähriger Anleger 20 Jahre lang Rente bezieht. Bei einem Endgehalt von 60.000 US-Dollar erhält ein Anleger mit Rentenansprüchen pro Monat 1.174 US-Dollar. Zinsen wir diese Leistung mit dem aktuellen inflationsbereinigten Satz für

US-Staatsanleihen ab, dann beträgt der Kapitalwert der Rente des Anlegers rund 270.000 US-Dollar. Da sich dieser Wert aber beim Tod des Rentners in Luft auflöst, revidieren wir den Wert anhand eines willkürlichen Abzinsungssatz auf 200.000 US-Dollar. (Darauf, *wann* Sie Rentenansprüche geltend machen sollten, komme ich noch.)

Gehen wir nun davon aus, dass unser Anleger über ein Investmentfondsportfolio im Wert von 1 Million US-Dollar verfügt und Benjamin Grahams klassische 50/50-Allokation einsetzt. Ungeachtet der Rente würde der Anleger also 500.000 US-Dollar in Aktien und 500.000 US-Dollar in Anleihen investieren. Doch wir wollen die Rente ja berücksichtigen.

Rentenbezüge und Vermögensstruktur

Addieren wir den unterstellten Wert der Rente von 200.000 US-Dollar zu dem Portfolio des Anlegers hinzu, beläuft es sich auf 1.200.000 US-Dollar. Doch unter Berücksichtigung der zugerechneten Rente steigt der anleiheähnliche Anteil des Portfolios auf 700.000 US-Dollar oder 58 Prozent – und der Aktienanteil fällt auf 42 Prozent.

Um also de facto eine 50/50-Allokation zu erreichen, müsste der Anleger 600.000 US-Dollar in Aktien und 600.000 US-Dollar in Anleihen halten (400.000 US-Dollar in Rentenfonds, 200.000 US-Dollar als Rente). Bei den Target-Date-Funds wird die Rente als Einkommensquelle in aller Regel ignoriert. Das bedeutet, dass die Anleger konservativere Portfolios halten, als ihnen möglicherweise bewusst ist. Die TDFs mögen die Rente als anleiheähnlichen Vermögenswert außen vor lassen – Sie sollten das nicht tun.

Aufgepasst: Wer die Rentenzahlung hinausschiebt, kann dadurch die Monatsrente, die er später erhält, erhöhen – allerdings auf Kosten der Jahre dazwischen, in denen er keine Rente bekommt. Der Anleger muss hier gut abwägen zwischen der Chance, spätere höhere monatliche Zahlungen zu erhalten, und dem Verzicht auf diese Zahlungen über ganze zehn Jahre.

Unser Beispielanleger mit einem Erwerbseinkommen von 60.000 US-Dollar würde bei einem Eintrittsalter von 62 Jahren 1.174 US-Dollar Rente im Monat bekommen. Schiebt er den Rentenbezug hinaus, bis er 72 ist, würden sich die monatlichen Zahlungen auf 1.974 US-Dollar erhöhen – eine deutliche Steigerung um fast 70 Prozent. Doch durch diesen Aufschub verzichtet der Anleger insgesamt auf 140.900 US-Dollar Rente. Er müsste die höheren monatlichen Leistungen 14 Jahre lang beziehen, bevor sich der Aufschub lohnt.

Altersvorsorge

Die Vermögensbildung für ein gesichertes, komfortables Leben im Ruhestand ist für viele, wenn nicht die meisten Anleger das wichtigste Anlageziel. Steuerbegünstigte Sparmöglichkeiten für die Altersvorsorge machen dieses Ziel leichter erreichbar. Sie sollten diese Möglichkeiten auf jeden Fall nutzen, müssen aber entscheiden, welche davon (oder welche Kombination daraus) für Sie die richtige ist. Hier ein kurzer Überblick über die verschiedenen Arten von Sparplänen für die Altersvorsorge in den USA:

Defined Contribution (DC) Plans werden von vielen Arbeitgebern angeboten. Damit kann sich der Beschäftigte/Anleger direkt Beiträge von seinem Erwerbseinkommen abziehen und auf sein Sparkonto einzahlen lassen. Der gängigste solche Sparplan trägt die Bezeichnung 401(k). Damit können Sie vor Steuern Geld für den Ruhestand zurücklegen, und die Beiträge werden vom Arbeitgeber häufig nach einer vorgegebenen Formel aufgestockt. Die Anlageerträge auf Ihr Sparvermögen steigen und werden nachgelagert besteuert – also erst bei Abhebung im Ruhestand.

Solche Pläne bieten oft die Möglichkeit, Kredit darauf aufzunehmen oder vorzeitig Kapital zu entnehmen, wenn es während der Erwerbstätigkeit zu finanziellen Engpässen kommt. Ähnliche Pläne gibt es auch für Mitarbeiter anderer Organisationen: den 403(b)-Plan für gemeinnützige Organisationen, den 457-Plan für Mitarbeiter bestimmter Non-Profit-Organisationen und den öffentlichen Dienst sowie den Thrift Savings Plan (TSP) für Beschäftigte der US-Bundesregierung.

Klassische IRAs kann jeder abschließen, der Lohn oder Gehalt bezieht. Die steuerlichen Vorteile des klassischen IRA gleichen denen eines DC-Plans – Ihre Beiträge sind gewöhnlich steuerlich abzugsfähig, können unversteuert anwachsen und werden erst nachgelagert besteuert, wenn Sie Kapital entnehmen. Der Jahreshöchstbeitrag liegt gewöhnlich bei 5.500 US-Dollar.

SEP-IRAs: Das Simplified Employee Pension IRA ist für Selbstständige und Kleinunternehmer gedacht. Steuerlich wird es ähnlich behandelt wie klassische IRAs, allerdings bei deutlich höheren Maximalbeiträgen.

Roth IRAs: Das Roth IRA wird steuerlich anders behandelt als andere Sparpläne zur Altersvorsorge. Die Beiträge sind nicht absetzbar (sondern werden voll besteuert), dafür sind die Auszahlungen nach Eintritt in den Ruhestand dann komplett steuerfrei – einschließlich aller aufgelaufenen Anlagegewinne. Anders als bei DC-Plänen und IRAs werden die aufgelaufenen Gewinne eines Roth-Kontos gar nicht besteuert. Roth-Beiträge können auch in viele DC-Pläne eingezahlt werden. Das Roth IRA ist vermutlich für die meisten neuen Anleger die bessere Wahl, doch wer schon in ein bestehendes klassisches IRA einzahlt, sollte sich darüber im Klaren sein, dass bei einer Umwandlung in ein Roth IRA erhebliche Steuern anfallen könnten. Rechnen Sie das mit spitzem Bleistift durch!

Wenn Sie das Kapital angreifen müssen

Bei einer Verzinsung, die für Anleihen derzeit bei rund 3 Prozent liegt, und einer Dividendenrendite auf Aktien von 2 Prozent (beides vor Abzug der hohen Kosten aktiv gemanagter Fonds) dürften die von Ihrem Ruhestandsportfolio generierten Renditen deutlich niedriger ausfallen als Ihr Finanzbedarf. Eine Faustregel besagt, dass Sie bei einer Entnahme von 4 Prozent des Jahresschlusswerts Ihres ursprünglichen Ruhestandskapitals im Jahr (aus Erträgen und Kapital), jährlich inflationsbereinigt, gut durchs Alter kommen. Garantiert ist das aber nicht.

Halten Sie sich daher nicht krampfhaft an Regeln wie 4 Prozent im Jahr. Gestalten Sie Ihre Finanzplanung fürs Alter flexibler. Wenn Ihre Entnahmeregel bei schlechter Marktlage einen zu großen Teil Ihres Portfolios aufzehren würde, sollten Sie den Gürtel enger schnallen und weniger Kapital abziehen. Entwickeln sich die Märkte gut, und Sie erhalten mit Ihrer festgelegten Quote höhere Zahlungen, als Sie eigentlich benötigen, sollten Sie den warmen Regen für eine stets ungewisse Zukunft wiederanlegen. Dadurch verhindern Sie zu große Löcher im Portfolio, wenn die Märkte fallen, und haben die Chance, Ihre Reserven aufzufüllen, wenn sie sich erholen.

Garantien gibt es nicht

Ich sage es noch einmal: Jede Strategie zur Vermögensaufteilung unterliegt zahlreichen Risiken – dem Aktienmarktrisiko, dem Auszahlungsrisiko, makroökonomischen Risiken und sonstigen Risiken, die in unserer fragilen Welt bestehen. Wir können nicht mehr tun, als wohlüberlegte Entscheidungen zu treffen und unsere Allokation und die Auszahlungen flexibel zu gestalten, wenn sich die Rahmenbedingungen ändern.

Wenn Sie mir nicht glauben …

Angesichts der ausgeklügelten Allokationsoptionen, die heute zur Verfügung stehen, bleiben die Vorzüge der einfachen 60/40-Regel für Mischindexfonds aus Aktien und Anleihen häufig unbeachtet. Anfang 2017 würdigte **Ben Carlson**, Autor von *A Wealth of Common Sense*, das Konzept in einem in *MarketWatch* abgedruckten Artikel mit dem Titel »A Lesson in Investing Simplicity: Why the Bogle Model Beats the Yale Model«:

»Die NACUBO-Commonfund Study of Endowments« weist jedes Jahr die Anlageerträge aus, die von »über 800 College-Stiftungen erzielt werden, die ein Vermögen von 515 Milliarden US-Dollar repräsentieren.«

Carlson verwendet das sogenannte »Bogle Model«, ein Portfolio aus 40 Prozent Indexfonds auf den gesamten (US-)Aktienmarkt, 20 Prozent Indexfonds auf den gesamten internationalen Aktienmarkt und 40 Prozent Indexfonds auf den gesamten (US-)Rentenmarkt. Die Tabelle zeigt, dass das Bogle-Modell in maßgeblichen Zeiträumen bis zum 30. Juni 2016 die durchschnittliche Universitätsstiftung beständig geschlagen hat. Für die ganzen zehn Jahre hat das Modell sogar besser abgeschnitten als das oberste Dezil der Stiftungsfonds.

Daraus folgert Carlson: »Dabei geht es nicht um aktive gegenüber passiver Kapitalanlage, sondern nur um einfache gegenüber komplexen, um operativ effiziente Anlageprogramme gegenüber operativ ineffizienten Anlageprogrammen und Portfolios mit hoher Wahrscheinlichkeit gegenüber solchen mit geringer Wahrscheinlichkeit. Es war schon schwer genug, Kapital gut anzulegen, bevor ein komplexer, ineffizienter Anlagestil mit geringer Erfolgswahrscheinlichkeit ins Spiel kam. Aus diesem Grund hat das einfache, effiziente Bogle-Modell mit seiner hohen Erfolgswahrscheinlichkeit auch die Nase vorn.«

ABBILDUNG 19.3

	Bogle-Modell	Durchschnitt Stiftungen	Oberstes Quartil Stiftungen	Oberstes Dezil Stiftungen
3 Jahre	6,4 %	5,2 %	6,3 %	6,6 %
5 Jahre	6,5	5,4	6,2	6,6
10 Jahre	6,0	5,0	5,3	5,4

Quelle: NACUBO-Commonfund Study of Endowments

ANMERKUNG: Der 60/40-Mischindexfonds, der in seiner Aktienallokation nur US-Aktien hielt, erzielte deutlich höhere Erträge als das »Bogle-Modell«: über drei Jahre 8,4 Prozent, über 5 Jahre 8,6 Prozent, über 10 Jahre 6,9 Prozent. Welche der beiden Strategien in den kommenden Jahren besser abschneiden wird, bleibt abzuwarten.

Zwanzigstes Kapitel

Anlageberatung, die sich langfristig bewährt

Im Sinne von Benjamin Franklin

Ich bin der tiefsten Überzeugung, dass die große Mehrheit amerikanischer Haushalte sehr gut bedient wäre, wenn sie ihre Aktien in Form eines Standard-&-Poor's-500-Indexfonds (oder eines Indexfonds auf den gesamten Aktienmarkt) und ihre Anleihen in einem Indexfonds auf den gesamten Rentenmarkt halten würden. (Anleger, die besonders hohen Steuersätzen unterliegen, sollten stattdessen ein ausgesprochen kostengünstiges indexähnliches Portfolio aus hochwertigen mittelfristigen Kommunalanleihen halten.) Auf die Gefahr, mich zu wiederholen:

Eine solche indexorientierte Strategie ist womöglich nicht die beste Anlagestrategie aller Zeiten, aber es gibt unzählige schlechtere.

Warren Buffett meint dazu:

> *»Die meisten Anleger, und zwar institutionelle Investoren ebenso wie Privatanleger, werden feststellen, dass es am besten ist, Stammaktien über Indexfonds zu halten, die minimale Gebühren berechnen. Wer diesen Weg einschlägt, schneidet unter dem Strich (also nach Gebühren und Kosten) auf jeden Fall besser ab als die allermeisten Profis.«*

(Und für die meisten Anleger stellt ein Indexfonds übrigens auch die ideale Möglichkeit dar, in Anleihen zu investieren.)

Trotz all der unvermeidlichen Ungewissheit im ewig dichten Nebel, der die Welt der Kapitalanlage umwabert, gibt es doch nach wie vor einiges, was wir sicher sagen können

Im Streben nach Anlageerfolg sollte Ihnen bewusst sein, dass wir nie genau wissen, welche Erträge Aktien und Anleihen in den kommenden Jahren bringen, und auch nicht, welche Renditen mit Alternativen zum Indexportfolio künftig zu erzielen sind. Doch nur Mut: Trotz all der unvermeidlichen Ungewissheit im ewig dichten Nebel, der die Welt der Kapitalanlage umwabert, gibt es doch nach wie vor einiges, was wir sicher sagen können:

- Wir *wissen*, dass wir so früh wie möglich anfangen müssen, zu investieren, und von da an regelmäßig weiter Geld zur Seite legen sollten.
- Wir *wissen*, woher die Erträge der Aktien- und Rentenmärkte kommen, und das ist äußerst aufschlussreich.
- Wir *wissen*, dass das mit der Auswahl einzelner Wertpapiere sowie mit der Auswahl von Fondsmanagern und Anlagestilen verbundene Risiko ausgeschaltet werden kann durch die absolut breite Streuung, die ein traditioneller Indexfonds bietet. Übrig bleibt einzig das Marktrisiko.
- Wir *wissen*, dass »den Markt schlagen« oder »den richtigen Ein- und Ausstiegszeitpunkt zu erwischen« generell ein Widerspruch in sich ist. *Das kann in wenigen Ausnahmefällen funktionieren, doch niemals für alle.*
- Und schließlich *wissen* wir noch, was wir *nicht* wissen: Wir können nie sicher sein, wie unsere Welt morgen aussieht, und noch weniger können wir sagen, wie sie in zehn Jahren dasteht. Doch mit intelligenter Vermögensaufteilung und vernünftigen Anlageentscheidungen können wir uns auf die unvermeidlichen Verwerfungen einstellen, die es geben wird, und sie unbeschadet überstehen.

Unsere Aufgabe ist und bleibt: uns den uns zustehenden Anteil der Gewinne zu sichern, die unsere Unternehmen in den kommenden Jahren so großzügig bereitstellen. So definiert sich nach meinem Verständnis eine erfolgreiche Kapitalanlage.

Der traditionelle Indexfonds ist die einzige Anlageform, mit der wir dieses Ziel garantiert erreichen. Passen Sie auf, dass Sie nicht zu den Verlierern gehören, deren Anlageerträge deutlich unter den Gewinnen bleiben, die auf dem Aktienmarkt realisiert werden. Wenn Sie sich nach den einfachen vernünftigen Leitlinien in diesem kleinen Handbuch richten, zählen Sie auf jeden Fall zu den Gewinnern.

John Bogle und Benjamin Franklin: die Parallelen ihrer Anlageprinzipien

Bei der Betrachtung meiner Anlageideen im Kontext anderer Konzepte, die ich über längere Zeit beobachtet habe, erkenne ich rückblickend erstaunliche Parallelen zu den Grundsätzen, aus denen die Weisheit von Benjamin Franklin spricht. Vergleichen Sie diese Sammlung an Aussagen – aus meiner und aus seiner Feder:

Zum Sparen für die Zukunft:

Franklin: Wenn Ihr reich sein möchtet, denkt ans Verdienen und ans Sparen. Denkt daran, dass Zeit Geld ist, denn verlorene Zeit lässt sich nicht wiederfinden.

Bogle: Wer nichts anlegt, wird todsicher nie das nötige Vermögen aufbauen, um seine finanzielle Zukunft zu sichern. Der Zinseszinseffekt ist ein Wunder. Die Zeit ist Ihr Freund. Nutzen Sie deshalb so viel Zeit wie möglich.

Zur Bedeutung der Kostenkontrolle:

Franklin: Nehmt Euch vor kleinen Ausgaben in Acht. – Ein kleines Leck versenkt ein großes Schiff.

Bogle: Einfache Arithmetik funktioniert. Ihr Nettoertrag besteht schlicht aus dem Bruttoertrag Ihres Anlageportfolios abzüglich der angefallenen Kosten. Halten Sie Ihre Anlagekosten daher möglichst gering.

Zu Risiken:

Franklin: Ohne Fleiß kein Preis. Wer einen Fisch fangen will, muss einen Köder auswerfen.

Bogle: Sie müssen investieren. Die größte Gefahr besteht nicht in dem kurzfristigen (doch nicht minder realen) Risiko der Marktvolatilität, sondern in dem langfristigen Risiko, Ihr Geld nicht mit großzügiger Rendite für sich arbeiten zu lassen.

Dazu, was wirklich zählt:

Franklin: Eine Investition in Wissen bringt immer noch die besten Zinsen. Der Fleißige lernt, der Umsichtige wird reich. Leert ein Mann seinen Geldbeutel, um seinen Kopf zu füllen, kann ihm das niemand wegnehmen.

Bogle: Ein erfolgreicher Anleger braucht Informationen. Informationen über die bisher erzielten Erträge von Investmentfonds – vor allem die kurzfristigen – besitzen zwar wenig Aussagekraft, doch Informationen über Risiken und Kosten sind unbezahlbar.

Über die Märkte:

Franklin: Ein Mann kann klüger sein als ein anderer, aber nicht klüger als alle anderen.

Bogle: Glauben Sie nicht, dass Sie mehr wissen als der Markt. Das weiß niemand. Und handeln Sie nicht aufgrund von Erkenntnissen, die Sie für exklusiv halten, über die aber gewöhnlich Millionen anderer ebenfalls verfügen.

Über Sicherheit:

Franklin: Wer über große Ländereien verfügt, kann mehr riskieren, doch ein kleines Boot sollte nah am Ufer bleiben.

Bogle: Ob Ihr Vermögen groß ist oder klein, Sie sollten ein Aktien- und Anleihenportfolio auf jeden Fall so breit wie möglich streuen. Dann bleibt nur noch das Marktrisiko. Anleger mit bescheidenen Mitteln sollten besonders vorsichtig sein.

Zu Prognosen:

Franklin: Zu sehen sind die Dinge leicht, vorherzusehen dagegen schwer.

Bogle: Um zu wissen, was wir nicht wissen, bedarf es Weisheit.

Zum Sorgen für sich selbst:

Franklin: Willst Du einen treuen und angenehmen Diener haben, so diene Dir selbst.

Bogle: Ihr eigenes wirtschaftliches Interesse dürfen Sie nie außer Acht lassen.

Und abschließend zur Ausdauer:

Franklin: Fleiß, Durchhaltevermögen und Sparsamkeit erweichen das Schicksal.

Bogle: Was auch passiert, halten Sie sich an Ihr Programm. Denken Sie langfristig. Geduld und Beständigkeit sind die wertvollsten Aktivposten für einen intelligenten Anleger. »Bleiben Sie auf Kurs.«

Ich gebe gern zu, dass Franklin im 18. Jahrhundert eleganter zu formulieren verstand, als Bogle im 21. Doch die Parallelen zwischen unseren Maximen lassen vermuten, dass sich die Grundsätze des vernünftigen Sparens und Investierens bewähren – vielleicht sogar auf ewig.

Der Weg zum Reichtum

Lassen Sie es mich noch ein letztes Mal wiederholen: Der Weg zum Reichtum bedeutet nicht nur, aus dem magischen langfristigen Zinseszinseffekt Kapital zu schlagen, sondern sich auch der Tyrannei der langfristig auflaufenden Kosten zu entziehen. Meiden sie kostenintensive opportunistische Marketing-Modalitäten mit hohem Umschlag, wie sie so typisch sind für das heutige Finanzdienstleistungssystem. »Bleibt nicht untätig – tut etwas!« ist ein Motto, dass den *Unternehmen* der Wall Street ausgesprochen gute Dienste leistet. Die *Anleger* sind aber weit besser bedient, wenn Sie genau das Gegenteil beherzigen: »Tut nichts. Bleibt einfach untätig!«

Wenn Sie mir nicht glauben

Die in diesem Schlusskapital ausgeführten Gedanken erscheinen mir absolut folgerichtig – und Ihnen vielleicht auch. Sollten Sie Zweifel haben, lassen Sie sich sagen, wie sich das aus dem Mund von **Clifford S. Asness** anhört, dem geschäftsführenden Gesellschafter von AQR Capital Management. »Im Grunde wissen wir, wie Investieren geht. Das lässt sich gut mit Abnehmen und Diätratgebern vergleichen. Wir alle wissen, wie man überflüssige Pfunde los wird und in Form kommt: Weniger essen und mehr Sport treiben … das ist ganz *einfach* – aber trotzdem nicht so *leicht*. Genauso verhält es sich mit der Kapitalanlage.

Zu den einfachen, aber nicht so leicht zu befolgenden Ratschlägen zum richtigen Investieren und zur Finanzplanung gehören im Allgemeinen: breit streuen … die Kosten niedrig halten … diszipliniert umgewichten … weniger Geld ausgeben … mehr sparen … weniger gewagte Annahmen zu künftigen Erträgen treffen … und wenn etwas angeblich nichts kostet, misstrauisch werden, solange nicht sehr überzeugende Argumente dafür sprechen – und dann alles noch einmal überprüfen.

Hören Sie auf, laufend die Aktienmärkte zu verfolgen … bei der Kapitalanlage ist weniger oft mehr. Und dann, ganz in Hippokrates-Manier: Auf keinen Fall schaden! Sie brauchen keine Wunderwaffe. Da beißt die Maus keinen Faden ab: Die derzeit zu erwartenden Erträge sind für eine große

Gruppe von Anlageklassen im historischen Vergleich niedrig. *Halten Sie sich daher diszipliniert an die Grundlagen.«*

Die einfachen Ideen aus diesem Buch funktionieren wirklich. Ich bin überzeugt, dass der klassische Indexfonds das Herzstück einer solchen Gewinnstrategie bilden muss. Doch selbst ich hätte mich nicht getraut, zu sagen, was der mittlerweile verstorbene **Dr. Paul Samuelson** vom MIT in einer Rede vor der Boston Society of Security Analysts im Herbst 2005 sagte: *»Dass John Bogle den ersten Indexfonds aufgelegt hat, ist vergleichbar mit der Erfindung des Rades, des Alphabets und von Wein und Käse.«* Diese Existenzgrundlagen, die für uns so selbstverständlich geworden sind, haben sich langfristig bewährt. Und das wird der traditionelle Indexfonds ebenfalls.

Dank

Beim Schreiben dieses Buches bin ich vom gesamten (dreiköpfigen) Team des Bogle Financial Markets Research Center enorm unterstützt worden – dem von Vanguard mitgetragenen Unternehmen, das seine Tätigkeit offiziell Anfang 2000 aufnahm.

Ganz besonders bedanken möchte ich mich an erster Stelle bei Michael W. Nolan, Jr., Senior Investment Analyst und Research-Experte, meinem Partner und hin und wieder auch meinem wandelnden Gewissen. Mike steht mir im Rahmen seiner 16-jährigen Karriere bei Vanguard jetzt schon seit sechs Jahren kompetent zur Seite. Er hat so ziemlich alles zu diesem Buch beigetragen, außer es zu schreiben: Themen recherchiert, Daten entwickelt, Quellen überprüft, den Text redigiert und mit dem Verlag zusammengearbeitet – und das nicht nur in herausragender Qualität, sondern mit so viel Gelassenheit und Humor, dass man es erlebt haben muss, um es zu glauben.

Emily Snyder, seit mittlerweile 27 Jahren meine Assistentin der Geschäftsführung (und seit 32 Jahren im Dienst von Vanguard), hat einen großen Teil meines Gekritzels zu einem formschönen Manuskript zusammengefasst, und das mit außergewöhnlichem Geschick, unerschütterlicher Finesse und stets gut gelaunt. Ich glaube zwar, dass sie innerlich zusammengezuckt ist, als ich ihr ankündigte, ich würde mein elftes Buch schreiben, aber sie hat mich trotzdem duldsam durch meine obligatorischen plus/minus acht Überarbeitungsdurchgänge begleitet, auf die es bei mir immer hinausläuft – alles im Interesse einer verständlichen, klaren, nachvollziehbaren und lesefreundlichen Sprache.

Kathy Younker ist ein Neuzugang in unserem kleinen Kreis, hat aber das Ihre zu dem endlosen Abtippen und Umschreiben beigetragen. Dabei ist es ihr mit bemerkenswerter Kompetenz, Geduld und guter Stimmung gelungen, meinen Schreibrhythmus in unserem hektischen Tagesgeschäft unterzubringen.

Ich sollte anmerken, dass ich die volle Verantwortung für die dezidierten Meinungen übernehme, die in diesem kleinen Handbuch zum Ausdruck kommen. Sie decken sich nicht unbedingt mit den Auffassungen des derzeitigen Managements von Vanguard.

Ich bin und bleibe Vanguard und den Mitgliedern unserer Mannschaft zutiefst verpflichtet und setze mich weiterhin unverbrüchlich für die Förderung der Werte ein, die ich dem Unternehmen mitgegeben habe, als ich es 1974 gründete – und in den 25 Jahren in meinen Funktionen als Chief Executive, später als Chairman und schließlich als Senior Chairman.

John C. Bogle